Clara Erskine Clement Waters

Egypt

Clara Erskine Clement Waters

Egypt

ISBN/EAN: 9783337240110

Printed in Europe, USA, Canada, Australia, Japan

Cover: Foto ©ninafisch / pixelio.de

More available books at **www.hansebooks.com**

ON PHILÆ.

BY
CLARA ERSKINE CLEMENT
Author of "A Simple Story of the Orient," "A Handbook of Legen-
dary and Mythological Art," etc.

WITH ONE HUNDRED AND SIX ILLUSTRATIONS.

BOSTON:

D. LOTHROP & CO.
1880.

of ROCKWELL AND CHU[...]
39 Arch St., Boston.

	PAGE
IN PHILÆ. *Frontispiece.*	
Papyrus	11
On the Edge of the Desert	17
Water-wheel on the Nile	21
The Nilometer, near Cairo	25
Shadoof	29
Ptah or Phtha	31
Approach to Assouan	33
Scribe	35
Pyramids of Sakkara, near Memphis	37
Distant View of the Pyramids	39
A Trip to the Pyramids — old style	41
Interior Views of the Great Pyramid	43
Stepped Pyramid	45
Landing Place at Assouan	47
Ascent of the Pyramids	51
Ladies at a Party	54
Lotus	55
Portico of Temple of Denderah	57
Women Weaving	60
Chem-Ket and Reshpu	62
Les holding Nosegays	64
Great Hall at Karnak	66
Atum	68

List of Illustrations.

	PAGE.
Canaanitish Immigration into Egypt	70
Black Slaves with their Families	72
Ancient Turquoise Mines	73
Pyramids of Gizeh	77
Egyptian Car and Horses	81
Harper in Tomb at Thebes	83
Bust of Cephren	85
Set, Ramses II., and Horus	87
Crocodiles on the Upper Nile	91
Thoth	96
Grottoes of Silsilis	101
War Chariot with Furniture.	106
Ancient Egyptian Coat of Mail	109
Golden Ewers and Basins	112
Box—in the Berlin Museum	114
Assault of a Fort	118
Propylon at Karnak	121
Columns and Obelisk, Karnak	124
Foreign Captives making Bricks	125
Remains of Temple, Abydos	129
Colossi of Thebes	135
Columns of Temple, Luxon	139
Mut	143
An Ethiopian Princess Travelling	148
Osiris, Isis and Horus	151
Bottles of Blue-glass	153
The Hall of Columns at Karnak	157
The Judgment Hall of Osiris	159
A Poulterer's Shop	161
Colossal Statue of Ramses the Great	163
Investiture of a High Priest	167
Phalanx of the Khita	173

List of Illustrations.

	PAGE
Ramses Slaying Captives	175
Great Temple at Isamboul	179
Palace of Ramses III., Medinet-Abu	185
Christian Symbols at Philæ	191
Dress of a King	192
Egyptian Palm Grove	195
Tombs of the Kings at Thebes	211
Pyramid at Assur in Nubia	217
An Egyptian Gentleman Fishing	219
Towing the Dahabieh	229
Pharaoh's Bed on the Island of Philæ	235
Portico of Temple at Philæ	239
Hypostyle Hall, Karnak	243
Portico and Temple at Esneh	246
Erment, or Hormonthis, near Thebes	253
Cataract of the Nile	259
Sarcophagus	262
Cleopatra's Needle	267
Pompey's Pillar	283
Nubian Serpent Charmers	291
Captive Jews in the Hippodrome at Alexandria	297
Female playing on a Guitar	301
The Monastery of St. Catherine	303
Windlass at the Convent	305
View from the Citadel of Cairo	315
Egyptian Girl	318
Egyptian Woman	321
Watching Fields in Egypt	333
Distant View of Cairo	337
Mosque of Saïd	339
Mosque of Mohammed Ali	342
A Roadside Well	343

Money-Changer at Siout	347
Camel Driver	351
A Shadoof	358
Sand-storm in the Desert	363
Nile Boat	369
French Army Passing the Great Sphinx	379
Bust of Cleopatra at Denderah	380
The Doum Palm in Nubia	383
Bringing Water from the Nile	386
In the Suburbs of Cairo	393
Bedouin Women Grinding Corn	398
Egyptian Fellaheen	411
Port Saïd	415
Crossing the River in Nubia	417
Cairene Water-seller	419
Fellaheen at work on the Canal	421
Map of the Canal	437
Town of Suez	439
Caravan starting from Suez	445

CHAPTER I.

KINGS OF MEMPHIS. 4400 TO 3300 B.C.

PAPYRUS.

EGYPT holds a most important place in history, for, if it was not absolutely the oldest nation of the earth, it was the source of civilization, art and letters to all the world, and it is impossible to show from what other nation, if any, Egypt derived its mythological religion, its philosophy and science. Nearly all the arts and sciences of the present day originated in Egypt—architecture and sculpture, medicine, chemistry, mathematics, astronomy, writing, and the use of paper, and many of the mechanical arts as now practised, are only such as were known and employed in Egypt ages ago.

When Greek history begins, Egypt was on the verge of its decline. Even in the days of Abraham, the Pyramids had been built and copper mines worked on Mount Sinai; and as, according to the Jewish tradition, he led his herds to drink in the Nile, he must have seen many of the monuments whose ruins now tell of the advanced state of Egyptian art at that time. Moses, we are told, was educated in all the learning of the Egyptians, and though we have no history of those times in books, their history was written in hieroglyphics, on temples and obelisks, long before the Greek alphabet was known.

Ancient Egypt was also the land of the greatest luxury. Even prior to the captivity of the Israelites, gold and silver ornaments, fine colors and embroideries were in common use, and at the time of the Exodus the luxury and magnificence of the wealthy almost equalled that of the great Cleopatra, the most luxurious queen the world has ever seen. Twelve centuries before the birth of Christ the Nile Valley was filled with cities and palaces, vast temples and magnificent tombs; and there is scarcely an article of comfort or luxury now in use that has not its counterpart in some of the pictures, still fresh and bright, on the walls of the Tombs of the Ancient Kings of Egypt.

> "Hail! Egypt! land of ancient pomp and pride,
> Where Beauty walks by hoary Ruin's side;
> Where Plenty reigns, and still the seasons smile,
> And rolls—rich gift of God!—exhaustless Nile.
> Land of the pyramid and temple lone!
> Whose fame, a star, on earth's dark midnight shone;
> Bright seat of wisdom, graced with arts and arms,
> Ere Rome was built, or smiled fair Athen's charms;
> What owes the past, the living world to thee?
> All that refines, sublimes humanity.
> The tall papyrus, whispering seems to say,
> Here rose the letters Cadmus bore away.
> The Greek to thee his Jove and Bacchus owes,
> With many a tale that charms, and thought that glows
> In thy famed schools the Samian learnt his lore,
> That souls, though wandering, lived for evermore;
> The giant structures piled on Gizeh's plain
> Speak of the sages watching heaven's bright train,
> Who first years, months divided—traced afar
> The comet's course, and named each glittering star.
>
> . . . .
>
> What though no more the priest on Isis calls,
> Or grand processions sweep from Memphis' walls,
> Praying the flood to rise o'er bower and field,
> Still swell the waves, and wonted blessings yield;

> And sweet the stream to traveller's thirsty lip,
> As when the Egyptian deemed it heaven to sip:
> And green the flags, and fair the lotus-flower,
> As when that babe, within his bulrush-bower,
> The embryo leader, Fame's immortal heir,
> Smiled on the royal maids who found him there."

To the history of what other country can one come with the delightful anticipations he may well bring to that of Egypt? To those who have visited that land, memory recalls its scenes with panoramic exactness and rapidity. To those whose journeys have been made by aid of books while sitting at their own firesides, imagination will present the pictures she has painted with magic power — pictures of groves of stately palms slowly nodding their feathery tops in the lazy breeze, which nothing less lofty than themselves can feel; and orange-trees, snowy with their bridal flowers or laden with golden fruit; pictures of the unbounded desert-sands, ever a striking emblem of a wasted life — no growth, no verdure, nothing telling of development or power, nothing reaching up towards heaven; — and there are trains of camels, stretching so far away that all shape and form is lost, while their towering burdens move steadily on; — pictures of swarthy men in fez or turban, with flowing garments and broad sashes of silk or cashmere, the ample folds of which conceal alike the sacred talisman, the precious jewel, and the glittering knife, while a sword or scimetar flashes by the side;—and veiled women, whose dark, dreamy eyes tell of that languid, Houri-like beauty peculiar to their race and clime;—pictures, too, of noble mosques, with marble courts and flowing fountains, and their graceful minarets springing lightly into air; of bazaars crowded with representatives of every nation that the sun shines upon; donkeys and donkey-boys, camels and their drivers; water-carriers, with full or empty goat-skins; women with their children perched astride their shoulders; elegant carriages, preceded by gayly-dressed runners, who clear the way with shining rods; sailors and soldiers, monks and sisters of charity, all jostling and crowding each other in these Cairene bazaars, while the merchants sit cross-legged on their cushions, and smoke their pipes, or sip their coffee with an air of solemnity and wisdom.

All these pictures may be seen in living, moving reality in Egypt, and beyond this manifest life lies the study of a past, full of wonder and mighty import.

Eighty years have now elapsed since the discovery of the Rosetta stone gave to the world the charmed key with which the secrets of the Egyptian monuments and writings have been unlocked, and their rich stores of historical truth made available.

This famous stone was found by M. Boussard, near Rosetta, in 1799. It is a slab of black basalt, about seven and a half feet in length by two and a half in breadth, and upon it is inscribed a decree in honor of Ptolemy Epiphanes. This decree was cut into the stone in three languages: the hieroglyphic, the demotic or enchorial, and the Greek; thus it furnishes the means of deciphering the ancient Egyptian inscriptions and papyri.

Since this inscription was deciphered, facts enough have been discovered, compared and verified, to afford a comparatively satisfactory history of Egypt, made up entirely from the incontrovertible testimony of the hieroglyphics, while the pre-historic age, with its gods, demi-gods and manes, still affords (and apparently always must do so) a mysterious realm, in which imagination may revel *ad infinitum*, and meet no refutation of its wildest fancies.

Geographically, Egypt is one of the most singu-

ON THE EDGE OF THE DESERT.

lar and interesting countries in the world. It embraces, at the largest calculation, but seventeen thousand square miles — about one-fourteenth of the size of the state of Texas.

Herodotus called Egypt "the gift of the Nile," and this name well expresses the importance of that river, which, entering Egypt near the island of Philæ, flows down to the Mediterranean, bearing and bestowing the entire prosperity of this wondrous land — for the Nile Valley, (a green belt from six to ten miles wide) and the Delta, (which lies between the two branches of the river, below Cairo) and the Fayûm, (which province owes its fertility to the irrigation from the Nile) make, in fact, all of Egypt; the remainder is desert sand or quarried mountain.

Wherever the Nile flows there is fertility; elsewhere, only desolation and sterility. The richness of the Nile deposit is such that it is only necessary to scatter the seed on the ground it has covered — no plough, no labor is required, and time only increases the richness of this soil. At present the loam near the first cataract has a depth of five feet, and that of the Delta four.

From its junction with the river Atbara (called also the Black River, on account of the richness of its deposit) the Nile flows fifteen hundred miles with no affluent. Alone it opposes a burning sun; alone it flows and overflows, and brings each year the seed-time and secures the harvest, as if a beneficent heart and controlling thought directed its course, and we can quite understand that to the ancients it was a sacred river, and the dwelling-place of a great god.

The rise of the river has been measured by means of nilometers, from the most ancient days, and it is probable that each important city had its own indicator of the height of the water. The most important nilometers are, that upon the Island of Rhoda, opposite Cairo, and one at Elephantine, near Assouan — the latter is in ruins. At Rhoda, the slender pillar upon which the measure is marked is in the midst of a square enclosure which formerly had a dome, and traces of Cufic inscriptions still remain. Here the rise of the river is carefully noted, and the people warned of any signs of a flood. The height of the water formerly regulated the amount of taxation, and Pliny says that a rise of twelve cubits brought famine; thirteen, starvation; fourteen, cheerfulness; fifteen, safety; and sixteen, delight. For this reason many of the statues of the Nile, of the

WATER-WHEEL ON THE NILE.

Roman period, are represented with sixteen children playing around the venerable god of the river.

In later years, the rise of the Nile has exceeded the average of many centuries. The regularity with which this river has risen at the same time to about the same height, has furnished one of the most wonderful physical phenomena of the world. Artificial irrigation is carried on by means of water-wheels and the shadoof, and the water is lifted in precisely the same way as by the primitive well-sweep; one well is close down to the river, another just above it, and so on until the top of the bank is reached, and the water is poured into ditches which divide the fields into square patches. The "shadoof" employs hundreds of men, women and children; their work begins with the dawn and ends only with the night. The motions of these people are slow and rhythmic, and they often sing a monotonous sort of chant while they dip, dip, dip, and the rude machinery creaks out a weird accompaniment.

In ancient times Egypt was called "the double land," and Upper and Lower Egypt were divided as they now are.

The former extended from Elephantine Island,

opposite the modern town of Assouan, on the right bank of the river, to the neighborhood of the Memphian district on the left bank — that is to say, the country now called Saïd by the Arabs.

Lower Egypt comprised the remainder of the country, and corresponded to the Delta of the Greek writers, called "the Behereh" by the Arabs. In the inscriptions, Egypt is called Kem or Kami, which signifies "the black land," a name probably taken from the color of the arable soil of the country. From the earliest times the whole country was divided into districts or nomes; Upper Egypt embracing twenty-two, and Lower Egypt twenty nomes. Each of these divisions had its own capital city, and its especial divinity, to whose worship the temples were dedicated. The nomes were separated by boundary stones, and great care was taken to preserve the limits as they were originally fixed.

The hieroglyphics show that though all the nomes were under the king, yet, in a sense, each one had its own independent government, and the office of captain or governor passed by inheritance to the eldest grandson on the mother's

[A table giving the names of the nomes and of their capital cities will be found at the end of this book.]

THE NILOMETER, NEAR CAIRO.

side, according to the ancient Egyptian law.

Feuds, of greater or less importance, frequently arose between these districts, and the entire country sometimes became involved in them; in fact, it occasionally happened that the ruling family was dethroned and the captain of a victorious nome made himself the king, and the founder of a new dynasty; thus the seat of government was changed from one city to another.

The earliest sovereign, of whom there is exact record, was Mena. His name signifies "the constant," and was written Min, Menis, Meines, Meinios and Meneres. He founded Memphis, the principal city of Lower Egypt, of which there now remain a few fragments of its temples and palaces, and a number of mounds, which yield nothing in return for their examination by the curious student of Memphian history.

Tradition says that Mena also constructed an enormous dyke, and turned the course of the Nile to the east, in order to build his city upon the former river-bed. It is the opinion of M. Linant-Bey, that this dyke is one with that of Cocheiche, which now, six thousand years after its construction by King Mena, serves to restrain the inundations of the Nile.

The existing personal accounts of this king are extremely brief. Is is said that he first introduced pomp and luxury into Egypt, and for this reason, in later years Tnephacthus ordered a curse against his memory to be engraved and set up in the temple of Amon-ra or Jupiter, at Thebes.

Mena established laws for the worship of the gods, and the temple was the first building to be erected. It formed the centre and the most important feature of the city, which, as it grew, had new temples added, each one making a point about which other edifices were clustered. Thus each quarter of the town had its own temple and its distinctive name. Other cities were laid out after the same plan and from their arrangement a confusion of names arises — Memphis, for example, was known as Anbu-hat or "the white wall," a name derived from the fortifications; Men-nofer or "the good place;" Chanofer or "the good appearance," and Macha-ta or "the land of the scales." Men-nofer is the name most used in inscriptions, and from this the Greeks made Memphis.

The principal god of Memphis, to whom its most celebrated temple was dedicated, was Patah, who, according to the Memphian doctrine, was the Father of all Gods, the Architect of the World,

SHADOOF.

and corresponded to the classical Hephæstus or Vulcan.

Mena also excavated a lake which lay without the city and was connected with the Nile by a canal.

As a warrior, he is credited with having made a successful campaign against the Libyan tribes.

Ptah or Phtha, King of the North and South.

He is said to have met a frightful death, being seized and killed by a crocodile.

In the thirteenth century of the Christian era, the ruins of Memphis were visited by Abd-ul-Latif, an Arabian physician, who gave a poetic and enthusiastic description of them, and an account of the so-called "green chamber," which was hewn out of a single block of stone, and measured about fifteen feet in height, by thirteen and a half in length, and ten in width.

After Thebes, Memphis is the city most frequently mentioned in Egyptian inscriptions, and many facts are given concerning its government and court, its laws and customs. Among its priests were princes of the royal family, who often exercised a powerful influence upon the welfare of the whole country.

The King, called Perao, (which means "of the great house," and is the origin of the bible Pharaoh), was frequently named as "his holiness," and seems to have stood before his subjects both as a god and a ruler. The deepest personal respect was shown him, his subjects prostrating themselves before him, unless graciously relieved from this homage by special favor. He commanded services from great and small alike, and rewarded them in a regal manner, with gifts of lands, slaves and maidens, and even by honorable decorations, such as the necklace of the gold nub.

The wife, daughters and grand-daughters of the king were called "prophetesses of the goddesses Hathor or Neit," and were confided to the lords of the court for care and instruction.

The court was respected by the people on

APPROACH TO ASSOUAN.

account of the wisdom and virtues of its members, as much as for its splendor. The nobles were charged with the superintendence of the treasury, the magazines of supplies, the buildings and works in stone, and even with the care of the king's household, the music, and other entertainments for the royal pleasure.

The army was led by experienced officers, and a commander-in-general organized and directed all military expeditions.

Scribe with his inkstand on the table. One pen is put behind his ear, and he is writing with another.
Thebes.

There were many learned men, as well as teachers of all kinds, and literary composers in Memphis. A great number of scribes were employed there, and were divided into various classes, according to their duties, which ranged from the writing of a sort of diary of domestic events up to the important work of the "pharaonic bureaucracy." All scribes were eligible for the highest rank of their order, which was given as the reward of intelligence and fidelity.

Order and exactitude characterized this ancient government, from the king down to the humblest man in the land, and this state of things was the legitimate fruit of the blind obedience, which was exacted alike from the royal secretary and the wretched worker, under the lash of the equally obedient overseer or task-master.

> "But Memphis' kings are less than ashes now,
> The crowns e'en dust, that decked each royal brow.
> Goshen, where Israel toiled, no trace retains
> Of all the towers they built, when scourged in chains.
> Memphis herself, as cursed for injuries piled
> On Judah's head, long, long hath strewn the wild.
> Where is the site to soft-eyed Apis reared,
> That sacred bull, kings, blood-stained chiefs, revered?
> Where Vulcan's fane? and gorgeous as a dream,
> The gold-roofed palace raised by Nilus' stream?
> No vestige meets the pilgrim's curious gaze;
> O'er Memphis' site the turbaned robber strays;
> Each wall is razed, each pillared shrine o'erthrown;
> The sands drift on, the desert breezes moan;
> Shades of the Pharaohs! rise from marble sleep!
> And o'er your lost, loved city bend and weep!"

The tables discovered at Sakkara and Abydus, together with the imperfect papyrus of Turin, furnish a list of the names of the sovereigns who followed Mena, but no other knowledge of them exists until the time of King Senoferu or "he who makes good." From his time the "speaking stones" reveal the history of their hoary long ago.

Senoferu lived about 3766 B. C., and is the first king to whom the inscriptions give four titles of honor.

This custom was ordained by law. The first title invariably began with a sign symbolical of the god, "the sun Hor," who dispensed life and light, prosperity and happiness — the other titles set forth the praises of the king of the "double country," in pompous words. Last of all, the name

PYRAMIDS OF SAKKARA, NEAR MEMPHIS.

which the king had received from his father, surrounded by a cartouche, was given.

Senoferu was known as "the lord of truth," "the vanquisher of foreign peoples," and by many other high sounding titles.

On the rocks of Wady-Magharah is clearly pictured a likeness of this king striking down an enemy — and the inscription speaks of him as the conqueror of the valleys of the mountains round

Sinai. These lands were very valuable on account of their copper ore and precious stones of blue and green color. At this day traces of miners may be seen in the caverns of this district, for the successors of Senoferu valued and maintained the rights which he had won and systematically profited by these treasures. The De Prisse rolls call Senoferu "a good king over the whole country, and it is believed that the pryamid of Meidoum contains his remains.

The tables of Sakkara and Abydos, with the Turin papyrus and the writings of Manetho, are not sufficient to furnish a satisfactory list of the kings of the fourth and fifth dynasties, about 3700 to 3300 B. C., and even the monuments differ as to their names and the order of their succession; but the tables of Abydos and Sakkara agree in calling Khufu the successor of Senoferu. Khufu was called Suphis by Manetho and Saophis in the Theban list of kings, but by the Greeks and in modern times he is called Cheops, Chemnis or Chembres.

The ancients represented Cheops as a tyrant and a brutal oppressor. They accused him of closing the temples lest the prayers of the people should shorten the time of daily labor, and it is even said

DISTANT VIEW OF THE PYRAMIDS.

that he was so detested, that no Egyptian would pronounce his name after his death.

The few "speaking stones" which tell of this king give him a more honorable character. By them

A TRIP TO THE PYRAMIDS — OLD STYLE.

he is named as one of the bravest, and most active pharaohs; an annihilator of his enemies, and the founder of several new towns. But everything else connected with this monarch sinks into insignificance when compared to the great pyramid which he erected, and which bears his name. No one who sees this monument can doubt that twenty years were consumed in its erection, or that it was considered an Herculean task even by this old nation of monument builders.

The process of building a pyramid was as follows: first the nucleus was formed by the erection of a small pyramid upon the soil of the desert. It was built in steps and contained a stone chamber well constructed and finished. Then coverings were added until the final size was reached, and at last all was enclosed in a casing of hard stone, deftly fitted together and polished to a glassy surface. The pyramid, thus finished, presented a gigantic triangle on each of its four faces.

The stone used for the inner structure was found near the place of erection, but as the work progressed, better material was brought from mountain quarries, and the vast labors thus accomplished are forcibly though silently told, by the numerous caverns in the Mokattam range, from which the finer stones were taken.

But the covering of the magnificent pyramid of Cheops, called in the inscriptions "Rhut" or "the Lights," was hewn out of the "red mountain" of

VIEW OF GALLERY IN THE GREAT PYRAMID.

Syene, or the modern Assouan, many weary miles from the wonderful monument it was to adorn.

This Syenite granite, hard as metal, and sprinkled with black and red, is capable of an exquisite polish, and was coveted by kings and architects as a crowning beauty to be added to their works. In the " red mountain " quarries the hand of the skilled workman may still be traced, by the marks

STEPPED PYRAMID.

of the chisel — the miner's hole — and, above all, by the giant statue, and mighty obelisk still hanging there as if spell-bound, half released and ever striving to escape from the unrelenting clasp of the stony nature which enfolds them.

On the borders of the desert more than seventy

such pyramids once stood, but that of Cheops so far exceeded all others in beauty, and so towered above them all* that we may well fancy that, like the sheaves of Joseph's dream, the lesser ones bowed before it. There it still stands, in the midst of pyramids and tombs, the everlasting witness to the power of that great monarch of the distant past, with the grim Sphinx not far away, as if to guard its secrets. It is a tomb entombed, for the yellow sand has been piled up about it by the winds of heaven, as if they would cover up and hide away this remnant of a people and a king, long since departed.

> "The shadow of the Pyramids
> Fled round before the sun;
>   By day it fled,
>   It onward sped;
> And when its daily task was done,
>   The moon arose, and round the plain
>   The weary shadow fled again.
>
> "The Sphinx looked East,
> The Sphinx looked West,
>   And North and South her shadow fell;
> How many times she sought for rest
>   And found it not, no tongue may tell.
>
> "But much it vexed the heart of greedy Time
>   That neither rain nor snow, nor frost nor hail,
> Troubles the calm of the Egyptian clime;

---

* 450.75 English feet high by 746 feet broad at base.

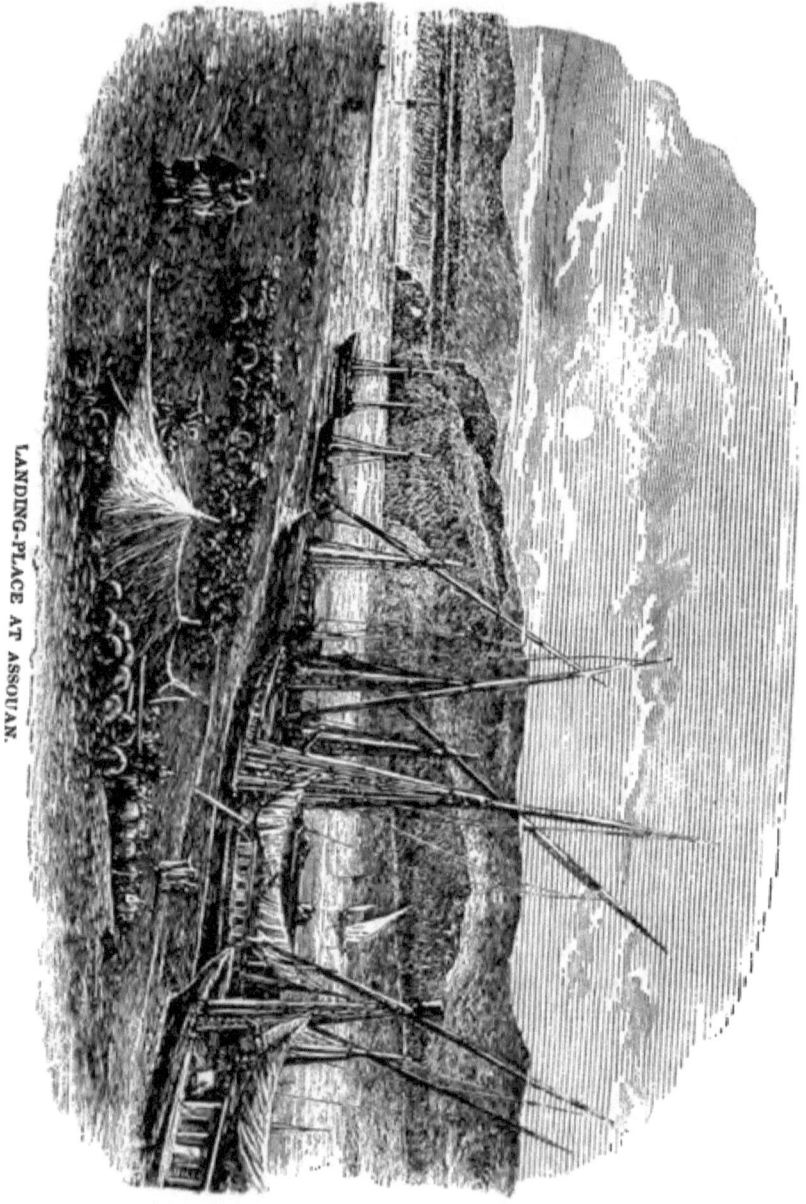

LANDING-PLACE AT ASSOUAN.

>   For these for him, like heavy iron flail
>   Against the palaces of kings prevail,
>   And crumble down the loftiest pile,
>   And eat the ancient hills away,
>   And make the very mountains know decay.
>   . . . .
>   He cursed the mummies that they would not rot,
>   He cursed the paintings that they faded not,
>   And swore to terrible Memnon from his seat;
>   But foiled awhile, to hide his great defeat,
>   With his wide wings he blew the Libyan sand,
>   And hid from mortal eyes the glories of the land."

The tables of Abydos and Sakkara name Ratatef as the successor of Cheops, and then follows Khafra, whose wonderful statues have recently been brought to light. Khafra was named by the Greeks Chephren, Kephren, or Chabryes. He has been named both the brother and the son of Cheops, but the monuments do not speak of this relation. His pyramid, near to that of Cheops, has been overshadowed by the discovery of a building in the desert, which is now associated with his name. It is constructed entirely of the stone of Assouan, and the glistening oriental alabaster; it contains passages, and halls, and smaller rooms, succeeding one another, all without inscriptions of any sort. The workmanship of this building is simply marvellous, as much so as the truth that no clue can be found to the discovery of its purpose or its maker. Eastwards, in a long chamber, a well was discovered containing several noble statues mostly in ruins, but that of King Khafra had suffered little injury. His name and titles are inscribed near his foot; the stone is of a green color and the whole work is that of a masterly sculptor.

This statue is a precious treasure and "teaches us that in the beginning of history their works were an honor to the artists."

The great Sphinx is not far distant from the pyramid of Khafra, and the name of this monarch is mentioned upon the slab or memorial stone which bears the inscriptions. This does not prove that the "Lion of the Night" (as the Arabs call the Sphinx) was made by command of Khafra.

The Sphinx has the form of a lion and the head of a man. It is cut out of the solid rock with the exception of the fore-legs, which were hewn out and added, and extend fifty feet from the breast. A memorial tablet records the fact that Thutmes IV. built a temple at the breast of the Sphinx, as a gift of honor. This temple has been excavated, but the desert sands soon bury it from sight. Pliny says that this Sphinx was without doubt a local deity, and was treated with divine honors. It is now known to be a representation of Hor-

ASCENT OF THE PYRAMIDS.

makhu, which is to say "Horus on the horizon," or the sun god of Heliopolis.

Two later kings than Khafra, belonging to the fourth dynasty, are mentioned in the table of Abydos, Menkaura or Mencheres, and Shepseskaf. The first was distinguished for his justice, kindness and piety, and after death he was honored with the institution of a special worship dedicated to his memory. Of Shepseskaf little is known and his name seldom occurs in the hieroglyphics.

The fifth dynasty (the last of the so-called Memphian kings, the most ancient sovereigns known in history), offers little of interest to the student of antiquity.

It comprised the reigns of eight kings, Uskaf, Sahura, Keka, Noferfra, Ranuser, Menkauhor, Tatkara and Unas. These rulers built pyramids, and made some conquests, but in truth left the kingdom much the same as they found it.

Some notable men lived in the time of the fifth dynasty. Among them was the occupant of the spacious tomb of Ti, remarkable for its numerous pictures illustrative of the manners and customs of the ancient Egyptians. This tomb is situated in the Necropolis of Sakkara, towards the north of the Serapeum, and is much visited by travellers.

The famous Prisse-papyrus was written by a son of king Tatkara, the Prince Patah-hotep. This document is in the National Library at Paris, and is called by the name of the man who bought it, at Thebes. It contains an old man's advice to young men, and instructs them as to the best manner of spending life and of making one's way in the world. It is very interesting, and, like all words of wisdom, is as well suited to the present time, as to that in which it was written.

Ladies at a party, talking about their earrings.

CHAPTER II.

FROM THE SIXTH TO THE THIRTEENTH DYNASTY.
3300 TO 2233 B.C.

LOTUS.

THE sixth dynasty forms the beginning of the second period of the ancient Egyptian empire, and the tombs of middle Egypt furnish much information concerning the history of this epoch.

There is some doubt as to the name of the first king of this dynasty. Uskara and Teta are both of this period, but the weight of testimony is in favor of Teta. One theory is that they were contemporary sovereigns, and each governed a portion of Egypt. M. Brugsch-Bey speaks of this as probable, but not positive. So little is known of these kings that one turns naturally to their successor, Meri-ra Pepi, whose name and renown are well maintained in the ineffaceable characters upon the rocks of Wady-Magharah, the ruins of Tanis, the temple of Denderah, in many quarries, and above all, upon a monument found in the grave of Una, in the burial place of Memphis, and now preserved in the Museum of Boulak. The great importance of this monument was first recognized by M. Rougé.

Una was a prominent man under King Teta, and served King Pepi in many important undertakings. "He was dearer to the heart of the king than all the dear nobles and all the other servants of the land," according to the text, and he was sent to Troja to obtain a sarcophagus, and many other stones for the construction of the pyramid of King Pepi, which was called "the good station" or "the good entrance." The cutting of these stones in the caverns of Troja and their transportation was a wonderful work and necessitated the employment of warriors, sailors and ships. The records go on to tell of Una as the leader of a campaign against the Amu and the Hirusha of Lower Egypt; another war against the land of Terehbah; and various other brave deeds, for which King Pepi conferred

PORTICO OF TEMPLE AT DENDERAH

on him great honors. The records in the tomb of Una are carried beyond the time of King Pepi, whose honors descended to his eldest son, Mer-en-ra, who made Una governor of Upper Egypt. He was the first man upon whom so high a dignity was conferred, and he was entrusted with the direction of all the public works, and the entire administration of the affairs of this important division of the kingdom.

An account of his many journeys in search of granite, alabaster and precious stones would be useless. Forests were cut down and vessels built to serve him on his expeditions, all of which he conducted to the full acceptance of "his holiness."

But for the records of Una nothing would as yet be known of the reigns of Teta, Pepi and Mer-en-ra. A second son of King Pepi, called Nofer-ka-ra, next sat on the throne, concerning whom little is known, and after his time an impenetrable veil conceals all vestiges of the acts of many sovereigns whose names are found upon the tables of Abydos and Sakkara.

To this period belongs the tradition concerning the beautiful, flaxen-haired queen, Nitocris, the noblest and handsomest woman of her time, and the builder of the third pyramid. It is related of her, that in order to revenge the death of her brother (who had been killed by his political enemies, who gave the kingdom to her), she constructed a vast, underground hall, and when she had invited the murderers to a feast there, the waters of the Nile were poured in through a canal

WOMEN WEAVING AND USING THE SPINDLES.

and all were drowned. Then Nitocris took her own life in order to avoid the vengeance which was sure to fall upon her. The inscriptions make the third pyramid belong to the reign of Menkara, the pious, who lived ten centuries earlier than this fabulous queen. However, Perring affirms that this pyramid has been **reconstructed, and some Egyptologists, Bunsen** and **Lepsius** being of the number, believe that Nitocris enlarged it, and covered it with the rich polished granite which made its claim to special notice.

The next king after **Nofer-ka-ra**, of whom the monuments tell anything of interest, was **Neb-kher-ra Mentu-hotep**, called also Ra-neb-taui He belonged **to a race of kings who** had fixed their capital upon the spot where the magnificent city of Thebes was built later. The simple brick pyramids of these sovereigns were at the foot of the western mountain of the Necropolis of Thebes, where some of their coffins have been found.

Near Philæ, on the island of Konosso, there is a bas-relief of this Ra-neb-taui, who is called the devoted **servant of the** celebrated Khem, the god of Coptos, and is credited **with the** conquests of thirteen foreign nations.

The last king of the eleventh dynasty was Sankh-ka-ra, and much interest is attached to the fact that under him the first journey was made to Ophir and Punt. This Punt, supposed to be the modern Somali, on the east coast of Africa, was, according to tradition, the original home of the gods, and

62 *From the Sixth to the Thirteenth Dynasty.*

thence had come forth a procession of sacred beings led by Amon, Horus and Hathor.

This marvellous land of Punt was rich in precious stones and metals, rare woods, incense, and balsam — birds with strange plumage, and animals,

Khem.   Ket.   Reshpu.

such as camelopards, panthers, apes and long-tailed monkeys.

Punt was the home of the god Bes, a powerful deity, who later gained dominion in Arabia and other parts of Asia, and even in the islands of Greece.

This god is represented as a short, deformed man with apish countenance, almost concealed by a lion's skin which gives him a Gorgon-like appearance. He has a curly beard, a head-dress of long feathers and a tail like an animal. Wilkinson believed that he represented Death, in a bad sense. Birch judges from his various representations that he had bad attributes, but Brugsch-Bey so far differs from this opinion that he calls him "no other than the beneficent Dionysos, who, as a pilgrim through the world, dispensed with hand rich in blessings, mild manners, peace and jollity to the nations."

It is well known that a road led from Coptos across the desert, to the coast of the Red Sea, and that from a land washed by the waters of the Arabian Gulf, precious treasures were received. The perilous voyages in frail barks, and the weary journey over parched sands, "where no water was," have furnished themes for prose and verse, and an attractive fascination lingers about those treasure-laden caravans, in spite of the painfulness of their way, and the hazards which they braved for the sake of the riches from the land of Punt.

Hannu was the noble sent by Sankh-ka-ra, on the first journey of this sort of which we have any record. The account of it is given in his own words, and ends thus:—"Never was there a like thing done since there were kings; never was anything like this done by any royal relation sent to these places since the time of the reign of the Sun-god, Ra. I acted thus for the king on account of the great friendship he has for me."

The same desert-path followed by this memor-

Bes holding nosegays.

able expedition, was used by all merchant caravans down to the time of the Ptolemies and the Romans.

It is not possible to say when the products of India were first brought to Egypt, but the tombs of Thebes give full assurance of the truth that some intercourse, either direct or through the medium of Arabia, existed between Egypt and India.

It is known that Solomon brought vast treasures from India, (2 Chron. viii.: 18, and 1 Kings ix.: 26-28) but this journey was made by Hannu at least fifteen hundred years before the reign of Solomon.

The twelfth dynasty, now to be considered, was characterized by the greatness of its kings, which was displayed in the wisdom of their home rule, and by their extensive conquests of foreign countries. The monuments and papyri give a comparatively full and clear account of this period, B. C. 2466 to 2266, and the beauty of the buildings and statues belonging to it show that Art received that intelligent patronage which insures its advance.

However, the first of these Theban kings, Amenemhat I., had much trouble in fixing himself securely upon the throne. He wrote a letter of instructions for his son and successor, Usurtasen I., in which he recounts the conspiracies which surrounded him; these were carried so far that those who sought his life even entered his bed-chamber at night.

The conquests of Amenemhat I. are attested by

GREAT HALL AT KARNAK.

various hieroglyphic inscriptions, all bearing witness to his success as a warrior. He was also zealous for the honor and worship of the gods, and founded the temple of Amon at Thebes, besides doing many works for the benefit of Memphis and cities of his kingdom.

An account also remains of the pyramid which he built, and the sarcophagus which he provided for himself. This last was made of a stone cut in the mountain of Rohannu, in the Wady Hammamat, which was so large that "never the like had been provided since the time of the god Ra."

During the last ten years of the life of Amenemhat I., his son, Usurtasen I., was associated with the old king in the government, and during the reign of the son, the kingdom regained its traditional order.

The works of Usurtasen I., which now exist, prove him to have been a mighty ruler. He secured the support of the priests by his zeal in paying honor to the gods, especially in erecting temples for them.

A very important one was that of Heliopolis or On, the city of the worship of the Sun-god, Atum, or Tum, and his wife Hathor-Jusas. This god was a local form of the great god Ra.

At Berlin there is a parchment which was brought from Thebes by M. Brugsch-Bey in 1858, which gives an account of the convocation of the officials of his court by Usurtasen, in the third year of his reign, for the purpose of a solemn consultation concerning the erection of a temple to the honor of the Sun-god. The king first addressed the assembly and expressed his wish to do this great work; he received the approbation and encouragement of his advisers, and immediately proceeded to appoint an overseer of the projected buildings, and to superintend in person the ceremonial of laying the foundations.

The inscriptions upon the Egyptian monuments

ATUM.

which set forth the praises of the kings, seem, in the present time, to be childish, unimportant and flattering to fulsomeness. The great obelisk of Usurtasen I., which stood in the grand entrance to the temple of the sun at On, bore the following words, four times repeated: —

"The Hor of the Sun.
The life for those who are born.
The king of the upper and lower land.
Cheper-ka-ra.*
the lord of the double crown,
the life for those who are born,
the son of the Sun-god Ra,
Usurtasen,
the friend of the spirits of On,
ever living
the golden Hor
the life for those who are born
the good God
Cheper-ka-ra,
has executed this work
in the beginning of the thirty years circle
he the dispenser of life for evermore."

These inscriptions are cut artistically in the red granite, and beside them no other information is given except the date of the erection of the monuments. Other obelisks in various localities bore the same praises of this king, who not only continued the work of his father upon the temple of Apetu, generally called that of Karnak, but he exceeded his predecessors by establishing a particular dwelling place for the so-called "seer of Amon," or the principal holy servant of that god.

The inscriptions in one of the tombs at Beni-Hassan praise Usurtasen as a warrior. These

---

* Cheper-ka-ra was one of the names given this king.

grotto tombs are hewn from the solid rock and are situated about a mile from the Nile, opening towards the West. The sculptures and paintings

CANAANITISH IMMIGRATION INTO EGYPT.
(From the tombs of Beni Hassan.)

here are remarkable and portray in a striking manner the occupations and amusements of the people, as well as their punishments, the collection of the revenues, and many other things.

From these tombs we learn that the manufactures of glass and linen, cabinet work, gold ornaments and other artistic objects were practised by the Egyptians of that day. Games now in use are there represented, such as ball, *mora* and draughts, and the animals, birds, and fishes of Egypt are all reproduced in pictures.

The grand and chaste architecture of these tombs is very noticeable, and the columns are especially to be praised. It seems that the Doric column must have been of Egyptian origin, and the pictures at Beni-Hassan, of buildings with arches, show that the arch is of very ancient date, for, although these decorative works were undoubtedly executed at different periods, yet the latest of them are very old.

The history of Ameni, an important official under Usurtasen I., is recorded upon two columns at the entrance of one of these tombs. After the manner of the ancients, he is represented as speaking to whoever reads the record; he goes on to recount his labors, which included a part in all warlike expeditions; the safe conduct to the king of all the booty; the superintendence of all the works for the palace of the king and other important services. Finally, he takes to himself the praise of having averted a famine, by his wise foresight in commanding the ploughing and planting of all available lands, and by his own provision of food for the poor.

The account of this great man is long, and continually interrupted by ascriptions to the king.

The chief information given in the story of Ameni is that which concerns the conquests in the land of Kush, which was to the south, and probably extended to Wady Halfa, where an ancient column of victory was erected.

Usurtasen I. was also energetic in profiting by the resources of his empire. In the caves and mountains of Sinai his colonists delved for turquoise and copper; in Nubia they sought for gold; he erected buildings in Tanis and at Abydos, and, in short, made his reign a proud period in Egyptian history, which still stands out in bright relief from the darkness and uncertainty which half conceals

BLACK SLAVES WITH THEIR FAMILIES.

many of his predecessors on the throne of the Pharaohs.

The successor of Usurtasen I. was Amenemhat II., and all that is told of him in hieroglyphics may be summed up by saying, that he well protected the interests of his kingdom, and fortified and strengthened the borders of the newly acquired

ANCIENT EGYPTIAN TURQUOISE MINES IN WADY MAGHARA.

territories. He carried on with energy the search for gold in Nubia, and restored many monuments which had been destroyed in the struggles for the establishment of this dynasty.

When Amenemhat II. had reigned twenty-nine years, he associated with himself his son, known as Usurtasen II., to whom the kingdom was left six years later, when the old king died.

The records concerning the reign of Usurtasen II. are disjointed scraps that only serve to show that the country was in a most prosperous condition, and all other inscriptions are unimportant when compared with that in the tomb of Khnumhotep at Beni-Hassan.

This tomb is of almost unequalled interest from its rich paintings, which not only show the manners and customs of ancient Egypt, as has before been mentioned in connection with all the rock-hewn tombs of this locality, but in this especial tomb, a historical representation enhances its value. It exhibits a Semitic family, consisting of thirty-seven members, who, in the reign of Usurtasen II., came into Egypt, and are shown as they presented themselves before the governor, Khnumhotep, to beg for a friendly reception in their adopted country. The strangers offer gifts; the whole train of loaded asses is seen, a few men making music, and doubtless singing praises of the king; and the texts explain that a part of their offerings consisted of the much valued paint of Midian, which was used for coloring the eyebrows and eyelids. This substance formed an important article in the traffic between the Shasu (or Arabs) and the Egyptians.

Upon the border of the hall of sacrifice of this magnificent tomb, there is a long inscription, in which Khnumhotep recounts many interesting facts concerning himself and the times through which he lived. From this it appears that beautiful towns then stood where now such desolation reigns; canals then gave a generous supply of water, which is now so scantily furnished by the shadoof; splendid temples, magnificent tombs and monuments were surrounded by a rich and industrious people, devoutly religious and proud of their flourishing grandeur.

Another text here gives a series of feasts, which shows by its arrangements of months and days that the Egyptians, 4380 years ago, had a knowledge of four different forms of years; what their calendrical relations were has not yet been explained.

The next sovereign was the famous King Usurtasen III. Under his reign all the conquests of

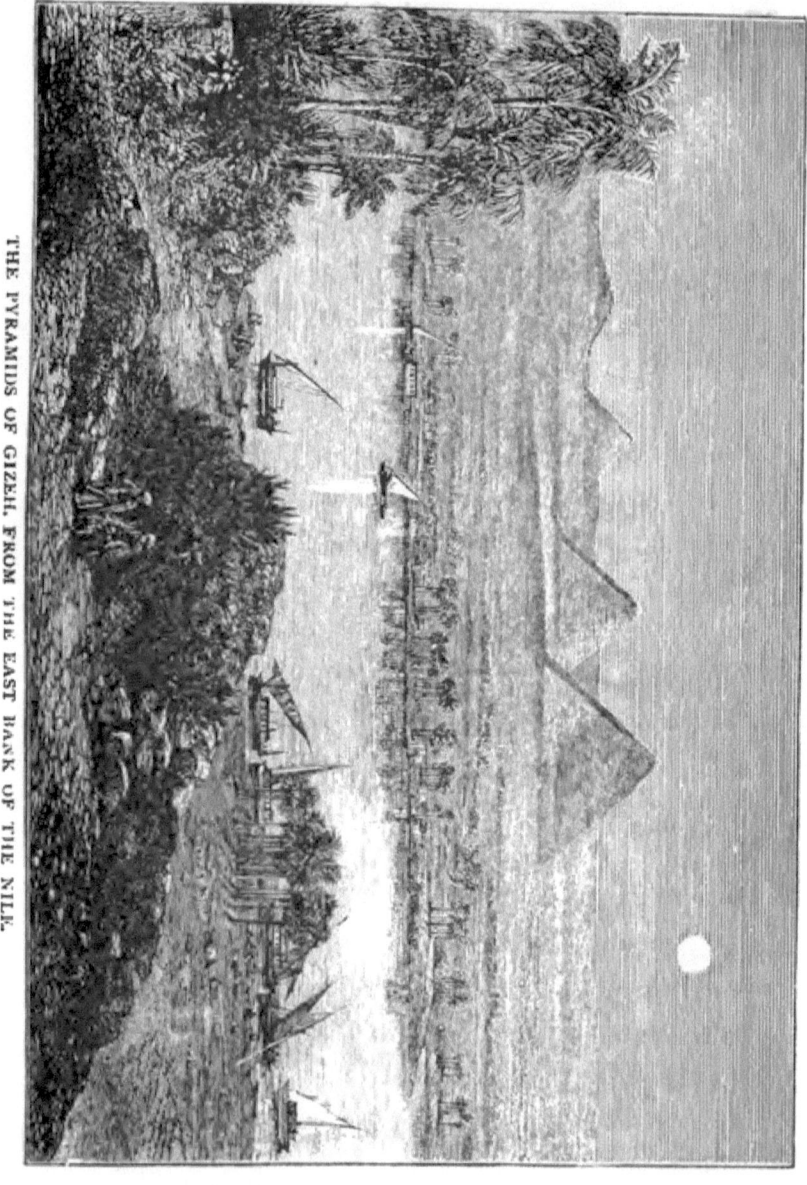

THE PYRAMIDS OF GIZEH, FROM THE EAST BANK OF THE NILE.

his predecessors were confirmed, and his boundary lines were carried as far south as the second cataract of the Nile, close below which he built fortresses, which commanded the country on both sides of the river. He also set up large boundary stones, as a reminder to the people he had conquered of his power and of the penalties they would incur if disobedient to him. One of these texts reads thus: "This is the frontier of the South, which was fixed in the year 8, in the reign of his majesty, King Usurtasen III., who gives life eternally. Let it not be permitted to any negro to cross it on his journey, except barks loaded with all kinds of cattle, oxen, goats, and asses belonging to the negroes, and except the negro who comes to barter in the land of Aken. To these, on the contrary, everything good shall be given. But otherwise let it not be permitted to a vessel belonging to negroes to enter on its road the country of Heh."

The wars of Usurtasen III. were cruel to the last degree; the women of the conquered tribes were enslaved, the crops burned, the cattle driven off, and the men killed. This story is confirmed by the pictures on the columns of victory of the sixteenth year of the reign of this king.

His successes so commended Usurtasen III. to the hearts of his countrymen, that he was honored with divine worship; sacrifices were offered to him and temples dedicated to his name and memory. Even Thutmes III., who is famed as the true Alexander of Egyptian history, fifteen centuries later than the time of Usurtasen III., dedicated a temple and standing altars to the memory of this warrior-king, and thus, as the text says, " caused to live again, monumentally, the memory of his glorious ancestor."

Amenemhat III., the succeeding king, rested his claim to the remembrance and gratitude of posterity upon another order of achievements. He it was who made that Lake Mœris, the benefits of which have furnished an inexhaustible theme for the ancient writers. During this reign so much attention was paid to the rise and fall of the Nile, and to its regulation, that now, after 4300 years have passed, we know what was the average height of the water, and what its greatest rise.

The enormous work of digging Lake Mœris is fully shown by a papyrus now in the Museum at Boulak, which gives a plan of the basin and its canal. This document gives much information and is of inestimable value.

EGYPTIAN CAR AND HORSES.

Other works attributed to Amenemhat III. are, the building of a fine pyramid, a wonderful labyrinth, and other astonishing labors of which the "speaking stones" say nothing, probably because

HARPER IN TOMB AT THEBES.

all these vast improvements were made in a province where the god Sebek was worshipped. The crocodile was sacred to this god, who was an abomination to the worshippers of Osiris, because he was a form of Set, or the Satan of Egyptian Mythology. Herodotus says in his account of the above-mentioned labyrinth, that it contained twelve covered courts, and three thousand halls and chambers, of which half were above, and half below, the surface of the soil in which it was built. Pliny says that some of the courts were made of Parian marble, and the columns of the red Syenite granite.

Some blocks of stone remain which furnish, by the remnants of their inscriptions, the only known relics of this great structure.

The last sovereigns of the twelfth dynasty were Amenemhat IV. and his sister, Queen Sebeknofrura, of whom the inscriptions say almost nothing.

CHAPTER III.

THE TIME OF THE HYKSOS KINGS AND A PORTION OF THE EIGHTEENTH DYNASTY.

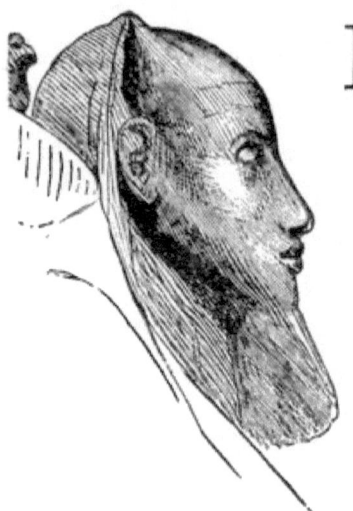

BUST OF CHEPHREN IN THE MUSEUM AT BOOLAC.

DURING the five centuries which succeeded the twelfth dynasty, the history of Egypt is shrouded in doubt and darkness. No perfect list of the rulers of that period is known to exist, and but few and scattering references are found in the hieroglyphic writings, to aid in clearing away the mists of the ages which have settled heavily down upon this epoch.

There are good reasons for believing that during

the thirteenth dynasty, civil dissensions arose in Egypt, and weakened that strong power which its previous unity had built up. At length the country became the prey of foreigners, and the sovereigns are known as the Hyksos or Shepherd Kings.

The theories and speculations concerning these strange rulers over Egypt are of great interest, but the size of this volume forbids an enumeration of them, and, were it not that the time of Joseph is believed to have been that of the close of this doubtful period, the Hyksos kings would be passed over here with a mere mention. Their monuments are found at Tanis, the Zoan of Scripture, and the pictures there represent them as of an Asiatic type, differing essentially from the Egyptians in features and characteristics.

It is certain that from the end of the twelfth dynasty the worship of Sebek or Set increased until he became the chief god of that time. To his other names that of Nub, or "the golden," was added, and his temples were at Zoan and Avaris, where were also many other monuments in his honor, especially Sphinxes made from the Syenite granite. The god Set is called the Son of the goddess Nut (Rhea).

As has been mentioned, he was thought to be the origin of all evil, both in the seen and unseen worlds. His name and likeness are found upon monuments as early as in the sixth dynasty, and his legend says that after the death of Osiris, Set and Horus (Apollo) were engaged in a contest which endured for three days and three nights, when these gods changed themselves into animals, probably lions. Set was overpowered, and all his companions were changed into beasts. Horus stabbed Set in the heart, and tore away a part of his organs. Set injured the eye of Horus.

One of the names of this god, given him by the Hyksos, was Sutekh or Sut. After his worship was once established he was the type of Northern, as Horus was that of Southern Egypt. The name Set may be translated by " limestone " and " fire." He is represented as a man, a lion, a hippopotamus, a boar and a serpent, all of which forms he is said to have assumed during the war of the gods. When represented as a man he frequently has the head of a crocodile, that animal being sacred to him, and worshipped with special honors at Coptos, Ombos, and Athribis or Crocodilopolis in the Thebaïd. In other parts of Egypt, as has been said, the crocodile was abhorred, and on a particular day, a solemn hunt of them took place; large numbers of them were thus killed, and were presented as sacrifices to the gods.

Opposite Manfalout, innumerable mummied crocodiles are found in mummy pits, which proves that another Crocodilopolis existed near that spot. Elian relates that where they were worshipped, their numbers so increased that great danger attended those who walked near the river, or attempted to bathe, or to draw water for any purpose. M. Brugsch-Bey has made the following formula of what he considers the present result of the search for facts concerning the Hyksos:

"1. A certain number of non-Egyptian kings of foreign origin, belonging to the nation of the Menti, ruled for a long time in the eastern portion of the Delta.

"2. The foreign princes had, besides the town Zoan, chosen as the capital of their power the typhonic place Hauar-Auaris, on the east side of the Plusiac arm of the Nile, within what was called later the Sethroite nome, and had provided it with strong fortifications.

"3. The foreigners had, besides the customs and manners, adopted the official language and the holy writing of the Egyptians. The whole arrange-

CROCODILES ON THE UPPER NILE.

ment of their court was formed on the Egyptian model.

"4. These same foreign kings were patrons of art. Egyptian artists made, according to the old pattern and according to the prescribed usage of their forefathers, the monuments in honor of the foreign tyrants; yet, in the statues of them, they were obliged to give way with regard to the expression of the foreign countenances, the peculiar arrangement of the beard, and the head-dress and other deviations of foreign costume.

"5. These foreign kings honored, as the supreme god of their newly-acquired country, the son of the heavenly goddess Nut, the god Set or Sutekh, with the additional name Nub, "gold," or "the golden," according to the Egyptian mode of viewing things, the origin of all that is bad and perverse in the seen and unseen world; the opponent of what is good, and the enemy of light. In the towns of Zoan and Auaris the foreigners had constructed to the honor of this god splendid temples and other monuments, especially Sphinxes, constructed of stone from Syene.

"6. In all probability one of the foreign lords was the originator of the new era, which most likely began with the first year of his reign. Up to the reign of the second Ramses, four hundred full years had elapsed of this reckoning, which was acknowledged by the Egyptians.

"7. The Egyptians were indebted to the stay of the foreigners, and to their social intercourse with them, for much useful knowledge. Especially the horizon of their artistic views was enlarged, and new forms and shapes were introduced into Egyptian art, the Semitic origin of which is obvious from a single glance at their productions. The winged Sphinx may be reckoned as a notable example of this new direction of art introduced from abroad."

One important and primal reason to be given in explanation of the paucity of the inscriptions concerning the Hyksos, is found in the fact that the native kings, who followed these foreigners, carefully endeavored to obliterate all traces of the hated interlopers, and destroyed the monuments they had erected, or so defaced the inscriptions upon them that they are almost indistinguishable.

Many accumulated reasons might be given for believing that Joseph lived during the last years of the reign of the Hyksos, but want of space allows but two of the most important ones to be noted here. First, by assuming that this was the time of Joseph, the dates which are now generally accepted as those of the emigration of Jacob into Egypt, and of the Exodus of the children of Israel will be in accordance with the Scriptures as found in Exodus xii : 40, and Genesis xv : 13.

Again, the inscriptions in the tomb of one Baba, at El-Kab, speak of a famine lasting many years, which is believed to be the same famine with that of Joseph's time. We again quote M. Brugsch-Bey : " The simple words of the Biblical account and the inscription in the tomb of Baba are too clear and convincing to leave any room for reproach on the ground of possible error. The account in Holy Scripture of the elevation of Joseph under one of the Hyksos kings, of his life at their court, of the reception of his father and brothers in Egypt, with all their belongings, is in complete accordance with the manners and customs, as also with the place and time."

There is an intense fascination in the study of the widely differing theories and speculations regarding these five mystic centuries, but so much well-attested fact is now at command concerning Egyptian history, that mere surmises should have no place beside it.

As the time of the Hyksos passes away, the monuments again take up the broken thread of their story, and a clear light is thrown on the succeeding reigns, commencing with that of Aahmes or Amosis, the first sovereign of the eighteenth

THOTH.

dynasty, who came to the throne about B. C. 1700. This king was not a Theban; his name signifies "Child of the Moon;" that of his mother, Aahhotep, "the moonly," and that of their descendant Thut-mes, "the child of Thut."

The god Thut or Thoth corresponded to the classic Hermes, and represented the moon as Ra did the sun; he was lord of the arts, and of the sciences of writing, and was invoked by the scribes; he presided over literature, and revealed knowledge to men; all inspired writings were attributed to him and said to be written by his own hand.

The ibis was sacred to Thoth, and he was represented with the head of that bird, one fable relating that under the form of the ibis this god had escaped the pursuit of Typho, or the evil one. Hermopolis was the chief city where Thoth was worshipped. Aahmes came to the throne when Egypt was much divided by internal dissensions, and though his first act was, by a short and decisive struggle to overcome Avaris and drive the foreigners as far as Sheruban, a town of Canaan,* and to fortify his Eastern boundary against the return of his enemies in this direction, he was soon forced to turn his attention to the restoration of peace within his kingdom.

During the occupation of the Hyksos many minor kingdoms had arisen; that is to say, the descendants of the old rulers had established themselves in certain towns, such as El-Kab, Thebes, Khmun or Hermopolis, and Khinensee or Herakleopolis. With these petty rulers Aahmes made a treaty, which left them certain powers while they acknowledged him as their Pharaoh.

By this treaty the king was able to unite the

* Joshua xix.: 6.

forces of the whole country in the work of re-subduing the negroes, who, during the foreign dominion, had thrown off the Egyptian yoke, and returned to the independence which the kings of the twelfth dynasty had so arduously taken from them. After many struggles, Nubia was again reduced, and Aahmes was free to devote himself to the rebuilding of the temples, and other works which flourish only in times of peace. The inscriptions relate that "in the twenty-second year of the reign of King Aahmes, 'his Holiness' gave the order to open anew the rock-chambers, and there to cut out the best white stone of the hill country An, for the houses of the gods of endless years' duration, for the home of the divine Ptah in Memphis, for Amon, the gracious god in Thebes, and for all the other monuments which his Holiness carried out. The stone was drawn by bullocks, which were brought and given over to the foreign people of the Fenekh." These words are found upon the rock-tablets of the quarries of Toora and Maassara, not far distant from Cairo.

The architectural works undertaken by Aahmes were continued for many years by his successors. The texts show that the exact time occupied in the re-building of the magnificent temple of the Sun at Edfou, was one hundred and eighty years, three months, and fourteen days.

The queen of Aahmes was one of the most renowned of Egyptian queens. Her fame is perpetuated upon many monuments. She is called Nofert-ari-Aahmes, "the beautiful companion of Aahmes," and "wife of the god Amon," which means the chief priestess of that god. When represented as the ancestress and founder of the eighteenth dynasty, she is called "the daughter, sister, wife and mother of a king."

It appears that when Aahmes died his son and successor, Amenhotep I., or Amenophis, was so young that Queen Nofert-ari acted as regent until he was of proper age to assume his kingly duties. This sovereign was famous for his campaigns and his extension of his dominions on the southern and northern borders of his kingdom.

In a tomb at El-Kab, where a soldier of Amenhotep I. recounts his services under that king, the enmity of the Libyans, who became such formidable opponents of the Egyptians, is first mentioned.

Amenhotep I. carried on the building of the great temple at Thebes, and did other works of a similar sort, and so endeared himself to his people that divine honors were decreed to him after his death.

Thutmes or Thotmosis I. is also famed as a great warrior; he even led his armies to the banks of the Euphrates, and although in later times the people of these lands endeavored to obliterate all traces of the Egyptian conquerors, the name of Thutmes I. still stands upon the inscribed stones near the falls of Kerman, near Tombos, between the twentieth and nineteenth degrees of latitude, and in these inscriptions his praises as a conqueror are spoken. These speaking tablets attribute to this king the opening of lands " which had remained unknown to his forefathers, and which had never beheld the wearer of the double crown;" and at last it is declared that " the land, in its complete extent, lay at the feet of the king."

It is plain that the importance of these conquests could scarcely be exaggerated. From the south must come to Egypt the ivory, ebony, gold, gems, balsam, resin, rare animals and skins, which so enhanced the luxury of the court of the Pharaohs. From the south came also those slaves, who, as prisoners, in the gold-bearing valleys of Wawa, with untold pains, washed out the precious metal,

GROTTOES OF SILSILIS.

and endured their heavy toils under the relentless rule of Egyptian overseers and soldiers.

The traveller in the Egypt of to-day must invoke the aid of the spirit of the imagination, and under the spell of his wand must let the grand old temples stand boldly forth, surrounded by their luxuriant, waving palm-groves, through which avenues of sphinxes stretch far away, — let flourishing towns and villages crowd the valley, — let the royal Nile-ship with its sails of costly byssus pass onward over the majestic, sacred river, — let pyramids, obelisks, statues and splendid tombs stand forth near and far, — then only can he understand, in part, why the dusky people sang such hymns as that one reads to-day in the grotto of Silsilis:

> "Hail to thee! king of Egypt!
> Sun of the foreign peoples!
> Thy name is great
> In the land of Kush,
> Where thy war-cry resounded thro'
> The dwellings of men.
> Great is thy power
> Thou beneficent ruler.
> It puts to shame the peoples,
> The Pharaoh! Life, Salvation, health to him!
> He is a shining sun."

Silsilis is a very interesting spot. There much of the stone was cut for the building of Thebes.

"The hundred gated queen
Though fallen, grand; though desolate, serene;
The blood with awe runs coldly through our veins,
As we approach her far-spread, vast remains.
Forests of pillars crown old Nilus' side,
Obelisks to heaven high lift their sculptured pride;
Rows of dark sphinxes, sweeping far away,
Lead to proud fanes, and tombs august as they.
Colossal chiefs in granite sit around,
As wrapped in thought, or sunk in grief profound.
Titans or gods sure built these walls that stand
Defying years, and Ruin's wasting hand.
So vast, sublime the view, we almost deem,
We rove, spell-bound, through some fantastic dream,
Sweep through the halls that Typhon rears below,
And see, in yon dark Nile, hell's rivers flow.
E'en as we walk these fanes and ruined ways,
In musings lost, yet dazzled while we gaze,
The mighty Columns ranged in long array,
The Statues fresh as chiselled yesterday,
We scarce can think two thousand years have flown
Since in proud Thebes a Pharaoh's grandeur shone,
But in yon marble court or sphinx-lined street,
Some moving pageant half expect to meet,
See great Sesostris, come from distant war,
Kings linked in chains to drag his ivory car;
Or view that bright procession sweeping on
To meet at Memphis far-famed Solomon,
When, borne by Love, he crossed the Syrian wild,
To wed the royal Pharaoh's blooming child."

The excavations at Silsilis are described by Eliot Warburton thus: "Hollowed out of the rocks are squares as large as that of St. James, streets as large as Pall Mall, and lanes and alleys without number; in short, you have all the negative features of a town, if I may so speak, *i. e.*, if a town be considered as a *cameo*, these quarries are a vast *intaglio*."

But if the days of toil were many for the Egyptian people, there were also days of feasts, when the masses were intoxicated by pageants — when the king scattered gifts, and dazzled by his splendor, the people applauded him and were proud of the spectacle, seemingly forgetful that their slavish lives and labors produced the wealth which was thus displayed before them.

The people of Western Asia, lying on the east of Egypt, were the ancient, hereditary and hated enemies of the Egyptians, and after Thutmes I. had carried out his plans in the south and made his power felt in Nubia and Kush, he made preparations for that war upon Asia which endured more than five centuries, under successive kings, and was, with few exceptions, fortunate for the Egyptians.

The countries against which this great struggle was carried on are known in the Bible and in the classics as Palestine, Cœle-Syria and Syria; these being again divided into small kingdoms, each of which are usually called by the name of some fortified or capital city. In the inscriptions all these lands are known under the one name of Ruthen-

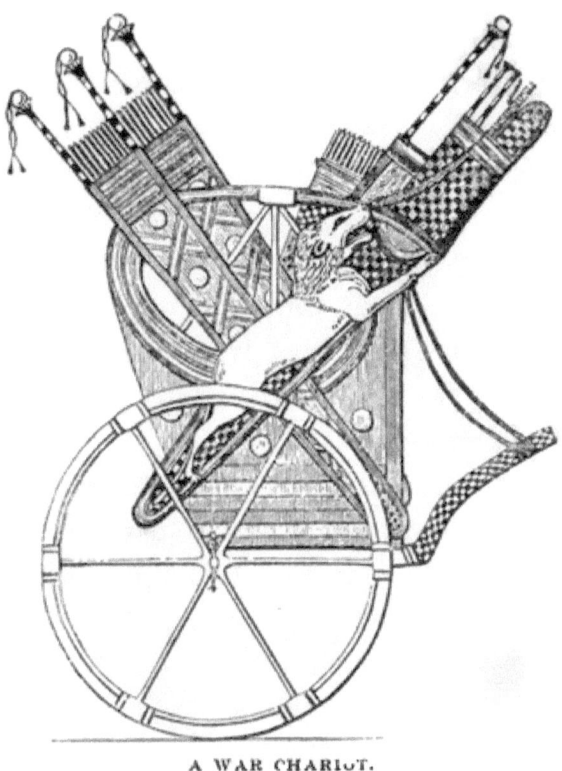

A WAR CHARIOT.

hir, which may be translated as Upper Ruthen or Luthen.

The texts frequently mention the land of Naharina or Naharain, and this is given as the bound to which Thutmes I. directed his efforts during his campaigns. There is little doubt that this was one with the "double-stream land," and was used for Mesopotamia, which lay between the Tigris and the Euphrates.

The inscriptions at El-Kab declare that Thutmes I. undertook this war " to wash his heart," that is, to be avenged for former injuries inflicted by the people of Naharain. He was victorious and took much booty, one important part of which was chariots and horses, which take their place in the battles of the Egyptians from this time. Many prisoners were also taken, and it may fairly be inferred that these men carried on in Egypt the arts of their own country which were hitherto unknown to the Egyptians, and thus the arts and trades of several nations were united. Again, this war inaugurated the system of commercial interchange among nations, which has proved of inestimable value to the whole world. "Trade and art went hand in hand. The descriptions of the chariots of war, which blazed with gold and silver, of weapons, from beautiful coats of mail to richly covered lances, of gold, silver, and brazen vases, of household furniture down to tent-poles and foot-stools, and of a thousand small objects, which appear as necessities to civilized men, allow us to cast a deep glance into the complete artistic skilfulness and into the direction of the taste of these early ages of history, and must ensure our deepest respect and admiration for the performances of the children of earth at that day." After the victorious return of the king, he erected at Thebes a tablet of victory, by the side of which Thutmes III., in his time, placed a second column. As an expression to the gods of his gratitude for their blessing upon his undertakings, Thutmes I. carried on with vigor the buildings at Thebes, and two granite obelisks before the western front of the temple of Karnak tell in their inscriptions of the piety and the power of this first king, who was called "Thut's child," to whom divine honors were paid after his death.

His successor, Thutmes II., ruled but a short time, and his reign was much disturbed by the jealousy of his sister, Hashop, who had been the favorite child of their father, and was allowed, before his death, to have some share in the government. The texts tell very little of Thutmes II. beyond the fact that he carried on two successful campaigns, and that with Queen Hashop he was much occupied in building at Thebes and at Medinet-Abu, and in the construction of the Tombs of the Kings.

After the death of Thutmes II. Hashop threw off her womanly attire, and clothing herself as a Pharaoh, she assumed the crown and all the royal insignia. Her brother, Thutmes III., was still so young that she was virtually sole monarch of

ANCIENT EGYPTIAN COAT OF MAIL.

Egypt. While she showed veneration for her father's name and memory, she used every power at her command to blot out the remembrance of her elder brother, and erased his name from many monuments.

Egyptian art reached a high point under Hashop, and the ruins of her works have a peculiar charm which bears witness to the excellence of her architect, Semnut. But the texts declare that she sought "to be a source of wonder to men, and a secret to the gods alone." As one means to this end she determined upon a voyage to the land of Punt, which, washed by the Indian Ocean, was the land of incense, ivory, and many precious things.

An entire history of this expedition, made in pictures and explained by texts, was put upon the eastern wall of the Stage Temple erected by this queen. Hashop was incited to this strange voyage by the oracle of Amon. Extensive preparations were made in the provision of ships, sailors, soldiers, ambassadors, and men of high degree, who attended on this august lady. Presents for the strangers she would visit were not forgotten, and all being ready, a prosperous voyage was made to the land of Punt, where the Egyptians disembarked, greatly to the surprise of the inhabitants of the country.

The pictures before mentioned represent the manners and customs which the Egyptians saw for the first time and the texts make many observations upon them; the amicable ceremonies, the exchange of gifts and the relations established, by which Hashop was accepted as the queen of this new land, are all clearly set forth, as well as the preparations for the return to Thebes.

Among the gifts which the queen brought home there were thirty-one incense trees, all packed in tubs and prepared for planting in Egyptian soil. May this not be considered the earliest essay in the culture of foreign plants?

The pictures forcibly portray the great labor of embarking all the treasures acquired by the queen, and the texts add that, " Laden was the cargo to the uttermost with all the wonderful products of the land of Punt, and with the different nut-woods of the divine land, and with heaps of the resin of incense, with fresh incense trees, with ebony, objects in ivory inlaid with much gold from the land of the Amoo, with sweet woods, Khesit-wood, with Ahem-incense, with holy resin, and paint for the eyes, with dog-headed apes, with long-tailed monkeys and grey-hounds, with leopard skins, and with natives of the country, together with their children. Never was the like brought to any queen (of Egypt) since the world stands." After the return to Thebes, all these riches were dedicated to the god Amon and grand festivals were instituted, at which the queen, the foreign princes whom she had brought with her, and the whole

Court appeared. The treasures were all weighed out by Hor, and a record made of them by Thut.

Soon after this, Hashop ordered another great ceremony to be observed, and on this occasion she dedicated the splendid Stage Temple, (that is built in stages connected with each other by flights of steps), at Der-el-bahri, to Amon and Hathor.

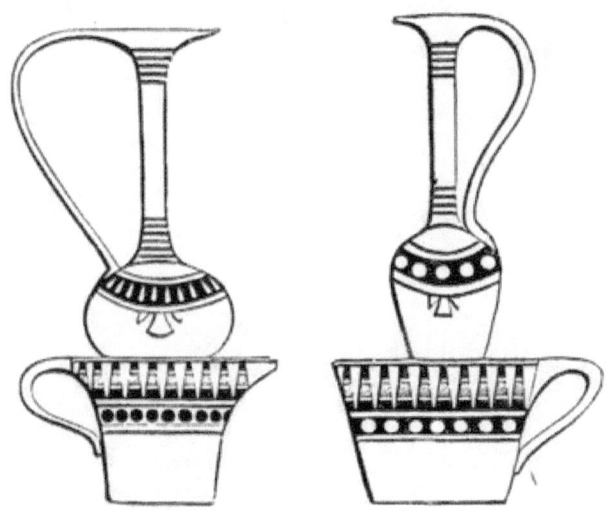

GOLDEN EWERS AND BASINS IN THE TOMB OF RAMESES III.

This festival was attended by numerous nobles and warriors who thronged to Thebes for this purpose, and everything conspired to make it a proud day for the vain queen, whose reign was peaceful and prosperous, undisturbed by dissensions or invasions.

During her entire reign Hashop had kept her younger brother, Thutmes III., quite out of sight. He was secluded in Buto without state or position, until having come to man's estate, he claimed his right to share the throne with his sister, whom he had hated for the part she had played towards him. His claim could not be set aside, and Thutmes III. was acknowledged king. From this time the texts are silent concerning Hashop.

CHAPTER IV.

THE REIGN OF THUTMES III., AND THE REMAINDER OF THE EIGHTEENTH DYNASTY, B. C., (ABOUT) 1600 TO 1400.

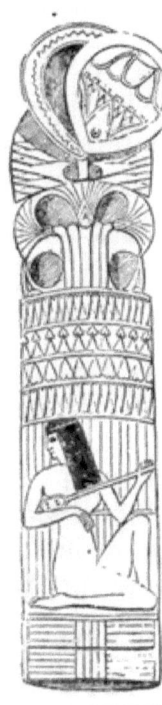

BOX IN BERLIN MUSEUM.

THE story of Thutmes III. or Men-kheper-ra, apparently cannot be told without exaggerated praise. As a warrior he was a marvel, and is well named the Alexander the Great of Egypt. He also did many wonderful works from which he gained artistic glory; he founded temples, and so increased the splendor and estimation of the service of the gods, that we scarcely wonder that he received divine honors while still alive, or that his name is seen at this day more frequently in Egypt than that of any other king.

He stood before his people as the personification of prosperity and good fortune, and his name was inscribed upon numberless small images, scarabei and amulets of all kinds, which were undoubtedly used as charms against the power of evil spirits and magicians.

If it be true that " the evil that men do lives after them," and that " the good is oft interred with their bones," then must this great king have been a perfect man. The sages of his nation and his time taught that the real life of a man is the remembrance of him when dead, and the character he bears with posterity; Thutmes III. must continue to live so long as great actions shall be respected and Art shall find appreciation.

The fourteen campaigns undertaken by this king within a space of twenty years gave him his first claim to reputation with the men of his own time. Under the reign of the vain Queen Hashop, the conquered peoples who paid tributes to Egypt had become restive, had left their dues unpaid, and some had even renounced their allegiance and declared themselves independent. About the same time the rule of the Arab kings in Babylon was established, and an entire change took place in the order of things from the river Euphrates to the Western Sea. Of all the peoples on that side who had been conquered by Thutmes I. only those of Gaza remained true to the Egyptians. Thutmes III. first turned his attention in this direction; he stormed city after city; crossed and re-crossed the rivers of hostile nations; led his troops to almost unequalled toils, and when victorious, returned to Egypt only to repeat the same labors in the subjugation of the revolted tribes on the south and west.

Full accounts of these wars were chiselled in beautiful characters into the walls surrounding the holy of holies in the temple of Amon, at Karnak. These inscriptions are now much injured; parts of them are scattered in the museums of various countries, but enough remains and has been carefully translated to afford a clear report of his campaigns, as well as of the booty captured, and the tributes paid later by the conquered peoples. These tributes included not only gold, silver, copper and precious stones, ivory, ebony, wheat and wine, etc., etc., but noble persons, and even kings' daughters, besides thousands of slaves or servants, which were sent into Egypt to appease the great conqueror and ease a little the burdens he imposed.

All the metals and other articles of tribute were

given over to the proper officials to be weighed, and estimated, and recorded in the books of accounts. The pictures which represent these weighers show that they used representations of animals in stone or metals, as weights are now employed.

The son of Thutmes III., called Nahi, was governor of the southern country of Upper and Lower Nubia, and received for the king all the taxes and tributes of these districts. In an inscription in the rock-temple of Ellesich he thus speaks : " I am a distinguished servant of my lord; I fill his house with gold and make joyful the countenance of the king by the productions of the lands of the south."

Before Thutmes considered the work of his campaigns completed he erected fortresses in order to protect what he had so hardly won — notably, that of **Men-kheper-ra U'af-shema**, which by translation reads, " Thutmes III., who has bound the land of the foreigners." This stronghold was in Phœnicia, at the foot of Lebanon, near the cities of Aradus and Simyra.

An idea of the extent of the conquests of this king may be formed from the fact that a single list gives the names of one hundred and nineteen towns which he conquered in the East, or Canaan; he sent living prisoners from all these places to

Thebes. The manner in which Thutmes III. carried on his wars was as follows: the towns he desired to have were summoned to surrender, and,

ASSAULT OF A FORT. THE TESTUDO AND SCALING-LADDER.

in case they obeyed, the inhabitants were well treated and only a moderate war-tax was imposed; but if a surrender was refused, an attack was made, and after conquest, heavy tributes were imposed. An obstinate resistance was punished by the destruction of the town and the crops, while all the treasures and many prisoners were borne away. It is difficult to appreciate, in this day, the effect which a triumphal return of the king had upon the old Egyptians. They were an excitable people, and gave themselves up to wild expressions of their emotions. The train of the conquering monarch was imposing to the last degree, embracing as it did, captive princes with their families, troops of horses, oxen, goats and many strange animals; splendid artistic works in ivory, gold, silver, and rare woods, and precious gems and many costly products of foreign skill and foreign soil. All these spectacles fixed the love and admiration of the people upon their young sovereign, and made them ready to aid him in realizing his grand desires for beautifying and enriching the cities of his own land.

His first care was to appoint, and celebrate with unequalled pomp, the feasts of victory. These were three in number, and each endured five days.

Of the sacrifices offered, the god Amon received the largest and richest share, and Thebes was the city most favored by the king, but other gods and other towns were not forgotten, and all these offerings amounted to a marvellous value.

It remains to consider this king as an architect or builder, and to review his mighty deeds in this wise, which are of more interest to the men of to-day than are the battles he fought. However could the temples have been built had the wars not occurred? for one of the great uses he made of his captives was to employ them as artisans and laborers, and thus add the glories of peace to his great fame. The following list gives the most important of his architectural works:

1. The Hall of the Pillars,* at Karnak, with the chambers and corridors belonging to it on the east, and the gigantic propylæ on the south. In this Hall of Pillars was placed that inscription known as the Table of the Kings. He also erected four obelisks and many statues at Karnak.

2. A Holy of Holies and a provision-house for the temple of Amon at Thebes.

3. Many gates and new doors of acacia-wood

---

* Square, not round as in the Hall of Columns of King Seti I.

PROPYLON AT KARNAK.

for the reconstruction of a temple at Thebes, which had fallen into ruin. No full account of this temple is now known to exist. Each one of its gates bore an inscribed name, such as, " Door of Thutmes III.; he exalted the greatness of Amon ;" or, " Gate of Thutmes III.; a great spirit is Amon."

4. Three statues in memory of his immediate ancestors; these were before the southern wings of the temple, and ruins of them are now seen.

5. An entirely new temple at Medinet-Abu.
6. Temple of Semne.
7. Temple of Kumne.
8. Temples at Ambos, El-Kab and Hermonthis.
9. Temple on Elephantine Island.
10. Also works at Abydos, Tentyra and Memphis, the exact extent of which cannot be told.

This list includes but a portion of his works, and it should be added that he richly endowed with splendid gifts the temples and the service of the gods in different parts of Egypt.

Upon the remnants of all these magnificent works many most instructive and interesting pictures and texts have been found, and, under the untiring labors of learned men, have been made available, to the great increase of the knowledge which formerly existed of these ancient times.

Among these are representations of the plants and natural curiosities which the Egyptians had

COLUMNS AND PART OF OBELISK AT KARNAK.

found in the lands they had visited. Water-lilies, cacti, fruits and flowers, melons and pomegranates, birds and animals, are all represented.

In one of the tombs of the hill Abd-el-qurnah

are preserved a series of pictures which the inscriptions beside them explain as representations of the captives whom Thutmes III. devoted to the building of the temple of Amon.

One of the overseers (Rois) thus speaks, " The stick is in my hand, be not idle."

Some of the workmen carry water in jugs; some

FOREIGN CAPTIVES MAKING BRICKS.

knead and cut up the earth; some shape the bricks with wooden forms, and lay them out to dry, while others are building the walls. The word-picture of Scripture * accords perfectly with the representations in this tomb.

* Exodus I. : 11, 13, 14, and Exodus v. : 12.

The numerous inscriptions belonging to the reign of Thutmes III. are most interesting to students of history. They are poetic and full in style; translations lose the delicate shades belonging to the original, but the following extract from an inscription on a granite tablet now in the Museum at Boulak, gives a good idea of the manner of the ancient writing :

"1. 'Come to me,' said Amon, 'and enjoy yourself, and admire my excellences.

"'Thou, my son, who honorest me, Thutmes the III., even living.'

"'I shine in the light of the morning sun through thy love.'

"2. And my heart is enraptured, if thou directest thy noble step to my Temple.

. . . .

"11. I make thy victories to go on through all nations; my royal serpent shines on thy forehead. And thy enemy is reduced to nothing as far as the horizon.

"They come and bring the tribute on their shoulders.

"And bow themselves.

"12. Before thy Holiness, for such is my will, I

make the rebellious ones fall down exhausted near thee.

"A burning fire in their hearts, and in their limbs a trembling," etc., etc.

Upon a stone found at Abydos, the king himself speaks. After recounting what he has done for the gods and their service, he continues thus:

"(I call upon) you, the holy fathers of this house, you priests and singers, you assistants and artists, as you are there, expend the gifts of sacrifice, with the tables of sacrifice (in your hand, lay) them down on the tables of the altars. Preserve well my memorial, honor my name, and remember my kingly dignity. Strengthen my name in the mouths of your servants, and let my remembrance remain preserved with your children, because I, the king, am a benefactor to those who are on my side, a severe lord against those who only remember my name in their speech. What I have done in this land, that remains in your knowledge. It does not appear a fable in your sight, and no man can dispute it. I have carved art-memorials to the gods, I have embellished their shrines that they may last to posterity, I have kept up their temples, I have taken care for that which was erected in former times.

"I teach the priests what is their duty; I turn away the ignorant man from his ignorance. I have done more service than all the other kings before me. The gods are full of delight at my time, and their temples celebrate feasts of joy. I have placed the boundaries of the land of Egypt at the horizon. I gave protection to those who were in trouble, and have punished the evil-doers. I placed Egypt at the head of all nations, because its inhabitants join with me in the worship of Amon."

These quotations give a hint of the richness of the monuments of this time, 1600 to 1565 B.C., which serve to fulfil the prophecy of this king that his "remembrance shall live in all times and to eternity." Another important way in which these words of his have been realized, is in the removal of the obelisks which he built. They have been taken to Alexandria, Constantinople, Rome and London.

Thutmes III. was succeeded by his son, Amenhotep II. In speaking of him, Brugsch-Bey says, "It is difficult and dangerous to be the son of a great father, for the good remains the enemy of the better, his own deeds vanish before the glory of the past, and the praise of men takes as the

REMAINS OF TEMPLE AT ABYDUS.

measure for the son the greatness of the father."

An eloquent American orator has said that "if the son is not much better than the father he is much worse, since the example which has preceded him should incite to still greater virtue."

But what could this son do to excel such a father?

Before the death of the old king, Amenhotep II. had shown himself to be a brave soldier, and had successfully conducted a campaign in the "red land," or the country between the Nile and the Red Sea. After the young king came to the throne he led his army against the eastern provinces, where, in Naharain, an insurrection had occurred and some of the subjugated towns had leagued together in order to throw off the Egyptian rule. The king put down the rebellion, and though he found no great booty in this field, which had already been stripped, he carried away seven kings, six of whom he hung on the walls of Thebes, and the seventh at Napata, in Nubia, as a warning to all his people of the fate which surely awaited those who attempted to free themselves from bondage.

Napata was the central point for the government of Nubia, and there Amenhotep II. added to the temples; he did other works at Amada and at

Kumne, but they were not remarkable for their beauty or for valuable inscriptions.

The next king, Thutmes IV., did not immortalize himself by grand inscriptions, and they say little more of him than that he made wars in Naharain, Libya and Nubia. He appears to have especially honored Hormaku; he cleared the sand away from the great Sphinx, and placed a memorial-stone before the breast of that old wonder. There is a legend of his having been commanded to do this work in a vision, but the chief interest of the tale is the fact, that more than three thousand years ago, this grim old monument was already covered up as it was when Lepsius and the Duc de Luynes, by dint of great labor and large expense, cleared away the desert sand and brought to the light of day the words of Thutmes IV. Again the ever moving sand has done its work, and again the tablet is hidden away.

The next king, Amenhotep III., was a glorious Pharaoh, of whom many stones recount brave deeds and devout acts. During his reign the broadest limits to which Egyptian rule had ever extended itself, were firmly maintained, and he even extended his kingdom on the south, or up the Nile, and "in the fifth year the king returned home. He had triumphed in this year, in his first campaign, over the miserable land of Kush. He placed his boundary wherever it pleased him. The king ordered that the remembrance of his victories should be preserved on this memorial stone. No other king has done the like, except him, the brave Pharaoh, who trusts in his strength, namely, Amenhotep III."

All this is from the memorial stone on the road from Syene to the enchanting island, Philæ. The names of six conquered nations follow, and on another stone at Semne, near the second cataract, there is the following catalogue of the prisoners whom the king captured in the land of Abeha:

Living negroes	150 heads.
Boys	110 "
Negresses	250 "
Old negroes	55 "
Their children	175 "
Total of living hands	740
Number of hands (cut off)	312
Total, with the living hands,	1052

The hands of the slain were carried home that all might see the number that were slaughtered

A statue of this king, which is now at Paris, bears on its footstool the names of thirteen peoples whom he subdued, and a tablet in Nubia adds still twelve others.

Under this king, Amenhotep III., the skilful architect, Amenhotep, son of Hapoo and the lady Atoo, flourished. He was so energetic as a workman and so faithful a servant, that to him the king erected a beautiful statue, much ornamented, and inscribed with high praises. This statue now enriches the Museum at Boulak. This great man is represented as himself speaking and enumerating the works which he had done. Among them all none are of greater interest now than the statues of Memnon, one of which was called the musical statue, and was said to hail the rising sun each morning.

Their height, as given by the architect in the hieroglyphics, was seventy English feet, and this accords with the actual measure of to-day, if 2.47 metres be allowed for the height of the head-dress, which is gone, and that is the exact height that a pshen crown should be.

These two statues are in a sitting posture, and represent king Amenhotep III. They now stand alone, for the temple which rose behind them is a

COLOSSI AT THEBES.

mass of ruins. These enormous figures were carved from single blocks of hard, red-brown sandstone, through which white quartz is mixed in small pieces. The execution shows a masterly control over this material, so hard, brittle and difficult to work. The statues are twenty-two feet apart, and that called the musical statue was partly thrown down by an earthquake, B.C. 27.

Many travellers, of all nations, have written their names upon these grim guardians of the desert, and many of the older ones declare that they heard the musical tones at the hour of the sun's rising. "The Quarterly Review" of February, 1831, and April 1875, have interesting articles explaining these sounds, by a theory that split or cracked stones, after cooling through the night, as soon as the sun again begins to heat them, emit a prolonged ringing or tinkling sound—" a peculiar, melancholy, singing tone."

The value of the legend of the musical Memnon is much lessened when it is known that it is of comparatively modern origin, and not a part of the antiquity to which the statue belongs.

This architect, Amenhotep, was a brave man. He came of noble stock, and his sayings were treasured and repeated as recently as the time of the

Ptolemies. He had not only to make these statues, but to move them from the quarries by boats, to land them, again to move them and fix them in their places. Even with all the power of steam, which now so well serves to move great weights, the achievements of this Amenhotep, the son of Hapoo, remain an inexplicable enigma.

These colossi and the temple near which they stood would have been works sufficient to satisfy the ambition of any sovereign but an Egyptian pharaoh. But Amenhotep III. also carried on the great national temple at Karnak to still fuller completeness, by raising an immense gateway before the western front, and erecting a new temple to the north, and still another to the south dedicated to the goddess Mut. He also built the temple of Luxor and united it to that of Karnak by an avenue of sphinxes in the form of rams *couchant* with the disk of the sun on their heads. The inscriptions declare that the temple of Luxor was erected at the end of a campaign when "the king had mounted his horse to reach the extremest boundaries of the negroes, and had scattered the people of Kush, and had laid waste their country," and also that the king himself "gave instructions

COLUMNS OF TEMPLE AT LUXOR.

and the directions, for he understood how to direct and guide the architects."

The sitting statues of Mut, when represented with a lion's head, are attributed mostly to this king and his time. Mut, or "the mother," was the second person of the great triad of gods of Thebes. She stood next to Amon and was of great importance. There is a doubt as to whether she was the same goddess as Buto, as some writers have said, but there is no doubt of her being (sometimes) the same as Sokhet, the wife of Ptah, and in this character the second person of the great triad of Memphis.

Other ruins at Elephantine, El-Kab, and various points in Nubia and the southern parts of his kingdom, bear witness in their inscriptions to the connection of Amenhotep III. with their creation or adornment. The records also prove that riches must have been showered upon him or he could not have bestowed them as lavishly as he did.

The great architect of this reign, the son of Hapoo, also built a temple on his own account, which was situated near the tombs of the women of the king's house, and was called the temple of Kak. A mandate of the king assured support to this temple and decreed that it should descend to the heirs of the noble architect for all time.

The marriage made by Amenhotep III. was not *en regle* for a Pharaoh. He took his wife from some race far removed from his own, and to this day her origin remains unexplained. She was of no royal family, but the daughter of a couple named Juao and Thuao. In his youth, this king was a great hunter, and the scarabei frequently relate how with his own hand, he speared two hundred and ten lions in the land of Naharain.

It would be a pretty story, if it should ever be told by the speaking stones, that he found his beloved in some danger, and having saved her by his goodly arm, made her his wife, that Queen Thi, to whom he was fondly attached, and who so often appears by his side. The results of this irregular marriage of Amenhotep III. were stupendous, for when his son Amenhotep IV. came to the throne, 1466 B.C., it appeared that he was not of the religion of his fathers, and indeed, so hated the great god Amon that he sent out his scribes with hammer and chisel to obliterate from the monuments the name of the great Amon-ra.

He changed his name and assumed that of Khuaten, or "the splendor of the sun's disk," and he called himself "a high priest of Hormakhu," and "a friend of the sun's disk."

The high priests of Amon and the people became so enraged at all this, that finally an open rebellion broke out, and the king determined to

Mut.

1. 'Mut, mistress of heaven.' 2. 'Mut, mistress of Asher.t.' 3. 'Mut-Uati.' 4. 'Mut, the soul mistress of Asher.' 5. 'Mut, pupil of the Sun, regent of the Earth.'

leave Thebes and to found a new capital, and there to institute his own religion and his own rule. He chose the place now called Tell-el-amarna, and there built a splendid temple to the sun-god Aten, upon a plan which in no wise followed that of the older temples. He made open courts with fire altars, and in many ways departed from the traditions of his fathers. The temple was surrounded by the houses of the royal family, until at length seven young princesses had their separate abodes, and an eighth was added for their aunt, a sister of their mother, Queen Nofer-it Thi.

In later days an attempt was made to utterly destroy this city, but the ruins prove that it was richly built and adorned with many beautiful monuments and sculptures.

His architect was one Bek, a grandson of the architect Hor-amoo, and a son of Men, who was a sculptor under the father of Khuaten. The gravestone of this Bek was sold at auction, not many years since, in the market-place of Cairo.

The inscriptions which preserve the prayers used in the service of the religion of King Khuaten are most interesting. These prayers appeal closely to Christians by their manifestation of a devout conception of a God. The following extract is a portion of one of these petitions:

"Beautiful is thy setting, thou Sun's disk of life, thou lord of lords and king of worlds. When thou unitest thyself with the heaven at thy setting, mortals rejoice before thy countenance, and give honor to him who has created them, and pray before him who has formed them, before the glance of thy son, who loves thee, King Khuaten. The whole land of Egypt and all peoples repeat all thy names at thy rising, to magnify thy rising in like manner as thy setting. Thou, O God, who in truth art the living one, standest before the two eyes. Thou art he which createst what never was, which formest everything, which art in all things; we also have come into being through the word of thy mouth."

The sculptures in the tomb of King Khuaten represent a happy, domestic life, in which the king, surrounded by his mother, his queen and their daughters, seems to be fully repaid by his peaceful happiness for any loss that could have resulted from his separation from the priests of Amon-ra.

This sovereign erected tablets, which still remain, as memorials of his love for his daughters; they were once destroyed by hostile Egyptians, but he replaced them with others which are now seen upon the living rock of the Libyan mountain, and in the valley to the south-east of Tell-el-amarna.

Other sculptures represent Khuaten as he presided over state ceremonies, arrayed in all the insignia of his rank and surrounded by such pomp as would impress the beholders with his power.

Khuaten had no son, and at his death the husband of his eldest daughter, one Sa'anekht, became king. His reign was very short, and he was succeeded by Tut-aukh-amon, the husband of the third daughter of King Khuaten. This king evidently threw off the worship of Aten. He returned to Thebes, and the priests consented to his rule, yet he never was considered as a legitimate sovereign. No blood of the Pharaohs ran in his veins, and all the pomp and circumstance with which he surrounded himself could never hide this fact, or blot it from the remembrance of his people.

One very remarkable souvenir of this Tut-aukh-amon remains in the tomb of Qurnah Murray. Here the king is represented on his throne, holding his court. Two governors of the South are present, and a negro queen, on a chariot drawn by oxen and surrounded by servants, comes to lay her rich gifts at the feet of her sovereign. The ruddy princes of the red land also bring their tributes and thus pray to the king: "Grant us freedom out of thy hand. Indescribable are thy victories, and no enemy appears in thy time. All lands rest in peace."

The representation of the gifts here presented to the king is calculated to impress upon the beholder the fact of the advanced state of the arts in that remote time. The art of ancient Phœnicia is of course admitted and fully appreciated, but the art of the negroes has scarcely been understood. The following extract from "Eygpt under the Pharaohs," by M. Brugsch-Bey, is of special interest. After speaking of the arts of the northern tributary tribes, he says, "If it may be allowed us, on the other hand, with equal certainty, to pass a judgment on the condition of culture and of handicraft in the lands of the negroes in the fifteenth century, B.C., from the colored representations of these sepulchral chambers, a knowledge of which was acquired to science from the Prussian expedition to Egypt under Lepsius, it becomes evident that here also—in spite of a peculiar direction of taste, which is seen, among other things, in furnishing the tips of the horns of the oxen with ornaments like the hands of men—a certain artistic spirit is observable in the composition and in the execution of the outward forms of the utensils. Passing over for a moment the costly golden vessels, set with precious stones, the manifold utensils of domestic life, the chariots, the ships, the weapons, and all the articles which the queen brings to Thebes, all these exhibit an unmistakable development of artistic power, which must without doubt be ascribed on the one hand to Egyptian influence, and on the other to the natural position of the so-called savage tribes, and to

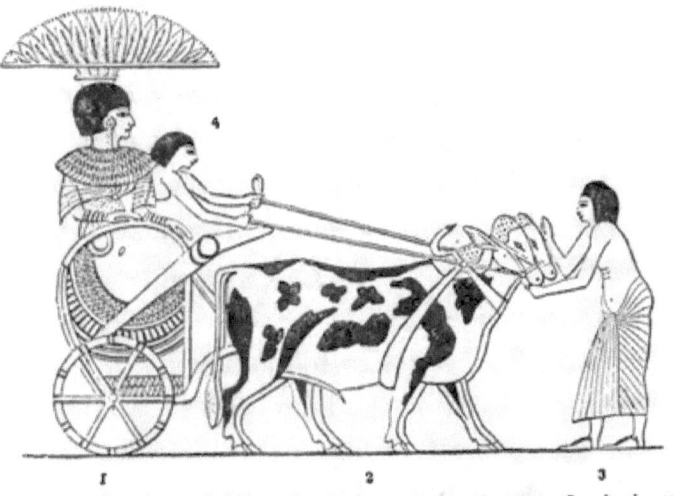

An Ethiopian princess travelling in a *plaustrum* or car drawn by oxen. Over her is a sort of umbrella. 3. An attendant. 4. The charioteer or driver. *Thebes.*

their powers of imitation. Even at this day, the prejudice that the negro is, both in taste and in art, an unprogressive son of Adam, can be refuted by hundreds of facts which prove the direct contrary in an incontrovertible manner in favor of our colored brethren. As representative of modern Egypt at the two universal exhibitions at

Vienna in 1873, and at Philadelphia in 1876, I had the much desired opportunity of exhibiting the most wonderful works in gold and silver, as examples of the finished artistic skill of the peoples of the Soodan, and of receiving prizes for black artists."

The reign of Tut-aukh-amon was not of great length and he was followed by " The Holy Father Ai." Whether he obtained the throne by force or cunning is not told, but he certainly had no claim to rule over Egypt as a king. He was the husband of the nurse who had suckled king Khuaten and he had served as " master of the horse" to that king. He had gradually been promoted to various high offices, and had been named " fan-bearer on the right hand of the king, and superintendent of the whole stud of Pharaoh." He was also a " scribe of justice," and must therefore have been learned in the law. There are texts which record the fact that he and his wife, "the high nurse and nourishing mother of the godlike one, the dresser of the king," had received great riches from the king, even to that degree that much gossip was the result ; these conversations remain in the hieroglyphics to this day.

Ai seems to have been fully accepted by the

priests or holy fathers, from whose number he had come forth. No farther mention is made of the "new teaching," and the old worship was fully restored. He was allowed to build his tomb among those of the kings, where to this day it remains, with his granite burial-case within. He carried on successful wars, and seems to have been a good king for the country. At his death, a great question arose as to who should succeed him. The choice fell upon Horemhib, called Horus by Manetho, the husband of Notem-mut, the sister-in-law of King Khuaten. This man was a devout servant of the god Horus, and dwelt in retirement at Ha-suten, near Tell-el-amarna. This city was the same with the Alabastronopolis of Ptolemy; on the monuments it is also called Ha-benu, the "Phœnix city," and Hipponon by the Greeks.

Horemhib had served as the first official of the court of his brother-in-law, and from his birth many remarkable circumstances attended him, all of which are set down in a document now preserved in the Museum at Turin. All the good fortune that came to him step by step; all the approbation of the gods for him, and many wonderful things are therein recounted, until all is crowned by his coronation in the temple at Thebes. The account then says, "There came forth from the palace the holiness of this splendid god Amon, the king of the gods, with his son before him, and he embraced his pleasant form, which was crowned

OSIRIS, ISIS, AND HORUS.

with the royal helmet, in order to deliver to him the golden protecting image of the sun's disk. The nine foreign nations now under his feet, the heaven was in festive disposition, the land was filled with ecstasy, and as for the divinities of

Egypt, their souls were full of pleasant feelings. Then the inhabitants, in high delight, raised towards heaven the song of praise; great and small lifted up their voices, and the whole land was moved with joy."

An inscription at Thebes, given in "Mariette's Karnak," also testifies to the good works of Horemhib in that city, and that he was a great warrior and personally bare arms in Soodan, is recorded in a temple which he built at Silsilis. He was the last king of the eighteenth dynasty.

CHAPTER V.

THE NINETEENTH AND TWENTIETH DYNASTIES.

BOTTLE OF BLUE GLASS.

RAMSES I., who succeeded King Horemhib, may have been the brother or the son-in-law of the last sovereign of the eighteenth dynasty, but the relationship cannot be traced. This Ramses is famous on account of being the founder of a dynasty, and as the father and grandfather of the famous kings, Seti I. and Ramses II. His reign was short, and no important account of him remains. He was succeeded by Seti I., B.C. 1366.

To speak of this king as a warrior of great

renown is to do him small justice, but to recount his campaigns would only afford a tiresome repetition of what has already been told in connection with older warlike kings. The theatre of his exploits embraced the east, west, and south of Egypt proper, and he carried his arms in all these directions as far as any Egyptian conqueror had previously gone, and returned laden with booty. He was received with shouts of praise, and celebrated the feasts of his victories in the orthodox Egyptian manner.

The texts give the following names of his conquests in the east, besides others not sufficiently distinct to be repeated:

1. Khita, the land of the Khita.
2. Naharain, the river-land.
3. Upper Ruthen, Canaan.
4. Lower Ruthen, Northern Syria.
5. Singar, the city and the land of Singara, the Sinear of Holy Scripture.
6. Unu, an unknown island or coast-land.
7. Kadesh, in the land of the Amorites.
8. Pa-bekh } both names require to be defined.
9. Kadnaf }
10. Asebi, the island of Cyprus.
11. Mannus, the city and land of Mallos.

12. Aguptha, the land of Cappadocia.

13. Balnu, Balaneæ, to the north of Aradus.

The following cities of Canaan were also conquered by King Seti I. :

Zithagael, Zor or Tyre, Inua'ne or Jamnia, Pa-Hir (Galilee?), and two cities of Judah of later times, called Bitha-'antha or Beth-anoth and Gartha-'anbu or Kiriath-eneb.

As a builder, Seti I. takes high rank, and much space would be requisite to a proper description of such works as the great Hall of Columns, at Karnak, and the tomb, now known as Belzoni's, which was that of Seti I. The temple of Osiris at Abydos, the Memnonium at old Qurnah, commenced by him, and other new temples and splendid additions to those which already existed at Memphis and Heliopolis, swell the number of his vast achievements. The Hall of Columns is three hundred and twenty-nine feet long by one hundred and seventy wide — originally there were one hundred and thirty-four columns, one hundred and fourteen of which were standing in 1868 when the writer visited Karnak. The columns are of enormous size, some of them being twelve feet in diameter, and sixty-six feet high without base or capital, which increase their height to ninety feet.

These columns are covered with paintings and sculptures, while the capitals represent the full-blown flowers and the buds of the papyrus plant.

The representations were doubtless intended by the king to show forth the greatness of the gods, and this they do, but the honor to the king himself is not to be ignored. He is represented as the familiar of the gods. He is seated among them, and even folded in their arms. He, the Pharaoh, is of colossal stature, while his subjects are dwarfs. He crushes his captives with one hand; in short, however much he desired to exalt the holy triad of Thebes he forgot not to say, "I am Pharaoh."

The tomb of Seti I. was not found by the Greeks, Romans or Arabs, and was only opened in 1817 by Belzoni, an Italian scholar and antiquarian, by whose name it is since known.

It is the finest tomb yet brought to light. It is entered by a staircase of twenty-four feet, which opens into a spacious passage, the walls of which are beautifully ornamented with sculptures and paintings.

From this passage a second staircase descends almost as much as the first, and leads to a hall from which a second hall opens. Beyond these are two still finer halls, a third staircase, two more pas-

THE HALL OF COLUMNS AT KARNAK.

sages, and a small chamber, and beyond all these the so-called great hall in which was found the alabaster sarcophagus of the king. This hall is about twenty-seven feet square, and beyond it are still other corridors and steps leading still farther into the mountain. In all, Belzoni's tomb is four hundred and five feet long with a descent of ninety-feet.

With the sarcophagus was buried a sacred bull,

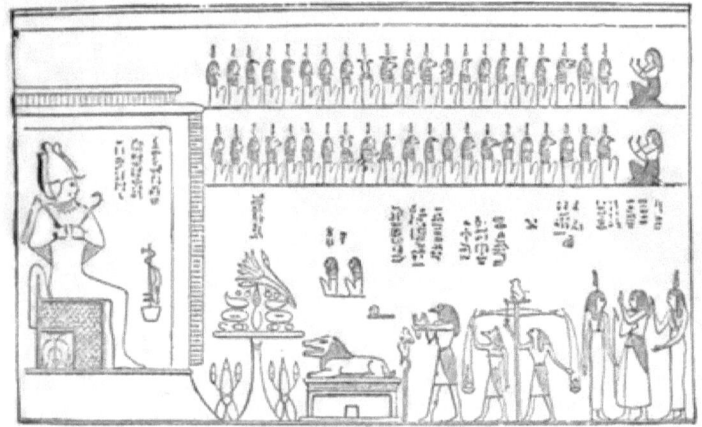

THE JUDGMENT HALL OF OSIRIS.

and hundreds of little images representing mummies were left about the sarcophagus by the mourners at the funeral.

The sarcophagus, as well as the walls of this tomb, are covered with representations of gods and men, and all possible or imaginary experiences which might attend the body in life or the soul after death, its trial before the gods, and many mysteries of the Egyptian faith.

Beside these religious representations, one sees illustrations of all the occupations and amusements of the people, kitchens in which all the operations of a good *cuisine* are going on, games of all kinds, boats and all belonging to them, armor and weapons, furniture richly ornamented and gilded, all the labors of the husbandman, long processions of captives, and culprits suffering punishment.

The colors of the pictures in this tomb are as fresh as when first used, and the richness of the decoration can scarcely be explained in words.

The Memnonium is one of the most celebrated works of Egyptian art. It is on the western plain of Thebes, about three miles from the river, and is in a comparatively good state of preservation. This seems to have been both a temple and a palace, and, like all such buildings, is adorned with many works of art. There was a library here, over the entrance of which was written "Medicine for the Mind." It is impossible to convey any accurate idea of the extent of these temples or the effect which they produce on the mind. The simple grandeur of their colossal halls and columns is indescribable, and wonder ever increases at the perfectness of what remains. There are no crumbling stones, no broken monoliths; some are fallen, and the columns or statues, which were made from several pieces, are separated but not broken. There are no fading colors, though the walls may

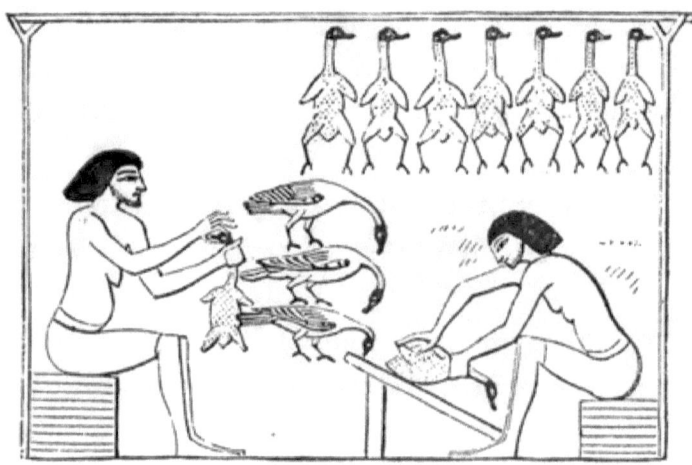

POULTERER'S SHOP.

be uncovered, and the pictures may have been exposed to all the atmospheric changes, and to the great heat of the sun for thousands of Egyptian summers. Seti I. dedicated this wonderful temple to his father, and before the magnificent entrance stood that famous statue which, according to Diodorus, was inscribed thus: "I am the king of kings, Osymandyas, if any one wishes to know how great I am and where I lie, let him surpass one of my works."

This statue, ruined as it is, excites a double wonder as to how it was made and put in place and how destroyed. It was sixty feet high and twenty-two feet across the shoulders; one toe is three feet in length. It is estimated to have weighed eight hundred and eighty-five tons, and was cut from a single block of stone, beautifully polished, and moved from the cataract of the Nile, a distance of about two hundred miles! As the son of Seti, Ramses II. was associated with his father before his death, and took care to carry out his father's designs after he was dead, it is not easy to know precisely where the work of the father left off. Much more might be written of the art of this period, but enough has been said to show how great an interest Seti I. had in it, and how well fitted the artists were to repay the patronage of such a king.

Another thing to which he gave particular attention was the development and working of the gold mines of the country, especially in Nubia. The king himself made a journey of inspection to the mines, and finding a scarcity of water he commanded a well to be bored deep into the rocky

COLOSSAL STATUE OF RAMESES THE GREAT.

ground. The inscriptions call down on him blessings for this work and declare that "Now can we travel up with ease, and reach the goal and remain living. The difficult road lies open before us and has become good. Now the gold can be carried up as the king and lord has seen. All the living generations, and those which shall be hereafter, will pray for an eternal remembrance for him."

King Seti I. did all in his power to propitiate the priests of Amon. Still he and his race worshipped foreign gods, especially the Canaanitish Baal-Sutekh or Set, from whom the king was named. His queen was also a descendant of Khuaten, which, though in accordance with the Egyptian laws of succession, was yet a hateful thing to the priests of the old Theban religion. It is allowable to believe that he distrusted their good will towards his son, since he associated him in the kingly office when he could have been but twelve years old, and many acts attributed to Seti were performed during this double reign, when the son was still too young to be recognized as having any influence upon affairs. The exact time of the death of the old king is not known. The ancients believed that his soul flew like a bird to heaven. It is a pleasant theory, to say the least, and who can dispute it? It was not found by Belzoni! But to speak seriously, he did not live to see the completion of his tomb, or the Memnonium, or of many other undertakings which he had inaugurated.

Ramses II. is known by several different names, and was the Sesostris of the Greek writers; the Sethosis and Ramesses of Manetho, and the Ses, Sestesu, Setesu and Sestura of the Egyptian records. He is also called Miamun I., and bears the title, A-nakhtu, or " The Conqueror."

He came to the throne as sole king about B.C. 1333, and so much is related concerning him in the remaining inscriptions that it is difficult to decide what should be chosen for a limited sketch of his career.

The first important act of his reign was the completion of the temple at Abydos, commenced by his father, Seti I. Upon one wall of this temple Ramses placed an inscription of great length, in which he addresses his father, and adds a reply which the dead king is supposed to make. The architectural works of the son are quite inferior to those of the father, and though they are many, his fame rests slightly upon them. It is as a statesman and soldier that he merits attention, and the

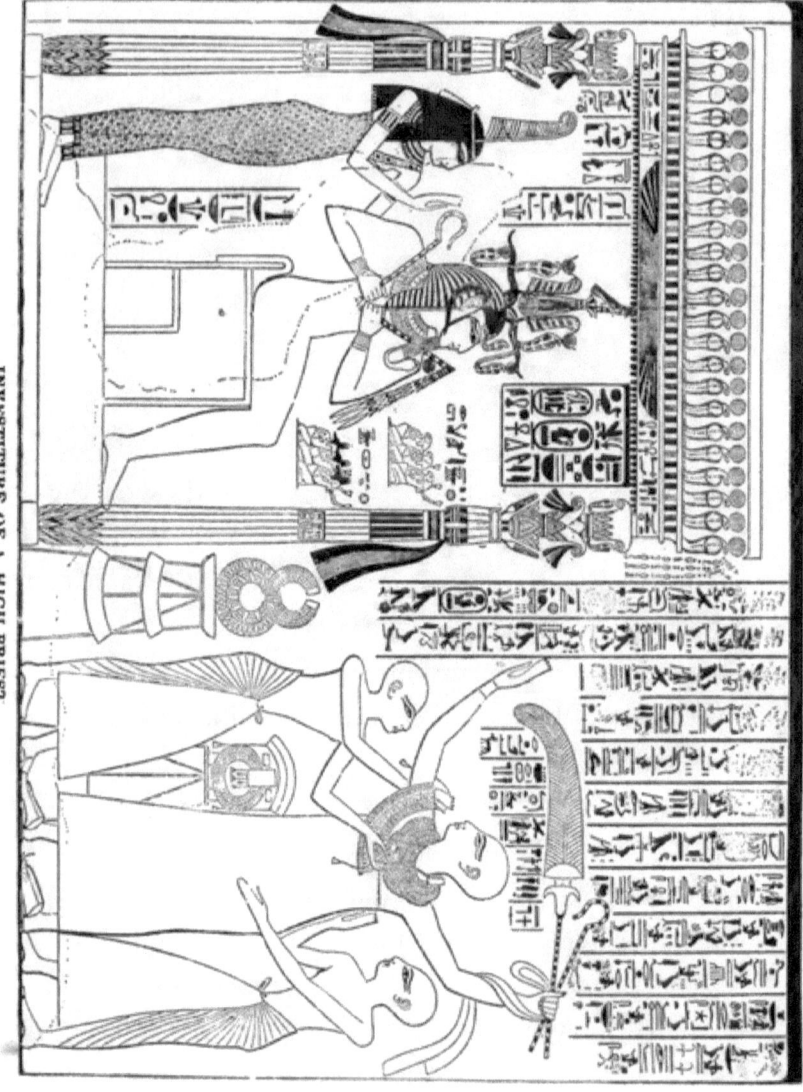

INVESTITURE OF A HIGH PRIEST

copious, boastful records which his vanity impelled him to make, now fulfil his desire to be made known through all times, to all nations.

It is not possible to speak of all the buildings of Ramses II., for their names are legion. The more important were the temple of Abydos, great additions to the temple of Ptah in Memphis, many works at Thebes, the completion of the Ramesseum, other works in different parts of Nubia, of which the great temple at Abu Simbel is the chief, and, more than all, the enormous labors which he caused to be executed at Zoan-Tanis, the city to which he removed his court, and where he founded a city within a city, called " the city of Ramses," and where he built up that place which from his time took on great importance. It was the city from which Moses led forth the children of Israel.

As a greater interest is connected with his works here than with those which more nearly follow the customs of his ancestors, the space we have will be given to them.

This city, situated on the eastern frontier of Egypt, was very important from its position on the Tanitic arm of the Nile, where it commanded the entrance of the two great roads to Palestine. Perceiving the advantages of this position, Ramses II.

established himself there, strengthened the fortresses, built a new temple-city within the old city, and instituted there the united worship of Amon, Ptah, Hormakhu, and Sutekh. He erected many statues and obelisks, and so glorified the city, called Pi-Ramessu, that it was henceforth the capital of the empire.

A description of it, given by an ancient Egyptian letter-writer says: " Nothing can compare with it on the Theban land and soil. . . . It is pleasant to live in. Its fields are full of good things, and life passes in constant plenty and abundance. Its canals are rich in fish, its lakes swarm with birds, its meadows are green with vegetables, there is no end of the lentils; melons with a taste like honey grow in the irrigated fields. Its barns are full of wheat and durra, and reach as high as heaven. Onions and sesame are in the enclosures, and the apple-tree blooms (?). The vine, the almond-tree, and the fig-tree grow in the gardens. Sweet is their wine for the inhabitants of Kemi. They mix it with honey. The red-fish is in the Lotus canal, the Borian-fish in the ponds. . . . The city-canal Pshenhor produces salt, the lake region of Pahir natron. Their sea-ships enter the harbor, plenty and abundance is perpetual in it

He rejoices who has settled there. My information is no jest. The common people, as well as the higher classes, say, 'Come hither! let us celebrate to him his heavenly and his earthly feasts.' The inhabitants of the reedy lake (Thufi) arrived with lilies, those of Pshenhor with papyrus flowers. Fruits from the nurseries, flowers from the gardens, birds from the ponds, are dedicated to him. Those who dwell near the sea, came with fish, and the inhabitants of their lakes honored him. The youths of the 'conqueror's city' were perpetually clad in festive attire. Fine oil was on their heads of fresh curled hair. They stood at their doors, their hands laden with branches and flowers from Pa-hathor, and with garlands from Pahir, on the day of the entry of king Ramessu-Miamun, the god of war Monthu upon earth, in the early morning of the monthly feast of Kihith. . . . All people were assembled, neighbor with neighbor, to bring forward their complaints. Delicious was the wine for the inhabitants of the 'conqueror's city.' Their cider was like . . . their sherbets were like almonds mixed with honey. There was beer from Kati (Galilee) in the harbor, wine in the gardens, fine oil at the lake Sagabi, garlands in the apple-orchards. The sweet song of women resounded to the tunes of Memphis. So they sat there with joyful heart, or walked about without ceasing. King Ramessu-Miamun, he was the god they celebrated."

Ramses is mentioned as a treasure city, Exodus, i.: 13, and it is believed that the Pharaoh who knew not Joseph, was none other than Ramses II., the Pharaoh of the oppression, and the father of that unnamed princess, who rescued the child Moses from his hiding place in the bulrushes.*

Because of these associations, the improvement of Zoan-Tanis is by far the most interesting to us of all the works of the great Sesostris.

Without entering upon any detailed account of the wars of Ramses II., such circumstances as are of the most use in elucidating the history of Egypt may be given.

In the early part of his reign a fierce war broke out between the Egyptians and the people of the Khita, which is to say, a land which was first in importance in the league of the cities of Western Asia, inhabited by a noble race, whose chivalry and superior character made them the peers of the

---

* The opinions on this point, as given by M. Brugsch-Bey, in his "Egypt under the Pharaohs," Chap. xiv., are well worth consideration.

Egyptians and an enemy which threatened to become a dominant race. It is most reasonable, from existing knowledge, to believe the people of the Khita to be the same with the Hittites of the Scriptures — that people so prominent from the time of Abraham down to the days of the captivity. The principal battle in the war against

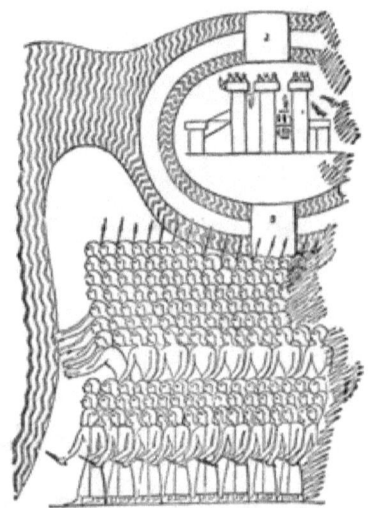

PHALANX OF THE KHITA.

the Khita, was that of Kadesh, on the bank of the Orontes. It was, in fact, a dreadful slaughter, and the courage of the Khita was so broken that they implored mercy from Ramses in the most abject manner.

At Abydos, Luxor, Karnak, and other places,

there are inscriptions which recount the story of this battle, and the pictures of it remind one of Pope's lines:

> "High on his car Sesostris struck my view,
> Whom sceptred slaves in golden harness drew;
> His hands a bow and pointed javelin hold;
> His giant limbs are arm'd in scales of gold,
> Between the statues obelisks were placed,
> And the learned walls with hieroglyphics graced."

A Homeric poem was written by the temple-scribe, Pentaur, which still exists, and is the oldest known heroic song in the world. It appears from all the testimony of those various writings, that the personal bravery and prowess of the king, on this occasion, is almost if not quite unequalled in history. We are told that, "when the king had halted, he sat down on the north-west of the town of Kadesh. He had come up with the hosts of Khita, being quite alone, no other was with him. There were thousands and hundreds of chariots round about him on all sides. He dashed them down in heaps of dead bodies before his horses. He killed all the kings of all the peoples who were allies of the (kings) of Khita, together with his princes and elders, his warriors and his horses. He threw them one upon another, head over heels, into the waters of the Orontes. There the king of Khita turned round, and raised up his hands to implore the divine benefactor."

The poem of Pentaur, which was first translated by Rougé and later by Brugsch-Bey, is such, even

RAMSES SLAYING CAPTIVES.

in a translation, that it commands the admiration of scholars now, as it must have done in the time of its author, when the appreciation of it was shown by its reproduction on the temple walls. How could a more flattering testimonial be made to any writer?

The tablets near Beyrout, well known to travellers of all ages and countries, prove that Sesostris must have extended his campaigns even to that point — and upon two occasions, separated by a space of three years' time.

Other successful campaigns, in the country later known as Galilee, the storming of Askalon, the subjection of cities in the "land of Kush," and other conquests in Libya, are all related in various well authenticated texts.

From the reading of inscriptions at Abu Simbel it is plain that this king carried on his wars by sea as well as land, though no detailed accounts of his naval engagements have yet been found.

After a time Ramses II. and the Khita made a treaty of offensive and defensive alliance, and became so important to each other in their joint opposition to the warlike tribes around them, that they confirmed their peaceful relations by the marriage of the great king with the daughter of the king of Khita. A memorial tablet was solemnly set up on this occasion in the temple of Abu Simbel (or Ibsambul) and the young queen was called Ur-maa Nofiru-ra.

Like his father, Ramses II. gave his attention to the greater developments of the gold mines of the kingdom; new wells were dug and all work connected with the mines vigorously pushed on, so that the slaves and prisoners employed as gold washers suffered pitiably under the Hir-pit or captain of the foreigners.

The extensive conquests of this king brought so many captives into Egypt that it is estimated that when they were added to the foreigners who were in the land before his reign, one-third of the entire population was not Egyptian. These captives were employed as seamen, soldiers, miners, builders, and so on, and were branded with the king's name, in order to guard against their escape, and to aid in their recapture in case of flight.

From this period, many Semitic words appear in the Egyptian language, which plainly shows the effect of so great a foreign element. In some respects the language gains in richness and fulness of expression, but when this mingling of tongues was freely indulged, it became offensive to good taste, and there exists a satirical letter, written about B. C. 1300, by a learned man to his pupil who had immoderately employed the foreign words and expressions.

Ramses II. had a long and prosperous reign — sixty-seven years in all, of which at least half must have been shared with his father. He had also a happy domestic life; three wives of his are named in the texts, Tsenofer, his favorite, Nofer-ari Mienmut, and the princess of Khita. He must also have had many concubines, since the list of his children on the temple of Abydos names fifty-nine sons and sixty daughters.

The tomb of Sesostris is so inartistic and unattractive as to merit no attention from travellers, and it is quite beyond explanation that so powerful an Egyptian king should have found so humble a burial-place. Mineptah II., the fourteenth in the list of the children of Sesostris came to the throne B. C. 1300. Under him no great wars or improvements were made, and the chief interest attached to him is, that he was the Pharaoh of the Exodus. In this connection we quote from "Egypt under the Pharaohs":—"If Ramses-Sesostris, the builder of the temple-city of the same name in the territory of Zoan-Tanis, must be regarded beyond all doubt as the Pharaoh under whom the Jewish legislator Moses first saw the light, so the chronological relations — having regard to the great age of the two contemporaries, Ramses II. and Moses — demand that Mineptah should in all probability be acknowledged as the

GREAT TEMPLE AT IPSAMBOUL.

Pharaoh of the Exodus. He also had his royal seat in the city of Ramses, and seems to have strengthened its fortifications. The Bible speaks of him only under the general name of PHARAOH, that is, under a true Egyptian title, which was becoming more and more frequent at the time now under our notice. PIR'-TO — 'great house, high gate' — is, according to the monuments, the designation of the land of Egypt for the time being. This does not of itself furnish a decisive argument. Only the incidental statement of the Psalmist, (Psalm lxxviii. 43), that Moses wrought his wonders in the field of Zoan, carries us back again to those sovereigns, Ramses II. and Mineptah, who were fond of holding their court in Zoan-Ramses.

.... the hope can scarcely be cherished that we shall ever find on the public monuments —rather let us say in some hidden roll of papyrus— the events, repeated in an Egyptian version, which relate to the Exodus of the Jews, and the destruction of Pharaoh in the Red Sea. For the record of these events was inseparably connected with the humiliating confession of a divine visitation, to which a patriotic writer at the court of Pharaoh would hardly have brought his mind.

Pre-supposing, then, that Mineptah is to be

regarded as the Pharaoh of the Exodus, this ruler must have had to endure serious disturbances of all kinds during his reign: — in the west, the Libyans; in the east, the Hebrews; and, let us at once add, in the south, a spirit of **rebellion,** which declared itself by the insurrection of a rival king of the family of the great Ramses-Sesostris. The events, which form the lamentable close of his rule over Egypt, are passed over by the monuments with perfect silence. The dumb *tumulus* covers the misfortune which was suffered."

In the review of the reign of Mineptah II. the literary element gains in importance, and many fine specimens of the Theban writings of this time yet remain; there are treatises upon theology, philosophy and history, as well as poems and stories.

The next king was called by two names, Seti II. and Mineptah III. He came to the throne B.C. 1266, and no records of his reign exist after the first two years, and in these no new thing worthy of note is recounted. His son, Setnakht-Merer-Miamun II., succeeded him in B. C. 1233, and but little is related of him in the remaining texts. He lived in troublous times and suffered from enemies in his own household as well as from those abroad.

In the end, he must have been conqueror, since

his son Ramses III. so declares in his record known as the "Great Harris Papyrus."

Ramses III. was the first sovereign of the twentieth dynasty, and bore exactly the same official titles as had belonged to the great Ramses II. He is therefore distinguished by the name Haq-on or "Prince of Heliopolis." The Egyptians called him Ramessu-pa-nuter, "the god Ramses," and the Greeks formed from this their title of Rhampsinitus.

Sufficient material for an account of his reign exists in the Harris Papyrus, given in his own words. He relates that the disturbances of previous reigns had so demoralized the caste distinctions that he was forced to set himself seriously to work to reform these abuses, from the caste of the councillors of the king down to the lowest caste of the common people.

Next he turned his attention to the enemies which surrounded him on all sides. In war he was successful, and added much to the resources of the country by the treasures of all sorts which he wrested from those whom he subdued. From a single victory he brought off twelve thousand five hundred and thirty-five hands and members, as a proof of the numbers slain — these were all counted out before the king.

The list of those whom he conquered was inscribed on his palace at Medinet Abu, and it includes seven kings, and many others of high rank.

Ramses III. also cultivated the arts of peace. He built "Ramessea" in at least ten Egyptian cities, and still others outside his own country, one being in the city of Canaan.

The finest ruins of the buildings of his time are those of Medinet Abu, upon which many valuable texts and pictures still remain.

Many temples erected by this Ramses were modest in their proportions, and the remains at Medinet Abu are the only ones which receive great attention from travellers in Egypt. The inscriptions here are of much importance, since they not only record matters connected with the king, but give lists of the feasts and other interesting facts.

The account of the riches which Ramses III. showered upon the temples indicates that the original "Aladdin's lamp" was his! It tells of gold in grains up to the weight of a thousand pounds, of bars of silver, of precious stones, including enormous quantities of the blue-stone of Tafrer, and the usual blue and green-stone of the

PALACE OF RAMESES III., MEDINET-ABOU.

country which was very valuable, and the real green-stone of Roshatha; of copper and lead ore in vast amounts, of all sorts of incense, and besides all these things in crude form, untold numbers of rings and other ornaments, vases, coffers, and images of precious substances.

Ramses III. also built a fleet of ships to be used in commerce with the land of Punt. He established, too, a caravan route for the merchants who passed and repassed from Egypt to the rich territories of the more distant East.

He sent out men to open up new copper mines, and much ore was brought back to him; he planted trees and shrubs in all the land to give shade to the people, and finally his kingdom was brought into the most prosperous and safe conditions of peace.

There also exists a full account of a wide-spread conspiracy in the Harem of this sovereign. In it many officers of his household were involved, while the excitement it occasioned was only allayed by the most solemn legal proceedings, followed by severe punishment of the guilty ones. The papyrus at Turin, which was first explained by Deveria, and called by him "Le Papyrus Judicaire," gives a detailed account of this affair. It is a most valuable document and throws much light upon the life of the women of that day, and shows the dangers from them to which the king was exposed.

The queen of Ramses III. was not an Egyptian. Upon the temple of victory, at Medinet Abu, are represented eighteen sons and fourteen daughters of this king — ten of the sons are called by their names, while the others are only represented by their portraits.

The eldest son, generally called Ramses IV., succeeded to the throne.

The only important circumstance of his reign, which is now known, is that he sent an expedition numbering eight thousand three hundred and sixty-five men into the valleys of Hammamat. The object of this enormous equipment was said to be the creation of monuments, none of which are now remaining. Nine hundred men died on the journey. The company embraced councillors of the king, the superintendents of the quarry and of the herds, the colonel of the war chariots, many scribes and superior officers of the courts, besides large numbers of soldiers and servants.

Ramses V. followed, of whose reign nothing can be said of importance. He was succeeded by the brothers Meritum and Ramses VI., who reigned conjointly. The tomb of Ramses VI. is very important, on account of the astronomical tables there inscribed, which are of great value to science. In no other way which commands attention has this sovereign been commemorated. His followers, **Ramses VII.** and **Ramses VIII.**, are also entirely unimportant when considered in connection with the monuments and writings of ancient Egypt.

Ramses IX., who came to the throne B. C. 1133, is the first king who is distinctly represented on the monuments as holding a position inferior to that of the priests of Amon-ra, who in later days exalted themselves to the throne. This king is pictured in the act of rewarding a priest who had done much for the honor of Amon-ra. The custom of the older time is here exactly reversed, for then the priests rewarded the king, by singing his praises and even paying him divine honors while he still lived.

During the reign of Ramses IX., a society of thieves was organized in Thebes, devoted to the opening and robbing of the tombs of the kings of the preceding dynasties. The tombs which thus suffered were those of the monarchs of the eleventh, thirteenth, seventeenth, and eighteenth dynasties. Several papyri exist which give accounts of the proceedings instituted for the detection of the offenders and of judicial matters relating to them.

Ramses X. and Ramses XI. may be passed with the bare mention of their names, while of Ramses XII., an unimportant, but curious story may be told. Ramses III. had built at Thebes a temple to the god Khonsu or "the preserver." This temple gradually became a sort of family shrine, and was, moreover, an oracle.

Ramses XII. had married a foreign princess of the land of Bakhatana, and a sister of the queen being ill, and suffering much, she was possessed by an evil spirit. The king, her father, then sent to Pharaoh, and begged that Khonsu might be sent into his country to exorcise this evil spirit, and thus cure the princess, the sister-in-law of **Ramses XII.** Consent was granted to this request and Khonsu was borne to a distant city, seventeen months being required for the journey.

When the princess was cured, the god was still retained in Bakhatana for some time, and then returned to Thebes, together with many rich gifts for his temple.

Ramses XIII. was the last king of the twentieth dynasty. A document, undoubtedly an autograph letter of this king's, is one of the riches of the Egyptian collection at Turin.

With the close of this dynasty the history of the priestly sovereigns begins.

CHRISTIAN SYMBOLS AT PHILÆ.

CHAPTER VI.

FROM THE TWENTY-FIRST DYNASTY TO THE CONQUEST BY ALEXANDER THE GREAT, B.C. 1100 TO 332.

DRESS OF THE KING.

THIS dynasty, which extended from 1100 to 966 B.C., was a time of much disturbance and great changes in Egypt.

The race of the Ramessids had been overthrown by the cunning of the chief-priest of Amon, who possessed himself of the throne and took the name of Siamon Hirhor. Besides being the chief priest of Thebes, he had been the chief fan-bearer, the chief architect, the chief general of the armies of the double country and the administrator of the granaries.

Naturally he had been in contact with people of all ranks and classes, and had improved his opportunities by attaching to his interest many powerful persons upon whose support he could rely, outside the priesthood, which he controlled under all circumstances. However, the well-laid plans of this cunning Hirhor were never fully carried out, for the new Assyrian power, which had replaced that of the Khita, was enlisted on the side of the Ramessids, who are believed to have been in exile in the Great Oasis. This fact laid great restraints upon the priest-king and positively lessened the extent of his kingdom since the Assyrians forbade him all control of the lands east of Egypt.

A descendant of the last Pharaoh, probably his great-grandson, and thus Ramses XVI., married a royal princess, a daughter of the Assyrian monarch, Pallasharnes. On account of this alliance the Assyrians marched into Egypt, and their attack, together with the dissensions which had arisen in favor of the exiled family, ended in displacing the priest-king, and placing an Assyrian monarch on the throne of Egypt.

This first Assyrian army which entered Egypt

was led by Nimrod, who was already king of Assyria, being associated with his father, Shashanq, who had married an Egyptian princess.

For this reason, when Nimrod died in Egypt, his mother had him buried at Abydos, and made a great provision of riches for the continual care and preservation of his tomb. In later years, when his father, Shashanq, visited this tomb he found that it had been neglected and the income belonging to it used for other purposes. The officials who had done this wrong were brought to justice and punished by death. The statue of Nimrod, formerly in his tomb at Abydos, is now in the Egyptian collection at Florence. It is headless, but the inscriptions upon it are sufficient for its identification.

An account of all the circumstances connected with the tomb of Nimrod exists upon a rock-tablet found at Abydos. It is of great interest, and a translation of it was first given to the world by Brugsch.*

After the death of Nimrod, his son Shashanq was made king of Egypt. He married the Princess Karamat, a descendant of the Ramessids, and thus

---

* "Egypt under the Pharaohs." Vol. II., p. 199.

EGYPTIAN PALM-GROVE.

the interests of the old and the new (the twenty-second) dynasties were united. On a wall of the temple at Karnak there is a long inscription concerning the restoration of this queen to her hereditary rights.

Shashanq, Sheshonk or Shishak made Bubastis his residence, and seldom visited the northern portion of his kingdom. The reign of this king was the most flourishing period in the history of this city, and Herodotus, in his time, declared that he had seen no more beautiful temple than that of the goddess Pasht or Diana, at Bubastis.

The reign of Shashanq is only remarkable for his war upon the kingdom of Judah. A full scripture account of this war is given in the first book of Kings, and another record of it is found in outline upon the temple of Amon, at Thebes.

When Jeroboam rebelled against Solomon, he fled to Egypt, and when, after the death of Solomon, a division arose in the Hebrew kingdom, one party adhered to Rehoboam, the son of Solomon, and the opposing party sent to Egypt, asking Jeroboam to return and be their leader. Thus it happened that Shashanq became an ally of Jeroboam, and made that famous expedition which ended in the taking of Jerusalem. The Egyptian pictures represent the king as colossal in size, dealing heavy blows with his club upon the Jewish captives. A list of the towns and districts conquered is given in hieroglyphics, as well as a speech addressed to the king by the great god, Amon. The Egyptian army engaged in the Judæan war was very large. The fabulous numbers of twelve hundred chariots and sixty thousand horses, with a grand army on foot, can scarcely be credited; but they achieved a great triumph, and bore home an enormous booty, including, it is said, the golden shields from the temple of Solomon.

Shashanq I. added to the temple of Karnak a hall, sometimes called that "of the Bubastids," because the names of several of his line are there inscribed. An account of the journey to Silsilis, in search of the stone used in the construction of this hall, is found in an inscription in that place, where, it is said that the king caused a new quarry to be opened.

From the time of Hir-hor it was the custom to make the eldest son of the king a priest of the Theban Amon. Shashanq I. conferred this office upon his son Auputh, and made him also commander-in-chief and general of his entire army. Auputh died before his father, and his younger brother ascended the throne under the name of Usarkon I. Nothing is known of his reign, and with him the importance of his line ended. The descendants of Shashanq became petty kings in various parts of a divided realm. Sometimes they were allies of the Assyrians — again they were leagued with the Ethiopian kings, and scarcely any remnant of them exists beyond the inscriptions upon the tombstones of the Apis-bulls, for they retained the city of Memphis where the bull was worshipped and performed the funeral rites whenever one of these sacred animals died. These inscriptions are more important on account of the information they give regarding the strange worship of this animal, than for anything that can be told of this dark time in Egyptian history.

Everything connected with the worship of the sacred bull is curious and interesting. The bull was considered a form of the great god Osiris. The following extracts from Wilkinson's "Manners and Customs of the Ancient Egyptians," give much information on this subject:

"Herodotus,[*] in describing him, says, 'Apis, also called Epaphus, is a young bull, whose mother can

---

[*] Herodot. iii. 28.

have no other offspring, and who is reported by the Egyptians to conceive from lightning sent from heaven, and thus to produce the god Apis. He is known by certain marks: his hair is black; on his forehead is a white triangular spot, on his back an eagle, and a beetle under his tongue, and the hair of his tail is double.' Ovid speaks of him as *variis coloribus Apis*. Strabo describes him with the forehead and some parts of his body of a white color, the rest being black, by which signs they fix upon a new one to succeed the other when he dies. Plutarch* observes that, 'on account of the great resemblance they imagine between Osiris and the moon, his more bright and shining parts being shadowed and obscured by those that are of a darker hue, they call the Apis the living image of Osiris, and suppose him begotten by a ray of generative light, flowing from the moon, and fixing upon his dam at a time when she was strongly disposed for generation.'† Pliny ‡ speaks of Apis 'having a white spot in the form of a

---

* Plut. de Isid. s. 43.

† It appears from the inscriptions at the Serapeum of Memphis, that Apis was produced by Ptah out of a heifer, and he was the incarnation of the soul of that god, being called "the second life of Ptah."— S. B.

‡ Plin. viii. 46.

crescent upon his right side, and a lump under his tongue in the form of a beetle.' Ammianus Marcellinus * says the white crescent on his right side was the principal sign by which he was known; and Ælian mentions twenty-nine marks by which he was recognized, each referable to some mystic signification. But he pretends that the Egyptians did not allow those given by Herodotus and Aristagoras.

"Memphis was the place where Apis was kept and where his worship was particularly observed. He was not merely looked upon as an emblem, but, as Pliny and Cicero say, was deemed 'a god by the Egyptians'; † and Strabo ‡ calls Apis the same as Osiris. Psammatichus § there erected a grand court, ornamented with figures in lieu of columns twelve cubits in height, forming a peristyle around it, in which he was kept when exhibited in public. Strabo says, 'Before the enclosure where Apis is kept, is a vestibule, in which also the mother of the sacred bull is fed; and into this vestibule Apis is sometimes introduced, in order to be shown

---

* Amm. Marcellin. xxii. 14.
† Cicero, de Nat. Deor. l. Plin. viii. 46.
‡ Strabo, xvii. p. 555. When Ælian (xi. 10) says, "They compare Apis to Horus, being the cause of fertility," he evidently means Osiris.
§ Herodot. ii. 153.

to strangers. After being brought out for a little while, he is again taken back. At other times he is only seen through a window.' The festival in honor of Apis lasted seven days; on which occasion a large concourse of people assembled at Memphis. The priests then led the sacred bull in solemn procession, every one coming forward from their houses to welcome him as he passed; and Pliny and Solinus affirm that children who smelt his breath were thought to be thereby gifted with the power of predicting future events.

"When the Apis died, certain priests chosen for this duty went in quest of another, who was known from the signs mentioned in the sacred books. As soon as he was found, they took him to the City of the Nile, preparatory to his removal to Memphis, where he was kept forty days; during which period women alone were permitted to see him. These forty days being completed, he was placed in a boat, with a golden cabin, prepared to receive him, and he was conducted in state down the Nile to Memphis."

It is said by some writers that the bull was only suffered to live twenty-five years, and when that time arrived he was led to the fountain of the priests and drowned with great ceremony. The reason for twenty-five being fixed as the number of years was, that it was the square of five, and the same as the number of letters in the Egyptian alphabet. His body was embalmed and he was buried with magnificent and expensive ceremonies, which were made especially impressive when Apis died a natural death within the prescribed time for him to live. The ceremonials attendant upon the discovery of a new Apis are described by various authors, all of whom agree as to their solemnity and importance.

"The Egyptians not only paid divine honors to the bull Apis, but, considering him the living image * and representative of Osiris, they consulted him as an oracle, and drew from his actions good or bad omens. They were in the habit of offering him any kind of food, with the hand: if he took it, the answer was considered favorable; † if he refused, it was thought to be a sinister omen. Pliny and Ammianus Marcellinus observe that he refused what the unfortunate Germanicus presented to him; and the death of that prince, which happened shortly after, was thought to confirm most unequivocally the truth of those presages.

* Plut. de Isid. s. 39. Amm. Marcellin. lib. xxii.
† Plin. lib. viii. c. 48.

"The Egyptians also drew omens respecting the welfare of their country, according to the stable in which he happened to be. To these two stables he had free access; and when he spontaneously entered one, it foreboded benefits to Egypt, as the other the reverse; and many other tokens were derived from accidental circumstances connected with this sacred animal.

"Pausanias * says, that those who wished to consult Apis first burnt incense on an altar, filling the lamps with oil which were lighted there, and depositing a piece of money on the altar to the right of the statue of the god. Then placing their mouth near his ear, in order to consult him, they asked whatever questions they wished. This done, they withdrew, covering their two ears until they were outside the sacred precincts of the temple; and there listening to the first expression any one uttered, they drew from it the desired omen.

"Children, also, according to Pliny and Solinus, who attended in great numbers during the procession in honor of the divine bull, received the gift of foretelling future events: and the same authors mention a superstitious belief at Memphis,

---

* Pausan. lib. viii.

of the influence of Apis upon the crocodile, during the seven days when his birth was celebrated. On this occasion, a gold and silver patera was annually thrown into the Nile, at a spot called from its form 'the Bottle:' and while this festival was held, no one was in danger of being attacked by crocodiles, though bathing carelessly in the river. But it could no longer be done with impunity after the sixth hour of the eighth day. The hostility of that animal to man was then observed invariably to return, as if permitted by the deity to resume its habits. Apis was usually kept in one or other of the two stables. But on certain occasions he was conducted through the town with great pomp. He was then escorted by numerous guards, and a chorus of children singing hymns in his honor headed the procession. The attention paid to Apis, and the care they took of his health by scrupulously selecting the most wholesome food, were so great, that even the water he drank was taken from a particular well set apart for his use; and it was forbidden to give him the water of the Nile, in consequence of its being found to have a peculiarly fattening property."

In 1851 Mariette Bey discovered the burial-place of the sacred bulls at Saqqarah, and information gained there has added much to the knowledge of the worship of Apis. Here are chambers in which bulls were buried from the time of Amenhotep III., down to the time of the Romans, and it appears that the so-called step-pyramid of Saqqarah was a very ancient Apeum.

The dynasty called that of the Bubastids was the twenty-second, the following one is called the Dynasty of Tanis, but its story only appears in snatches, as the struggles now with Assyrians and again with Ethiopians are described, and the kings of Egypt of this time appear to have done no great deeds of war abroad, or to have wrought the works of peace at home.

According to Manetho, King Bocchoris or Bokenranef stood alone in the twenty-fourth dynasty. The little told of him by the texts will be related in connection with the twenty-fifth or Ethiopian dynasty.

The Ethiopian sovereigns were descended from the priest-kings, who, when their power at Thebes was overthrown, had gone South into that land of Kush, which the older kings had so hardly won, but which now, when the Assyrians approached, was left to free itself, and only waited a strong leader to declare a new government. This was most opportune for the priests of Amon, who hastened to place themselves at the head of the whole South. The northern boundary of their new kingdom was at Syene, and Mount Barkal (where a fortress had been built by Amenhotep III.) was chosen for the royal residence, and the capital city was called Napata, or the "City of the Holy Mountain."

The old worship of Thebes was established here, together with the writing, divisions of time, and all the Theban manners and customs, and in the course of events their former home became their own — the old priests again ruled at Thebes, while Lower Egypt was ruled by the Assyrians, and Middle Egypt was a bone of contention between the two powers. Both governments embraced numbers of petty sovereignties, whose rulers paid tribute to the so-called great kings.

The struggles between the two powers were unending, and sometimes even the capital cities fell into the hands of the dominating power. A campaign of more importance than usual occurred about B. C. 766, in which the Ethiopian king, Piankhi, came off victorious over Middle and Lower Egypt. He set up a memorial tablet at Mount Barkal, where, not many years since, it was discovered. The inscription is long and very curious, and has been translated and published separately, by Canon Cook, of Exeter, England. The king who stood as the leader of the war against Piankhi, and the head of the satraps and princes of Lower Egypt, was named Tafnakhth.

The inscription of Piankhi relates at great length how completely he reduced all his enemies, how humble they were before him, and how they brought to him their treasures, so that he sailed up the Nile with "ships laden with silver, gold, bronze, stuffs, and all the good things of Lower Egypt, with all the products of Phœnicia, with all the woods of the Holy Land."

No record of the subsequent incidents remains, but it is certain that the fruits of this great conquest were not long enjoyed by the Ethiopian kings.

The son and successor of Piankhi, named Miamun Nut, lost all power in Lower Egypt, and made a campaign against that country in person, but the king of this portion of his dominions yielded his allegiance to King Nut, as soon as he appeared to claim it, and paid his tributes without bloodshed.

Such unsatisfactory accounts as these already

given, are a fair example of all that is known concerning these descendants of the priest Hir-hor — that first priest who aspired to be a king. Other information concerning them comes from the Assyrian cuneiform inscriptions, which only repeat more tales of wars between the Ethiopians and Assyrians. From these last-named inscriptions it appears that Bocchoris, whom Manetho called a Pharaoh of Saïs, of the twenty-fourth dynasty, was, in truth, one of the petty sovereigns above mentioned. At length, the rival claims which had so long disturbed the land of the double crown, ever since the beginning of the reign of Hir-hor, a period of more than four centuries, were all merged in a single interest through the marriage of Psamethik I. (the first king of the dynasty of Saïs, and the grandson of that Tafnakhth whom the Egyptians had conquered,) with the Ethiopian princess, Shep-en-apet, the great-grand-daughter of the conqueror of Piankhi. This union between the North and South restored peace to Egypt.

Brugsch says of this period, "We are standing beside the open grave of the Egyptian kingdom, The array of kings, whose names are enrolled in these last dynasties — some of them natives and some foreigners — appear as the bearers of the old decaying corpse, whose last light of life flickered up once more in the Dynasty of Saïs, only to go out soon and forever. The monuments become more and more silent, from generation to generation, and from reign to reign. The ancient seats of splendor, Memphis and Thebes, have fallen into ruin, or, at all events, are depopulated and deserted. Only the strong bulwark of the 'white citadel' of Memphis serves as a refuge for the persecuted native kings and their warriors, in their times of need. The Persian satraps dwell in the old royal halls of the city. The whole people has grown feeble with age, disordered to the marrow, and exhausted by the lengthened struggle of the petty kings and the satraps of the mighty power of Assyria."

Psamethik I. succeeded in overcoming great obstacles, and placed himself and his descendants on the throne of this broken Egypt as sole monarchs of the entire kingdom. His name may be traced upon the "speaking stones" from one end of Egypt to the other, but the glory was departed— the old gods of Egypt seem to have turned away in weariness and sorrow from the melancholy changes upon which they have looked.

Neith, whose place of worship was at Saïs, by

the sea, (which now became the court city) was the last of the ancient deities to be reverenced, and her temple the last one to be maintained with any attempt at the ancient splendor.

From this time no connected history of Egypt can

TOMBS OF THE KINGS OF THEBES.

be given from its own monuments or papyri—it must be sought in the history of the other nations with whom it was involved: the Assyrians, Persians, Macedonians, Jews, Greeks and Romans.

The government had never been such as to draw

out the love or command the devotion of the people, they were but abject slaves to each power in turn, only slaves once for all, and what difference could it make as to the nationality of the master? From this period there is on one hand more certainty and more doubt connected with what is told of Egypt. More certainty in some cases as to grand events, which are related in the histories of several nations, but more doubt as to minor matters chiefly related by curious foreign travellers, who neither understood the language nor comprehended the customs and modes of thought of the Egyptians.

There were six sovereigns of the twenty-sixth dynasty:

Psamethik or Psameticus I.
Neku or Necho.
Psamethik or Psameticus II.
Uahabra or Hophra.
Aahmes or Amasis.
Psamethik III.

It endured from B. C. 666 to 527, when Cambyses conquered the country and established the first Persian dynasty.

Many of the monuments of this age are especially beautiful, but show a change of style and the effect of foreign manner. The museums of Italy are rich in sculptures and statues belonging to this period.

In the time of the first Psamethik some attempt was made to return to the traditions of the earlier days both in religion and art, and the term, Egyptian Renaissance, may be fitly used (in several senses) in describing this age.

But the truth that one cannot touch pitch without defilement is here illustrated. Stronger fancies had crept in from the various peoples and religions which had been in contact with the sons of Kemi, and demons and genii and all sorts of fabulous creations look out from the stones once sacred to the great triads and their descendants only. In truth, the last Egyptian monarch, Nakhtnebef, appeared in the character of a magician and exorcist rather than as the " Son of the Sun ! "

The Persians, Cambyses and Darius I., as well as some of the Ptolemies or Lagidæ, continued the worship of the Apis-bull, and provided for the grand funerals of these sacred animals, and some of the Apis tablets furnish most important historic aid in the matter of fixing dates and so on. It is from these tablets that it appears beyond contradiction that Cambyses conquered in 527 rather than 525

B. C., thus increasing the length of his reign to six years in place of the four years which has been generally accepted. The fact, recorded by the inscription, that Cambyses prepared a burial-place for the Apis, and the representation upon the stone of that king as kneeling in worship of the sacred bull, is a strong refutation of the oft repeated tale of his having slain an Apis with his sword.

When Cambyses came to the throne he found no difficulty in enlisting in his service those who had held prominent positions under his predecessors. One of these men, who had been the commander of the fleet under two preceding kings, served under Cambyses also. His name was Uza-hor-en-pi-ris, and his statue, now in the Vatican, bears an important inscription, besides being a beautiful specimen of the art of his time. He is represented in an upright position embracing a shrine which contains the mummy of Osiris. Under Cambyses, and later, under Darius, this man was the president of the physicians, and it is well known that the Persians placed a high estimate upon the services and the skill of the Egyptian physicians. The inscription upon this statue represents this nobleman as speaking, and he presents Cambyses under quite a different character from that in which he ordinarily appears. He recounts how this king, after he had been instructed by Uza-hor-en-pi-ris, forbade all desecration of the temples of Saïs and restored the proper ceremonies of the religion of their gods, and replaced the sacred property of all the gods of Saïs as it had been formerly.

Darius I. (he also declares) provided for the instruction of the scribes and the training of young priests, "because he knew that such a work was the best means of awakening to new life all that was falling into ruin, in order to uphold the name of all the gods, their temples, their revenues, and all the ordinances of their feasts forever."

King Darius I., and probably Darius II., were the builders of the temple of El-Khargeh in the Great Oasis, at a city called Hib or Hibe in the texts, and Hibis by the ancient writers. The decoration of this temple was carried on down to 360 B.C.

Darius I. also attempted to connect the Red Sea with the Nile by a canal. Several inscriptions, some in hieroglyphics and some in cuneiform characters, makes this an undoubted fact. *

It is said that Darius relinquished this bold

---

* The great scholar, Jules Oppert, has fully translated the cuneiform inscriptions, and thus rendered to history a great service.

project because he was assured that the level of the Red Sea was so high as to render it a danger thus to bring its waters into Egypt.

Xerxes I., who placed his brother as satrap over Egypt, was less esteemed than his predecessors had been, and as the Greeks had gained some victories over the Persians and weakened their power, the Egyptians took the opportunity to revolt, and after several attempts the Pharaohs once again gained the throne, which they retained during two dynasties, the twenty-ninth and thirtieth, which endured only about sixty years, and embraced the reigns of seven kings, as follows:

Dynasty **XXIX.**, of Mendes.
Naif-an-rot or Nephorites I.
Hagar or Akoris.
Psa-mut or Psamuthis.
Naif-an-rot or Nephorites II.
Dynasty **XXX.** of Sebennytus.
Nakht-hor-hib or Nectarebes.
Zi-ho, Teos or Tachos.
Nakht-neb-ef or Nectanebus.

A granite sarcophagus, now at Berlin, is one of the authorities concerning the families of these last remnants of the mighty kings of the " double land." The monuments, however, are so silent concerning them, that it is almost as if they had never lived.

The thirty-first dynasty was under three Persian kings. Ochus, Arses, and Darius III., the last of whom was overcome by Alexander the Great, who, B.C. 332, added Egypt to the list of his conquests.

PYRAMID AT ASSUR IN NUBIA.

CHAPTER VII.

EGYPT UNDER THE PTOLEMIES.

THE conquest of Egypt, by Alexander the Great, cannot be ranked as a great achievement for that mighty warrior.

The rule of the Persians had been odious to the Egyptians, and when it was known that Alexander had overthrown the power of Darius III., the Egyptians made little resistance to their new conqueror, and the city of Pelusium, the first point of his attack, was easily overcome.

Leaving a garrison at Pelusium, Alexander commanded his fleet to join him at Memphis, to which city he made a triumphal march. At his approach, each town threw open its gates and yielded to him without a struggle. Near Heliopolis he crossed the river and entered Memphis without taking a life in its conquest.

Memphis was held at that time by Mazæus, an officer under Darius, who not only surrendered the city, but also eight hundred talents in gold, and all the furniture and effects of the late sovereign.

Alexander manifested deep wisdom in the

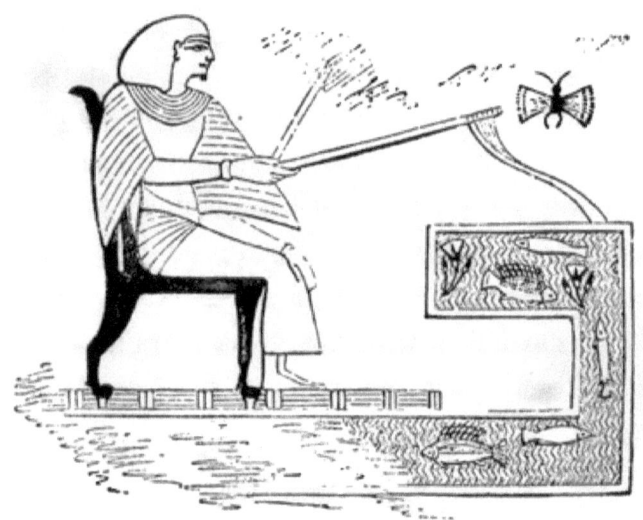

AN EGYPTIAN GENTLEMAN FISHING.

course which he followed in Egypt. He recognized the truth that the only hope of strengthening the weakened country, of which he had possessed himself, was by restoring its old religion and customs, rather than by attempting the introduction of new ones.

He was, for this reason, careful to observe the time-honored ceremonies in his coronation, to sacrifice to the Apis-bull, and he determined to pay his devotions at a shrine of the great god Amon-ra. He also entertained and propitiated the Egyptians with games and music performed by the Greeks.

Why Alexander went to the temple in the Oasis of Ammon rather than to the great temple at Thebes, is not known, but it is reasonable to suppose that the length of the journey to the more famous city and temple, and want of time to take it, must have given the other direction to his pilgrimage.

The most important result of his visit and devotion to the shrine of Amon-ra, was, that he landed at Rhacotis, then a small village, but so advantageously placed that the monarch determined to erect on its site the city which should control the land of Egypt. He immediately commanded the improvement of the harbor, and the laying out of a city, and soon that Alexandria arose which has since been so important in the history of Egypt and the world.

The Oasis of Ammon, from which the salt of ammonia is named, was the most northerly of the three oases of the Libyan desert, and in its midst stood the temple of Amon-ra. Here the treasures of the merchant caravans were deposited while the weary camels were allowed to rest in this grateful valley, and the figure of the god had been adorned, by those who thus sought the protection of his sanctuary, with many precious jewels.

Alexander tarried only long enough to pay his devotions, leave his gifts, and thus gain the right to be called the "Son of the Sun," and then return to Memphis.

During his absence his generals had established his authority in various parts of the country, and Alexander regulated the affairs of the government preparatory to leaving Egypt. He appointed two native judges, Doloaspis and Petisis, to administer the civil departments of the government; he left the garrisons in the command of Greeks, and appointed over all, two prefects, Apollonius over Libya and Cleomenes over Arabia. This last was a cunning and dishonest man, and in various ways disobeyed the orders of Alexander and departed from the policy that he had decided to pursue in the government of Egypt.

In spite of this the people were much happier and more prosperous than they had been under the Assyrians or Persians. Alexander devised many ways of increasing his revenues and his power in his new possessions. He introduced colonies of Samaritans into the Thebaid, who cultivated the lands which had fallen into disuse during the decline of Upper Egypt, at the same time that they formed an element in the land favorable to the conqueror, in case of any rebellion against his rule.

Alexander soon left Egypt, but not until he had made all possible provision for the building up of Alexandria. Some authorities even say that the king drew the plans with his own hand, at all events, he appointed the great architect, Dinocrates, who had superintended the building of the temple of Diana at Ephesus, to be the builder of the city of Alexandria.

Alexander did not live to see the pride of the city he had founded. He died at Babylon, eight years later, and was followed in the government of Egypt by the Ptolemies, or the family of the Lagidæ.

Ptolemy Soter, or "the Preserver," the first of this line of sovereigns, was said to be the half-brother of Alexander the Great, or the son of Philip and Arsinoë, who was married to Lagus, a Macedonian of humble position. At all events, Philip, before his death, advanced Ptolemy to positions of trust, and he also served as a general under Alexander. After the death of the great conqueror there was much trouble concerning the division of his kingdom, all of which will not be recounted here. Suffice it to say that after first serving as the governor, Ptolemy was finally the king of Egypt.

When he assumed the government as the representative of Philip Arridæus, (the half-brother and successor of Alexander the Great), one of his first acts was to put Cleomenes to death.

It is said that a prophecy had declared that the city which should be the burial-place of Alexander, should rise to be the seat of power and of the government of all his vast conquests. This gave rise to a rivalry among all the cities which had any claim to this honor.

Perdiccas, the former general, who had become the regent of the kingdom of the minor sovereign, commanded that the body should be conveyed to Æga, in Macedonia. But Ptolemy persuaded the general Arridæus, who had charge of the funeral train, to allow the body to rest in the temple of Jupiter Ammon, in the Great Oasis, where Alexander had made his vows in person.

Therefore, when, more than two years after the death of Alexander, the funeral *cortege* reached Syria, Ptolemy met it with an army and bore the much coveted remains to Memphis, where he retained them until a fitting tomb could be erected in Alexandria.

Perdiccas, acting as regent for the two young princes (Philip Arridæus, who was unequal to the care of the government, and Alexander Ægus, the posthumous son of Alexander the Great,) now thought it time to check the course of Ptolemy, in whom he saw the desire and ability to grasp the whole power and make himself an independent ruler. He therefore advanced from Egypt with the Macedonian army; Ptolemy met him at Pelusium and forced him to retire; in short, the whole campaign was disastrous to Perdiccas, who was finally killed by one of his own soldiers. Before his death such discontent had arisen in all ranks of his army that the supplies sent them by the far-seeing Ptolemy were accepted and hostilities ceased.

Both the young princes had fallen into the keeping of Ptolemy, and he must have been tempted to retain them, and thus be master of all by right, as their guardian.

But he had other plans, and recommended to the Macedonians that they should appoint as regents two generals, Python, who, under Alexander, had held the same rank as Perdiccas, and that Arridæus who had consigned to him the remains of Alexander. This advice was acted upon, but in reality the control of Macedonia was the only power that was left to these regents, for, as soon as possible, Ptolemy conquered Cœle-Syria and Phœnicia, overcoming Jerusalem, and thus making himself master of all the coast-country between Cyrene and Antioch, twelve hundred miles in extent. It was now possible to make Egypt felt as a naval power, for the forests of Lebanon and Anti-Lebanon were of her possessions, and the Egypt with this command of timber and seaports was a very different country from the ancient Egypt, of which Thebes was the centre, and the Nile the only scene of its navigation.

It is not necessary to recount all the vicissitudes of conquest and re-conquest which attended upon the efforts of Ptolemy to bring Egypt into the foremost rank as a naval power. He finally possessed himself of Palestine, Phœnicia, Cœle-Syria, and the Island of Cyprus, the last being of great value on account of its large and safe harbors.

Alexander had said that whoever held Cyprus held command of the seas. The exact date of the first conquest of this island by Ptolemy is not known, but he appointed a governor and banished the former rulers, and gained final and absolute possession of it B. C. 294 or 293, from which time it remained an Egyptian province.

At times Ptolemy had control of Cilicia, Caria and Pamphylia, and even of the important cities of Corinth and Sicyon in Greece; but he never allowed himself to be so involved in foreign wars as to weaken himself at home.

Ptolemy Soter was most certainly ambitious, but he knew where to direct his ambition, and how to limit it with wisdom.

After the attack by Perdiccas, B. C. 306, as related above, he was assailed by Demetrius and Antigonous, B. C. 306, and was threatened again by Lysimachus and Seleucus.

In the early part of his reign Ptolemy had established his power over Cyrene, but B.C. 313 a revolt occurred there, which was not ended until five years later, when Ptolemy fully occupied the country and made his son Magas governor there.

In truth, however, the most important features of the reign of this first Ptolemy, were the building of Alexandria, and the founding of its institutions. This king was fond of learning, and wrote a history of the wars of Alexander; the book is now unknown, but Arrian praised it heartily.

Ptolemy founded a great library at Alexandria and connected it with his own palace; he encouraged learned men to make this city their home; his college became so famous that Alexandria has been called the "University of the East;" and though it was too late to make Egypt the home of the best Greek art, yet, an appreciation of it, and great attainments in science and literature, made a fame more enduring for Alexandria than that which rose from its possession of the last of the Seven Wonders of the World, which the Pharos was reckoned to be.

The "Museum," as the University was called, comprised rooms for the Professors, a common dining-hall, a corridor for exercise, a theatre for spectacles and disputations, a botanical garden and a menagerie. No modern academy can claim to have done more for learning than was done there. The courses of study were four in number, viz.: Poetry, which included Criticism, Mathematics, Astronomy and Medicine. The names of the learned men who were contemporaneous with the

Lagidæ are such as would immortalize any age ; in art, Apelles and Antiphilus, who executed many pictures for the court of the Ptolemies ; Euclid and Apollonius of Perga in mathematics ; Hipparchus in astronomy ; Manetho in history ; Eratosthenes in chronology and geography ; Philetas, Callimachus and Apollonius of Rhodes in poetry ; Aristophanes of Byzantium and Aristarchus in criticism, besides many others who made their era one to be remembered for all time.

While Egypt derived so many benefits from the scholarship and culture of Greece, she conferred a boon in return, by the knowledge of papyrus and its uses, the value of which could not be estimated.

From his scholarly tastes it may be justly inferred that the Library and Museum were the two things most dear to Ptolemy Soter, but he did not forget to do many other noble works, such as the Heptastadium or causeway which connected the Island of Pharos with the shore ; the temple of Neptune ; the royal palace ; the Mausoleum of the kings, called "the Soma ;" the Hippodrome or race course ; and the temple of Serapis, which was unfinished at the time of his death. He also rebuilt the inner chamber of the great temple at Kar-

TOWING THE DAHABIEH.

nak, besides many smaller, but very useful works not here mentioned.

The character of Ptolemy Soter stands out from that of his age in bright relief. He was simple in his mode of life, brave and generous in war, and faithful to his plighted word. He gained the love and respect of the Egyptians by his forbearance, and the Thebans, who were fast losing their ancient prestige, were perhaps more ready to submit to a stranger than to a native of Lower Egypt.

In his domestic life this king was most unfortunate. He first married a Persian princess, who seems to have borne no children; his second wife, Eurydice, was the mother of Ptolemy Ceraunus, " the Thunderer," and several other children; and his third wife was Berenice, whose son, Ptolemy, (Philadelphus) was chosen by Ptolemy Soter as his successor, and was associated in the government two years before the death of the old king, who died B. C. 283, aged eighty-four years. Ptolemy put away Eurydice in order to marry Berenice, and his choice of the younger son, to the exclusion of the elder, made Ceraunus so bitter an enemy of his family that he engaged in intrigues which ended in bloodshed. This preference of the younger son has been attributed to the influence of Berenice over her husband in his dotage. It was the picture of this queen that the poet of Samos, Asclepiades, mistook for that of Venus, and consequently wrote:

> "This form is Cytherea's; nay
> 'Tis Berenice's, I protest:
> So like to both, you safely may
> Give it to either you like best."

Ptolemy Philadelphus was but twenty-six years old when his father died, and being already in power no disturbance occurred, and few sovereigns have commenced their reigns with brighter prospects than opened before him. The long reign of his father had brought the whole country of Egypt into a flourishing and firm position. Alexandria had the largest commerce of any city in the world, besides being one of the special seats of art and learning.

Though not a great soldier, Ptolemy Philadelphus succeeded fairly in the three wars in which he was engaged; the Macedonian, Cyrenæan, and Syrian. However, two of his enemies, Magas and Antiochus II., were largely influenced by marriages which reconciled their interests; the first became the father-in-law of the son of Ptolemy, and the second became the son-in-law of the king.

The public works of this reign were of great importance. The light-house on the Island of Pharos was completed; the canal between the Nile and the Red Sea was perfected, and the city of Arsinoë built on the present site of the city of Suez. Plotemy Philadelphus also built two other seaport cities, both called by the name of Berenice, both on the east of Africa, but separated by eleven degrees of latitude; the second was called the Troglodytic Berenice. From the most northerly of these cities he built a road to Coptos, over which the merchants passed for centuries with their caravans, laden with the products of India, Arabia and Ethiopia, which thus found their way into Europe and established a great commerce.

The new city of Ptolemais in the Thebaid was the chief emporium of the Ethiopian trade, which consisted largely in ivory; elephants were also brought there alive, and were used in the service of the army.

The revenues of this king, chiefly from customs, are said to have been more than three and a half millions of pounds sterling, besides tributes of grain and other products. But his army and navy must have exhausted immense sums, since they are estimated at two hundred thousand foot soldiers and forty thousand horse, with chariots and elephants in addition, and fifteen thousand vessels, and one thousand transports with more than five hundred and fifty thousand rowers.

However, the principal, lasting fame of this Ptolemy, like that of his father, rests upon what he did for letters. He added immensely to the Library of Alexandria. Learned men found a Paradise at his court. There Manetho wrote, and there under the patronage of the king, the translation of the Hebrew Scriptures into Greek was begun. He also added much to the adornments of the capital, architecturally, and by ornamental works of art. The temple of Serapis, mentioned before, was, when completed, the largest building in Alexandria. It was built upon an artificial mound, raised one hundred steps above the rest of the city; it was very beautiful within, while the porticos with which it was surrounded added much to its outward effect. It was built to receive the statue brought from Sinope, a city of Pontus, by Ptolemy I. Serapis, whose worship became so popular, and was later followed at Rome, was sought out by Ptolemy on account of a dream in which he saw the god, and was commanded to remove it to another place. The character of this deity has

PHARAOH'S BED ON THE ISLAND OF PHILÆ.

never been satisfactorily established, since the different nations who worshipped him gave him different attributes. But it is certain that he was a Greek, not an Egyptian deity, and as his temple was an abomination to the native Egyptians, it was placed outside, frequently near the burial-places of the old Egyptian cities, as that of Memphis was near the tombs of the Apis-bulls. It is said that under the Ptolemies and Romans forty-two temples were erected to this god in Egypt.

The characteristics attributed to Serapis were those of Osiris and Apis in conjunction, his infernal character made his likeness to Osiris, who was called the judge of the dead and the ruler of Hades. Again, Serapis was likened to Æsculapius, and again to the Sun.

His worship was abolished by the Roman senate on account of its licentiousness. A temple of Serapis is one of the most interesting of the ruins at Pozzuoli, near Naples. The temples of this god were oracular, and his votaries consulted him by sleeping and dreaming in them.

He is represented with the attributes of a Cerberus, a dragon or a snake. His head or figure, engraved on certain stones, was thought to possess mystic charms, and representations of him are common in museums.

It should be remembered that the beautiful temple of Philæ, dedicated to Isis, was commenced in the reign of Ptolemy Philadelphus. No more lovely spot than Philæ exists in Egypt. The statues originally here were all intended for representations of Arsinoë, the sister whom Ptolemy II. made his queen, and on whose account he was called Philadelphus or "the sister-loving."

The priests who lived in this temple were never allowed to leave the island, and none but priests were permitted to set foot upon the sacred spot. This is the most ancient monastic life of which history speaks, and these monks mortified themselves by chastisement, and even by cutting themselves with knives.

The character of Philadelphus was most cruel and unlovely. His slaughter of four thousand Gauls, who served him as soldiers, and whom he distrusted, fades into insignificance before his murder of his two brothers and his incestuous marriage with Arsinoë, who had before been the wife of his half-brother, Ptolemy Ceraunus. He was tenderly attached to this queen, and erected the Arsinoëum at Alexandria, as a magnificent

PORTICO OF TEMPLE AT PHILÆ.

monument to her memory. The coins which bear the images of this king and queen are beautiful and numerous. Philadelphus died, B. C. 247, at the age of sixty-two, after a sole reign of thirty-six years.

Arsinoë bore no children to Philadelphus, and he was succeeded by Ptolemy Euergetes, or Ptolemy III., a son of Philadelpuhs by his first queen, Arsinoë, who was a daughter of Lysimachus, and was banished to Upper Egypt when Philadelphus wished to make his sister his queen.

Euergetes or "the Benefactor," was the most ambitious of his family in enlarging his kingdom. His prosperity was such that he hesitated not to act on the offensive, and during his reign the Egyptian empire reached its greatest extent. In his Syrian war, Rome, with which republic Philadelphus had made a treaty of friendship, offered him assistance, which he declined.

This Ptolemy also did much for art and letters, and while he added few new buildings to Alexandria, he built a new temple at Esneh, rebuilt one at Canopus, and made large additions to the great temple at Thebes. During his wars he recovered many of the images of the Egyptian gods which had been borne away by former conquerors, these he restored to their original places, and thus won much favor in his empire.

It is probable that Egypt reached her highest prosperity during the reign of Ptolemy Euergetes, and with his death, B. C. 222, her decline began. He married Berenice, the daughter of Magas, who bore him three children.

The time of the first three Ptolemies extended over one hundred and one years, a brilliant period, under the leadership of comparatively good men, for of the nine Ptolemies who followed, six were detestably vile, two contemptibly weak, and but one, Philometor, had any claims to respect.

Ptolemy IV. was strongly suspected of having taken the life of his father, and it is believed that he chose the title of Philopator as a denial to these suspicions. Whether he killed his father or no, he made haste when once in power to murder his mother, his brother Magas, and his uncle Lysimachus. He only reserved the same fate for his sister, Arsinoë, until she should be his wife and the mother of his son, when her murder was added to his crimes, and he gave himself up to a licentious life.

The command of the government was left to Sosibus, who successfully conducted the war with

HYPOSTYLE HALL, KARNAK.

Antiochus III., of Syria, and was afterwards harassed by the intrigues of Agathocles, and a revolt of the native Egyptians.

Although Philopator was so vile a wretch, he in some measure maintained the traditions of his family. He especially favored Aristarchus, the grammarian, and so admired Homer that he built a temple in his honor. He also took time, at some period of his life, to compose poems and tragedies, which last style of composition one would judge him to be well prepared for.

Philopator died B. C. 205, aged forty years, leaving his son, Ptolemy V. or Epiphanes, as his successor. The boy was but five years old, and the infamous Agathocles made himself regent, but was so hated by the people that he was put to death, together with his mother and sister, and their vile supporters in the villanies they had perpetrated.

Next Sosibus, son of the minister of the same name mentioned above, held the regency, but the people were so demoralized that the country seemed likely to fall under the power of some new foreign conqueror, when the Egyptian rulers asked protection from Rome, and M. Lepidus was sent by the Roman senate to act as guardian to the young

Ptolemy. Lepidus was succeeded as regent by the general Scopas, and later the wise Aristomenes was at the head of the government. At length, when Epiphanes was but fourteen years old, he was crowned as king, and left to rule as best he

PORTICO AND TEMPLE AT ESNEH.

could. Few facts are known of his reign, but it is certain that all the foreign conquests of the Ptolemies were lost, except Cyprus and Cyrenaïca; the power thus weakened was never regained.

The decree inscribed upon the famous Rosetta stone, which has been of inestimable value in our day, was issued upon the occasion of the coronation of Ptolemy Epiphanes, B. C. 196.

This king was married to Cleopatra, daughter of Antiochus the Great, by whom he had three children. He died from poison when but twenty-nine years old. He left a demoralized army, an unmanned navy and an empty treasury, over which his son, Ptolemy Philometor, was declared king at the age of seven years. His mother was a woman of strong character, and during her regency of eight years, she was vigorous and successful in her administration of the government.

After her death Philometor was led into a war against Antiochus, when, but for the aid of the Romans, all Egypt would have been lost. The rise of the Roman power in Egypt may be dated from this time. The affairs of Egypt were now discussed in the Roman senate, and the decisions of that body, though not always final, were of great importance.

In the year B. C. 169 the younger brother of Philometor, who called himself Euergetes II., but is better known as Physcon, "the bloated," was associated in the government. After four years dissensions arose, and Physcon obtained the power while Philometor went to Rome to seek aid. After much discussion a division of the territory and the power was made, and through the offices of the

Roman deputies peace was restored between the brothers. Libya and Cyrene were allotted to Physcon, but after a few years his restless ambition drove him to Rome to demand further power. The senate added Cyprus to his territory and seemed to look for implicit obedience from Philometor, but he refused to concur in their arrangements, and when at last all preparations were made, and Physcon appeared ready for battle, Philometor was victorious and took Physcon prisoner, and showed great forbearance in sparing his life, and restoring to him the government of Cyrene.

At length Philometor was killed in a battle against the Syrians, which was fought near Antioch B. C. 146.

The wife of Philometor, Cleopatra, was his full sister, and bore him three children; a son who took the name of Eupator and two daughters, both named Cleopatra; one of whom became the wife of Demetrius II., of Syria, while the other remained unmarried.

The Ptolemies were now much less esteemed by the Egyptians than the first kings of their race had been. The policy of Ptolemy Soter and Philadelphus, who had regarded the customs of the country, and had in many ways consulted the prejudices of of the Egyptians, was forgotten. In the time of Philometor acts were perpetrated and allowed, which greatly incensed the Egyptians and engendered bitter hatred of the royal family. At this period, too, there was a marked decline in the literature of Alexandria. Criticism, such as that of Aristarchus, took the place of composition, and Hipparchus, the mathematical astronomer, was the most important scholar of his time.

The death of Philometor was followed by serious disturbances in Egypt. His son, Ptolemy VII., called Eupator, was declared king, but the Romans interfered and placed Physcon or Euergetes II. on the throne, and stipulated that he should marry the widow of Philometor. This he did, and his first act was the murder of Eupator, the son of his bride.

His cruelty was such, and his revenge upon those who had not favored him so dreadful, that nearly all the foreigners, especially the literary men, fled from Alexandria, and the depopulation was so great that this tyrant was forced to ask new colonists to settle in his capital. Cleopatra bore a son, who was called Memphitis, as a compliment to Memphis. After this the king repudiated the mother and took her daughter, also called Cleopatra, for his wife. The murder of Eupator and the repudiation of the queen, greatly incensed the Romans against Physcon, and his cruelties became so unendurable that a revolt broke out and he was forced to fly to Cyprus. By this time his mode of life had induced extreme corpulency, and he could not walk. After the flight of the king, his first queen, the widow of Philometor, was placed upon the throne and a war ensued between Physcon and herself, by which she was forced to appeal to the Syrians for aid. Here she made a grave mistake, for the Egyptian pride so revolted against asking a favor from their Syrian enemy, and the danger of falling into Syrian power was so much feared, that a revolt followed. Cleopatra was forsaken, and took refuge in Syria, while Physcon was reinstated in power.

It was in the beginning of this war between Cleopatra and Physcon that this monstrous father had slain his own son, Memphitis, and had sent the head and hands of the murdered boy to his mother.

After Physcon's return to the throne, fewer crimes are attributed to him, indeed, he is said to have become an author, and to have encouraged letters. The scholars who had fled from Alexandria had settled in various cities and were shedding the glory which had been so long peculiar to that city upon many other places. Pergamus appeared as a growing rival in the size of her library, and about this time the use of parchment was introduced, on account of a law made by Physcon forbidding the export of papyrus, as by this means he hoped to prevent book making, and the enlargement of the library at Pergamus. From that time date two words, now in the English language: parchment,— from Pergamus, and paper, from Papyrus.

Physcon died B. C. 117, and his eldest son, Ptolemy IX., called Lathyrus succeeded him in Egypt, while Apion, his natural son, received the kingdom of Cyrene, as a bequest from his father. Apion, realizing his danger from the nations surrounding him, made a league with the Romans, who promised to protect him while he lived, upon the condition that his kingdom should belong to Rome after his death. Thus he ensured himself a quiet and prosperous reign which endured twenty years, at the end of which he died, and Cyrene passed from the grasp of the Egyptians forever, and became a Roman province.

The reign of Lathyrus lasted thirty-six years,

but during that time the kingdom was divided by political storms, and he often ruled Cyprus alone. During the first ten years, his mother, Cleopatra Cocce, was in truth the ruler, while Lathyrus was called king of Egypt, and her younger son, Alexander, called Ptolemy Alexander, reigned in Cyprus. At the end of this time, Cleopatra, who was almost the worst member of her wicked family, became enraged against Lathyrus on account of his kindness to the Samaritans, who were the enemies of her allies, the Jews. She first raised a revolt against Lathyrus in Alexandria, then took Selene, his wife from him, and finally banished him to Cyprus, and placed Alexander on the throne.

Lathyrus remained eighteen years in Cyprus, while his mother and Ptolemy Alexander ruled together in Egypt. Meantime, Lathyrus successfully defended himself against the attempts of his mother to dispossess him of his power. He also gave aid to the Syrians, and at last, when Cleopatra Cocce and Ptolemy Alexander quarrelled, and the son murdered his mother, Lathyrus was recalled and became sole monarch of Egypt, as Alexander had been forced to flee, and had gone to Lycia.

Lathyrus was not long at peace, for Alexander

ERMEUT, OR HERMONTHIS, NEAR THEBES.

attempted to re-establish himself in Cyprus; he did not succeed, and fell in battle. Then a revolt broke out in Upper Egypt, and Thebes held out three years against a siege before it was overcome and laid in ruins, never again to resume its place among the cities of the East.

After the reduction of Thebes, Egypt was tranquil while Lathyrus lived, and he was of some account as an ally of the Greeks, Egypt being at this time the only country west of Persia that had not submitted to the power of the Romans.

Lathyrus died, B.C. 81, and left but one legitimate child, a daughter, called Berenice. She ascended the throne and reigned alone six months, when she married her cousin, Ptolemy Alexander II., who claimed the throne of Egypt, and was supported by the Romans. It was understood that the queen should share the government with Alexander, but three weeks after the marriage she was murdered by her husband, who fell in his turn, the victim of the fury of the Alexandrians, who slew him in the public gymnasium.

Fifteen years of contention for the power, and great disorder, followed this tragedy, and this period of Egyptian history requires a separate volume to make it clear or do it justice, and no account will here be given of the ups and downs of Auletes, "the Flute-player," the illegitimate son of Lathyrus, who at length attained the power, B.C. 65, and whose reign is ordinarily reckoned from B.C. 80, at which time his struggle for the throne began, though he was not recognized by the Romans until B.C. 59, when Julius Cæsar was made Consul.

The life of Auletes, his revels and his debauchery, so disgusted the Alexandrians, that when he increased the taxes, a rebellion arose and he was driven into exile, and his daughters, Tryphæna and Berenice, were placed on the throne. The former soon died, but Berenice continued to reign until Pompey sent a strong force to Egypt under Gabinius for the purpose of reinstating Auletes.

After the return of the king his first act was to murder Berenice, because she had resisted his authority and attempted to retain her position as queen.

By the aid of the Romans Auletes reigned until B.C. 51, and may be credited with having done all in his power to merit the hatred of his subjects and to degrade his country.

Auletes was the father of the last and most famous Cleopatra, and he left the kingdom to her and her brother Ptolemy, upon the condition that they should marry, and rule together. When Auletes died Cleopatra was seventeen years old, and Ptolemy four years younger; they had another brother, also called Ptolemy, and a sister, Arsinoë, both of whom were quite young children.

Cleopatra was very beautiful, and even at the age of fifteen made an impression upon Antony, who accompanied Gabinius to Egypt. She had a spirit which brooked no control, and soon quarrelled with her brother, and made herself so disliked by the Egyptians that she was driven to seek safety in Syria, where she attempted to raise an army of allies, who would replace her in her authority. But Cæsar arrived in Egypt and undertook to arrange a peace between Cleopatra and her brother. She had heard of Cæsar's susceptibility to such charms as hers, and by some intrigue she met him and made him her slave. In order to replace her on the throne the Roman fought bravely, and in the course of the ensuing war Ptolemy was killed — it is said that he was drowned in the Nile.

By the efforts of her lover she was again a queen and ruled with absolute authority while he remained near her, although, with the motive of propitiating the Egyptians, he had her nominally married to her younger brother.

When Cæsar was forced to go to Rome she followed him with her so-called husband, and the Romans were much scandalized at the open connexion between Cæsar and the queen, for she lived in apartments in his house and he loaded her with honors. She bore him a son called Cæsarion, who was later put to death by Augustus.

After the death of Cæsar, B. C. 44, Cleopatra returned to Egypt and passed through a stormy period of warfare, until Antony was sent to Asia Minor, B. C. 41. He soon yielded his implicit allegiance to her, and one of her first deeds under his protection was the murder of her sister, Arsinoë, who had once preferred a claim to the throne. To this she swiftly added other murders, tearing her victims from the sanctuary of the temples in order to slay them, for so blind was Antony to her faults, that he regarded neither religion or any voice of pity where her wishes were at stake. When Antony was with her in Egypt, she gained such power over him, that though he returned to Rome and married Octavia, and was later engaged in the Parthian expedition, he yet returned to "that accursed Egyptian," as Augustus called her.

CATARACT ON THE NILE.

Augustus so excited the Romans to hatred of Antony that at length a war was declared against Cleopatra. We will not follow the course of the struggle. Suffice it to say that when she believed the cause of Antony weak, and saw that Augustus must triumph, she turned traitor to the former, and tried to use her charms upon the latter. But her course was run, and at length, when Antony was dead, she preferred to take her own life rather than to be carried to Rome to grace a triumph in the Eternal City.

> "This mortal house I'll ruin,
> Do Cæsar what he can. Know, sir, that I
> Will not wait pinion'd at your master's court,
> Nor once be chastis'd with the sober eye
> Of dull Octavia. Shall they hoist me up,
> And show me to the shouting varietry
> Of censuring Rome? Rather a ditch in Egypt
> Be gentle grave to me! rather on Nilus' mud
> Lay me stark naked, and let the water-flies
> Blow me into abhorring! rather make
> My country's high pyramids my gibbet,
> And hang me up in chains."

CHAPTER VIII.

EGYPT AS A ROMAN PROVINCE, FROM B. C. 30 TO A. D. 450.

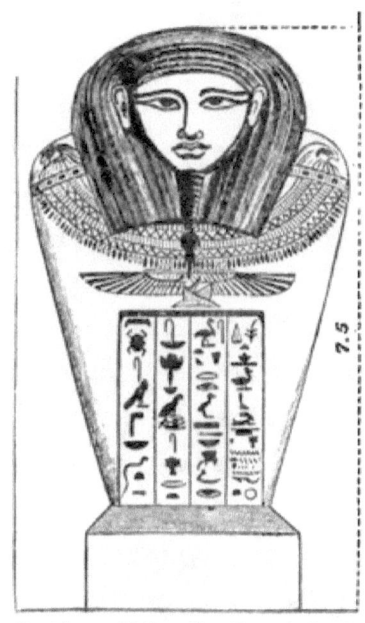

Sarcophagus with the goddess Nut on the breast.

WHILE Egypt remained a province of Rome it was governed by a Roman prefect or governor, of the equestrian rank, and during that time the history of Egypt is so much involved in that of Rome, that in a sense, the history of the latter is that of the former, and here an outline only will be given, filled in with the most important occurrences which essentially concerned Egypt.

Under the Emperor Augustus (as Octavianus

called himself after he came to the throne) the governor of Egypt was responsible to him alone; not even the Roman senate had a right to interfere in the government of this province, and under the governor all offices of importance were given to Romans, native Egyptians receiving only the most subordinate places, being treated essentially as slaves, and raised only to the rank of the emperor's freedmen.

Augustus pursued a very different course in his government of the Egyptians from that followed by Alexander the Great. Instead of adapting himself and his laws to their customs as far as was practicable, he studied how to degrade and wound them. He refused to visit the Apis-bull; he founded a new city, called Nicopolis, on the spot where he had conquered Antony, and made himself master of Egypt, and to this new and strange place he removed the sacrifices and the priesthood of Alexandria. Finally, when he left Egypt to return to Rome, he carried with him an immense amount of movable treasures, precious metals, ornaments, rare articles of all sorts, the double crown of Egypt, works of art, and in due time the two obelisks were removed to the Eternal City, which stand on Monte Citorio and in the Piazza del Popolo.

At Rome he graced his triumph with these spoils, which were drawn on wagons, while the two children of Antony and Cleopatra were led in the procession, loaded with chains, rejoicing, no doubt to remember that their mother had preferred death before this humiliation.

While in Egypt, Augustus introduced the reckoning of time by the so-called Julian year. The imperfectness of that reckoning was exposed and remedied by Gregory XIII., but the astronomers of Egypt were so learned in their science that they distrusted it from the first, and never used it; the result was that three kinds of years were in use in Egypt, viz.: the old form, with the first day of the year on or about July 18th; the Julian year beginning the 29th of August, and the astronomer's year, which was movable.

Early in the new reign in Egypt the old canals were cleared and the new Nilometer built at Elephantine, and these works were of great value to the Egyptians as well as to their masters, since so much more country was covered by the Nile overflow, and the crops largely increased.

It was with the third Roman governor, Ælius

Gallus, that Strabo made his journey up the Nile, of which he wrote a most entertaining and instructive account. It requires the largest exercise of the imagination before one can believe that the wonderful Alexandria which he saw from the top of the temple of Pan, or the flourishing vineyards which produced the fruit from which the Mareotic wine was made, could have existed where the unattractive modern city and the desolate Egypt of to-day now lies.

The treasures borne to Rome were not the only reminders of Egypt to be found there. Many religious opinions and customs were carried home by the Roman officers and soldiers, and at length even the beggars on the banks of the Tiber asked alms in the name of Osiris. The Egyptian belief in the immortality of the soul, the rewards of good and evil at the judgment day, and many other like points, were most welcome to men, who, like the Greeks and Romans, could be said to have no faith, and the worship of Isis and Serapis so gained among the Italians, that Augustus made a law, forbidding under pain of severe penalties the use of any Egyptian ceremonies in his kingdom.

The change from the rule of Augustus to that of Tiberius was not perceptible in Egypt, and under the latter many improvements were made. The temple of Sebaste or Cæsar's temple, was completed, and two obelisks were removed from Heliopolis, and set up in front of this building, in honor of Tiberius, and called Cleopatra's needles. One of these obelisks was presented to the British nation by Mehemet Ali; the other is soon to be erected in New York, and is a gift to America from the late Khedive. It is a monolith of red granite of Syene, seventy feet in height; it is covered with hieroglyphics, and bears the cartouch of Thotmes III.

The Sebaste was the loftiest building in ancient Alexandria. It had a library, and was ornamented with many works of art; it was surrounded by porticos, and stood in the midst of a sacred grove, near the harbor, so that it was one of the most impressive objects of the city as approached from the sea.

During the reign of Tiberius the great portico was added to the temple of Denderah. The architecture of this portico is imposing and grand in style, like that of the older Egyptian structures, but the sculptures are much inferior to those of ealier artists. Much speculation has been expended upon a curious zodiac upon the ceiling which

CLEOPATRA'S NEEDLE.

apparently embraces Egyptian, Babylonish and Roman elements in its plan.

Under the Ptolemies there had been much disturbance in Egypt concerning the Jews, but at last many privileges had been granted them, and at the time of the Roman conquest about one-third of the Alexandrian population was Jewish. Living as they had, in the midst of Greeks and Egyptians, some of their customs had been modified, but they were never treated as equals by the other races, although Cæsar had declared them citizens and engraved his decree upon a pillar in a public place.

Upon the accession of Caius or Caligula an edict commanded that his statue should be worshipped in every temple, and when the Jews refused to comply with this, a persecution arose against them, which was sanctioned rather than condemned by the prefect Flaccus, until finally they were deprived of all rights as citizens. Their houses were plundered and burned, their wise men scourged in the theatre, and the most humiliating indignities heaped upon them. It happened that in the midst of this excitement, Agrippa, the king of the Jews, landed at Alexandria, being on his way from Rome to his own kingdom. He sent such an account of the state in which he found his people in Egypt to Caligula, that the emperor sent immediately to arrest Flaccus and depose him from his office. The persecution of the Jews, however, did not cease here. Though they had made themselves felt as a power in letters in Alexandria, and through their philosophy and the earnest elegance of their style, had come to be regarded as the first writers of the Alexandrian school, they received no justice at Rome, and their emissary, the learned Philo, withdrew from his audience with Caligula, saying, "though the emperor is against us, God will be our friend."

When Caligula died and Claudius became emperor, he restored to the Jews all the rights they had enjoyed under the Ptolemies and Augustus, and the reign of this emperor was such that scholarship and the pursuits of peace were resumed with a new sense of content. The Claudian Museum was founded where the emperor insured some notice of his own attainments by commanding that on certain days of the year his histories of Carthage and of Italy should be publicly read.

Many reforms of the civil service in Egypt were inaugurated by Claudius, and the coins made in his time are of great use to the student of history, because they are dated with the year of the emperor's reign, and are covered with such designs as afford a knowledge of many things connected with the native Egyptians.

During this reign the value of the Eastern commerce was immense, and for the first time the Greeks and Romans seemed to fully comprehend and appreciate the importance of the route from Egypt to India. The journey from Alexandria to the coasts of Arabia or to the Eastern coast of Africa, near the equator, and back, required nearly a year's time; many dangers of desert and of sea attended it, but for fourteen centuries from the time of Claudius it was the only route from Europe to India, and the wildest imagination would not suffice to conjure up all the wonderful riches which were carried over it, nor half the human suffering which was endured in its passage, nor the agonies of the heavily laden creatures that died of thirst and starvation in the desert, between Coptos and Berenice, on the Red Sea; a fearful journey, which could be made only by night, and required twelve of these, each way.

Pliny made the estimate, that four hundred thousand pounds sterling in silver and gold was sent annually from Alexandria to India, and that the goods purchased were sold in Rome for one hundred times the amount paid for them, or forty millions of pounds sterling!

Under the reign of Claudius, the beautiful temple of Latopolis, which was commenced under the Ptolemies, was greatly improved, and his name is found in several other temples of Upper Egypt.

The reign of Nero was marked by but one important event in Egypt, which was the introduction of Christianity. Where the doctrines of Christ were first preached, they were only embraced by the ignorant and humble, and no historian has given a full account of these beginnings, but it is probable that St. Mark went to Alexandria at about the time when Nero ascended the throne, and then, when he joined St. Paul in Rome he left Annianus, generally accounted the first bishop of Alexandria, in charge of the growing church in that city. It is related of this good man, that he was converted by a miracle performed by St. Mark, the healing of a cobbler who had been so sorely wounded in his hand that it was useless, which wonderful thing done before the sight of Annianus, convinced him that God alone could give such power, and moved him to devote himself to the same work as that of Mark.

Marvellous things are told of the effects of the preaching of St. Mark in Alexandria, and of the number of converts he there made, as well as of the faithfulness of the new Christians and the rapid increase of their numbers after he left them.

Following Nero, were the emperors Galba, Otho, and Vitellius, whose united reigns were of such short duration as to have no effect on Egypt.

Vespasian, the Syrian general, was next exalted to the purple, and he landed in Alexandria, A. D. 70, on his way from Cæsarea to Rome. When he reached the city he was met by the officers of the government, and by the scholars and philosophers, all of whom united to pay him honor. Vespasian soon became the friend of Apollonius of Tyana, the most celebrated scholar then in Alexandria; a man who claimed the power of working miracles, which power was soon attributed to Vespasian also; in short, this friendship between the emperor and the philosopher seems to have been founded upon the hope of benefits resulting from it to both parties.

The Alexandrians had felt that on account of their readiness to acknowledge and honor Vespasian he would show his appreciation of their good will by making their taxes less, or removing some of their burdens, but these hopes were wofully disappointed, and they called him "the scullion," in order to express their contempt of his meanness and greed.

Titus, the son whom Vespasian left in Egypt when he went on to Rome, was more politic and far-seeing, and attempted to strengthen his father's power by pleasing the Egyptians. To this end he attended the consecration of a new Apis-bull, on which occasion he appeared in royal magnificence and wore the state crown.

Under Vespasian the great temple of Kneph at Latopolis was finished, and though the names of many sovereigns are there inscribed, that of Vespasian holds the place of honor. This emperor carried to Rome a statue of the Nile, surrounded by sixteen children, and placed it in the temple of Peace. The number of the children is typical of the number of cubits desirable in the rise of the Nile.

During the reigns of Titus, Domitian, Nerva and Trajan, nothing of importance occurred to change the usual aspect of affairs in Egypt. Some of the writers of the day, like Juvenal, held everything up to ridicule; others, like Plutarch, found good in everything, but a comparison of many authorities gives the conclusion that in Egypt at this period a most peculiar religious and moral (or immoral) atmosphere pervaded everything.

The earnest Egyptians clung with tenacity to their old faith, and their zeal was so impressive that it gave an air of solid reality even to their wildest superstitions, so that the Greeks and Romans, in large numbers, had half adopted them and wore mysterious rings and other charms about the person.

Domitian even believed in astrologers, and fortune-tellers, and built temples for the worship of Isis and Serapis at Rome. The artists of Rome, in that time, multiplied their representations of the mother Isis with the child Horus in her arms, as industriously as the Italian painters of later days have attempted to portray the Holy Mother and the child Jesus, and Juvenal declared that the Roman painters lived upon the goddess Isis. The pictures of Isis, in her character of the goddess of the Dog-Star or Sirius, (to which planet it was said that her soul was transferred after death), remind one surprisingly of the representations of the Virgin as our Lady of the Immaculate Conception, with the moon beneath her feet.

Next to the devout, native Egyptians, came the

Greek philosophers, who may be described by the single word, Platonists. They were numerous and had much influence in Egypt. Third in importance came the Jews. As has been said, the learned Jews had made themselves so prominent as scholars, that any belief which they cherished, must at least be respected. The Jews were very numerous in Egypt, and many of the important writings now known as Jewish only, emanated from the Jews of Alexandria.

Added to all these came the Christians, who had, since the days of St. Mark's preaching, striven to build up their church and faith. The Christians of Alexandria, at this time, were men of low degree, but even so, they formed an element not to be ignored, and there were some among them well able to hold their own in the continual disputations which occurred in public places.

It requires little discrimination to see that all these religious beliefs so tempered and shaded each other, that it may safely be said that in the full sense of the terms there was neither an Egyptian, Jew or Christian in Alexandria.

In the sixth year of his reign, A. D. 122, the Emperor Hadrian visited Egypt. He was accompanied by Antinous, who was so dear to the emperor that when an oracle declared that the prosperity of Hadrian could only be secured by the loss of that which was most precious to him, Antinous was so sure of his place in the emperor's heart, that he did not hesitate to drown himself in the Nile, in order to secure the good he desired for his master and friend. For this sacrifice he was commemorated by Hadrian in the building of a city called Antinoöpolis, where divine honors were paid to Antinous, as to a god. Coins were also struck in his honor as "the Hero Antinous."

Hadrian interested himself much in the Museum of Alexandria, and made many improvements in the city. The following letter, which he wrote to the consul Servianus, records some of his observations in this strange country:

"Hadrian Augustus to Servianus the Consul, greeting:

" As for Egypt, which you were praising to me, dearest Servianus, I have found its people wholly light, wavering, and flying after every breath of a report. Those who worship Serapis are Christians, and those who call themselves bishops of Christ are devoted to Serapis. There is no ruler of a Jewish synagogue, no Samaritan, no presbyter of the Christians, who is not a mathematician, an augur, and a soothsayer. The very patriarch himself, when he came into Egypt, was by some said to worship Serapis, and by others to worship

Christ. As a race of men they are seditious, vain, and spiteful; as a body, wealthy and prosperous, of whom nobody lives in idleness. Some blow glass, some make paper, and others linen. There is work for the lame, and work for the blind; even those who have lost the use of their hands do not live in idleness.

"Their one god is nothing; Christians, Jews, and all nations worship him. I wish this body of men were better behaved, and worthy of their number; for as for that they ought to hold the chief place in Egypt. I have granted everything unto them; I have restored their old privileges, and have made them grateful by adding new ones."

Gnosticism, though not entirely new in Alexandria, was at this period very flourishing under the leadership of one Basilides, who may be called the founder of Egyptian Gnostics. Any clear definition of Gnosticism and of the essential differences between the great number of diverging Christian schools, all of which claimed this name, would be impracticable here, and the Gnosticism of Egypt only will be partially explained.

Under Hadrian the most noted Gnostic teacher was Saturninus of Antioch, the founder of a special school in Syria. As Basilides is said to have been taught in Antioch, he was probably a follower of Saturninus.

Basilides taught that matter was eternal; that

in order to be saved one must be fated or elected to salvation, and one so elected could not be lost through sin; that Deity had begotten seven Æons or natures out of himself, and these, together with the deity, formed the sacred Ogdoad or combination of eight; he named the seven Æons as Mind, Word, Understanding, Power, Excellences, Princes and Angels; and these in their turn, were divided and sub-divided until three were three hundred and sixty-five emanations; hence the mystic nature of the number three hundred and sixty-five on the symbolic or ABRA-SAX stones of the Gnostics. ABRA-SAX may be translated, " hurt me not." These three hundred and sixty-five emanations each governed a world, and the lowest emanation of all governed the world of matter, and became the Jehovah of the old Scriptures, and in order to counteract the bad influence which he had exerted, by endeavoring to make "his chosen people" the rulers over all others, the first Æon, or intelligence or *Nous* was sent, who entered into the man Jesus at his baptism, and endeavored to teach men that their final and greatest good should be to return into the supreme good; that the *Nous* or true Christ did not suffer crucifixion, but stood by, laughing, while Simon of Cyrene suffered in his form, and he then returned to Heaven—and lastly, he taught a purgatorial transmigration of souls in case of the very wicked.

Other Gnostic sects arose in Egypt, differing from the followers of Basilides, but as few of their writings remain, we can only judge them by the reproaches of those who wrote against them, and the legitimate conclusion is, that they were an emanation from the lowest superstition and sensualism, tinged by a ray of truth, and perhaps, struggling feebly towards the truth; a transition phase between the worship of beasts, fishes and birds, and the acceptance of Christian truth.

Marcus Aurelius was the next emperor who visited Alexandria. He went there on account of the rebellion in which Cassius joined, but did not arrive until it was ended. This visit took place about A.D. 175, when the Library of Alexandria was at its greatest glory, and the city stood prominently out, the centre of the learning of the globe.

Marcus Aurelius forgave the children of the traitor Cassius, but his son, Commodus, when he became emperor, put them to death.

Upper Egypt was now so unimportant that little or no mention is made of it by any writer, and so complete was its desolation that prisoners were banished to the neighborhood of Thebes, as they had formerly been sent to the wilds of the desert.

Caracalla visited Egypt, A. D. 211, and there enacted one of the most ruthless tragedies of history. The emperor had heard that the Alexandrians had amused themselves by laughing at his eccentricity of dressing like Achilles and Alexander the Great, which, to say the least, could not have been becoming to his very moderate stature. They had also expressed their horror at his murder of his brother Geta and other fearful crimes which he had perpetrated. Though he gave no outward sign of rage, the heart of Caracalla was full of revenge, which he wreaked upon the Alexandrians by murdering, in cool blood, thousands of the young men of the city whom he had collected on a neighboring plain, under the pretext of selecting those who were fitted to be enrolled in an Alexandrian phalanx, which he declared his intention of forming upon the model of the already existing Spartan and Macedonian corps.

The troops of Caracalla encircled the whole plain, and as he moved among the admiring youths, saluted by their cheers, and smiling upon them, the soldiers gradually closed their ranks so that the young men were completely hemmed in, and at a signal, given by the emperor himself, they fell upon and slew the unarmed boys, as well as many of their freinds who had come out to witness the proposed review. Many were driven into the canal, and the Nile flowed to the sea, a river of blood.

Caracalla next consecrated, in the temple of Serapis, the sword with which he had slain his brother Geta, and then returned to Antioch, well pleased with the manner in which the jokes of the Alexandrians had been avenged! From this moment the Alexandrians were treated as enemies rather than subjects of the Roman power.

The interval between the time of Caracalla and that of Quintillus, A. D. 217–270, was that of the rise of the kingdom and strength of Palmyra, while the history of Egypt was that of every province under a declining power, as was that of Rome in the East, at that time, until finally rebellions, sieges, war, and every sort of unhappy fate befell it, and in the last named year, Zenobia, queen of Palmyra, was acknowledged as queen of Egypt by the whole nation.

Zenobia made Egypt a province of Syria, and the effect upon the people of Upper Egypt was to

POMPEY'S PILLAR.

elevate them in their own opinion, and to render them ever after more rebellious against the Greeks of Alexandria.

However, the reign of Zenobia in Egypt was of short duration, for Aurelian overcame her army in 272, took her prisoner, and carried her to Rome, where, after gracing his triumph, she was permitted to pass her life in that quiet which must be the most acute torture to a woman like Zenobia.

> " City of Solomon ! whose fame and power,
> And wondrous wealth, began in earth's young hour;
> How, mid her fallen pomp, thought wanders back
> O'er vanished days,—a sad yet dazzling track.
> Arabia's fierce and desolating horde,
> Rome's conquering eagle, Babylonia's sword,
> All we behold, but chief one form appears,
> Rising all radiant from the gulf of years:
> Proud is her step, her dark eye varying oft;
> Now flashing fire, now languishingly soft;
> The jewelled crown well suits that brow serene,—
> 'Tis great Zenobia, Tadmor's glorious queen.
> Beauty hath oft put war's dread helmet on,
> Since her who ruled earth-conquering Babylon;
> Yet not Semiramis, who boasts her bays,
> Nor Gaul's bold maid, who graced these latter days,
> Swayed the rough hearts of men with wilder power,
> Or met more bravely battle's dreadful hour,
> Than she on whom pleased fame and fortune smiled,
> The dark-haired mistress of the Syrian wild.
>
> But now the conqueror's brighter hour has passed,
> And fair Zenobia's star goes down at last.

The Roman comes,—his legions file around,
Doomed Tadmor's walls, to deafening trumpets sound.
Aurelian bids the desert princess yield,
But hark! her answer—clashing sword and shield!
Girt by her chiefs, her proud plumed head she rears,
Defies the foe, and each faint spirit cheers;
Her milk-white courser prances round the wall,
Her gestures, looks, and words inspiring all.
Through opened gates her troops are sallying now,
Still in their front appears that dauntless brow:
Where'er her silver wand is seen to wave,
There rush the boldest, and there fall the brave,
And when borne back by Rome's immense array,
She fights retreating, pauses still to slay.

But ceaseless war, and famine's tortures slow,
Wear bravery out, and bring Palmyra low.
'Twas then the Queen, to crush the despot's might,
Passed from the gates beneath the veil of night,
Hers still the hope from Persia aid to call,
Save her loved land, and stay Palmyra's fall.
With fluttering heart, but calm and fearless eye,
Across the trackless desert see her fly!
On swept the camel with unflagging speed,
As though he knew that hour of deadly need;
Her Syrian guards o'er Arab steeds might lean,
But not keep pace with her, their flying queen.
What recked she drifting sand or scorching sun?
What recked she pain or toil, that mission done?
Come hunger, thirst,—on, on her course must be,
Each swift-winged hour brought, Tadmor, doom to thee!

Lo! on their track, through clouds of rising sand,
Bright helms were seen, now glittered spear and brand:
Then horsemen forward dashed,—a long-drawn row,—
'Twas Rome's dread troops, the fierce pursuing foe!

They saw, and hailed,—across the waste was borne.
The hoarse, deep note of many a trumpet-horn;
And on they came, like winds careering fast,
Not half so fearful sweeps the simoom blast;
They brought for her who scoured those desert plains,
Woe and disgrace, captivity and chains.
But still Zenobia flew, the steeds that bore
Her guards had sunk,—those chiefs could aid no more;
And now that camel shaped his course alone,—
He reared his head as louder blasts were blown,
And strained each nerve his soft black drooping eye
Telling of suffering, fear and agony;
Unhappy, faithful thing! that still would brave
Toil, peril, death, his royal charge to save.

'Twas vain: as hounds at length chase down the deer,
The Roman horsemen drew more near and near;
Though some fell back, or sank upon the way,
Yet others, slowly gaining, reached the prey.
They halted, wheeled,—their armors' dazzling sheen
Formed a dread wall round Syria's fated queen;
Hope fled her breast,—she yielded,—ruined now,
But still majestic shone that high-born brow.
Ah! as they led their prisoner o'er the plain,
No more to rule, but grace a tyrant's train,
And, exiled, pine where wooded Anio sweeps,
Far from her desert home and palmy steeps,
The sun of Syria's power went down in night,
On Freedom's tree there rained a withering blight.
Glory to proud Palmyra sighed adieu,
And o'er her shrines Destruction's angel flew."

Soon after Zenobia's fall the Egyptians endeavored to assert themselves by setting up as their ruler Firmus, a Syrian, who took the title of emperor, and leading the Arabs and native Egyptians against **Alexandria, undertook its overthrow.** No reliable account of this rebellion exists. The new government was organized, and Coptos and Ptolemais selected as its capital cities, but the Romans were greatly disturbed by this movement, fearing the loss of the tribute of Egyptian corn, and Aurelian hastened to attack Firmus, made him a prisoner, then tortured and finally murdered him.

This unsuccessful revolt was the first manifestation of the independence which the Arabs and Blemmyes of Upper Egypt were beginning to feel. Their troops were so constantly engaged in rebellions on one hand or the other that a better discipline was reached, and they began to assume a character ill suited to the slaves of Rome. At length, in the fourth year of the reign of Diocletian, A. D. 288, a serious rebellion broke out, and one Achilleus was declared emperor. This new movement assumed such proportions that in A. D. 292 Diocletian, in person, led his army into Southern Egypt and destroyed Coptos and Busiris, after they had sustained long sieges.

But a short time elapsed ere the city of Alexandria declared itself in favor of Achilleus, and Diocletian again led an attack in Egypt. Alexandria held out against a siege of eight months, at the end of which Diocletian entered as its conqueror. Fortunately for the Egyptians his horse stumbled as he rode into the city, and he taking this for an augury, and interpreting it to mean mercy, did not subject the Alexandrians to the fate they might reasonably have feared. It was in honor of this clemency that the so-called Pompey's Pillar was erected, and was, in all probability, surmounted by a statue of the horse which saved the city from pillage and destruction.

But that which marks the reign of Diocletian with a stain, so scarlet that at this distance of time it is clearly discerned upon the ever moving roll of history, is the edict of persecution against the Christians, which was carried out to the extremist letter in the province of Egypt. The story belongs to the history of the church, and its recital causes a double wonder at the pertinacity with which the Christians endured, and at the fertile invention of sufferings and torments with which the Romans were endowed. So important was this persecution that the habit of reckoning from the era of Augustus was abandoned, and time was reckoned from the first year of Diocletian, and called by Christians the Era of Martyrs.

From this time to that of the reign of Constantine many different beliefs arose in Egypt, the most important being that called Manicheism, a Persian form of Gnostic doctrine.

The succession of Constantine, as sole emperor of Rome, A. D. 313, made a revolution in the religion and character of the whole empire. He became a Christian, and his reign was marked by quarrels between different sects of Christians, rather than those between Christians and Pagans. The council at Nicæa, and the great Arian controversy occurred during the reign of Constantine.

The building up of Constantinople robbed Alexandria of its prestige as a seat of learning, and gave it a blow from which it never recovered. But Alexandria continued to be famous as the fountain of all true knowledge in religious matters for some time, until finally even this precedence was lost, and asceticism, magic and astrology did their deadly work, taking the place of the paganism and idolatry which gradually died out, so that even the advent of the pagan Julian, and all his zeal for its resurrection, only served to show how dead it really was.

NUBIAN SERPENT CHARMERS.

About 370, when paganism was quite extinct, the monasteries of Egypt had risen to their best estate. The laws of the empire acknowledged them and protected their property and rights. Pachomius founded an order which then numbered more than seven thousand, although his rule was most severe. Another order was under the leadership of Anuph, who boasted that he could obtain anything for which he chose to pay.

Serapion was at the head of a thousand monks in the Arsinoite Nome, and a large company withdrew to the desert of Scetis, the spot sanctified by the penance and triumph of St. Anthony, and the devotion, self-denial and endurance of these men form a story almost exceeding belief.

Many solitary hermits and monks were scattered through Egypt, leading the severest penitential lives. Some of these monks wrote such things as have rendered their fame immortal, but others, and the larger number, were simple, devout men, devoted to their doctrines, which, in many cases, were anything but such as a true Christian should believe.

St. Jerome gives an account of St. Mary of Egypt, which is essentially as follows: A woman named Mary, whose wickedness far exceeded that of Mary Magdalen, dwelt at Alexandria, and after seventeen years of the most abandoned life, in the year 365, as she walked one day near the sea, saw a vessel about to depart for Syria, well filled with pilgrims who were going to Jerusalem. On inquiry she found that they went to keep the feast of the True Cross. She was seized with an irrepressible desire to go with them, and having no money for the voyage she sold herself to the sailors and pilgrims, and thus accomplished the journey.

Arriving at Jerusalem she approached the church with the others, but when she would enter some invisible power restrained her, and as often as she essayed to cross the threshold so often was she driven back.

Then a sense of all her wickedness came over her — sorrow overpowered her — she fell to the ground and prayed for pardon and peace. Instantly the restraint was removed, and she entered the church on her knees.

When she came out she bought three loaves of bread and went into the desert, even beyond Jordan, where she remained in deepest penitence. She drank only water, and subsisted on roots and berries and her three loaves, which were constantly renewed by a miracle.

Her clothing wore out and dropped off, then she prayed God to clothe her, and her hair became like a thick cloak about her, or, as others say, an angel bore her a heavenly garment.

When she had thus passed forty-seven years she was found by Zosimus, a priest. She begged him to keep silence concerning her, and to return at the end of a year, and bring with him a holy wafer that she might confess herself and receive the holy sacrament before her death. Zosimus did as she asked, and when he returned was not able to cross the Jordan, and Mary was miraculously assisted to cross to him. After receiving the wafer she requested him to leave her, and to return at the end of another year.

When that time had passed and the good priest came again he found her dead, and in her hand a paper, upon which was written: "O, Father Zosimus, bury the body of the poor sinner, Mary of Egypt! Give earth to earth, and dust to dust, for Christ's sake!" When he endeavored to do this he found himself unable, for he was old and feeble. Then a lion came and assisted him, digging with his paws; and when the body of Mary was placed in the grave the lion went quietly away, and Zosimus returned home, praising God for the mercy he had shown to the penitent woman. *

St. Macarius, of Alexandria, another hermit saint, was very famous in Egypt for his scholarship, as well as for his piety. The following singular story is told of him, and it is illustrated by a painting in the Campo Santo at Pisa. He was once walking among the Egyptian tombs when he saw a skull. He turned it over, and asked to whom it belonged. It replied, "To a pagan." He then said, "Where is thy soul?" and the skull replied, "In hell." The saint then demanded, "How deep?" "The depth is more than the distance between heaven and earth," answered the skull. Then Macarius asked, "Are any deeper than thou?" "Yes, the Jews are deeper still," was the reply. "And any deeper than the Jews?" again questioned the hermit. "Yes, in sooth, for the Christians whom Christ Jesus hath redeemed, and who show in their acts that they despise his doctrine, are deeper still," replied the skull.

---

* St. Mary of Egypt is mentioned by Southey, in Roderick, the last of the Goths, as—that Egyptian penitent whose tears fretted the rock and moistened round her cave the thirsty desert.

Chaucer mentions her, in the Canterbury Tales, line 4,922, and she is one of the penitents who intercede for the soul of Margaret, in Goethe's Faust, second part, Act v., Sc. 7.

CAPTIVE JEWS IN THE HIPPODROME AT ALEXANDRIA.

The monasteries of Egypt were visited by many strangers, and the monks were believed to require no learning to aid them to speak divine truth, since God had endowed them with the power of miracle-working, and revealed all holy knowledge to them, through the Holy Spirit.

When Theodosius came to the throne in 379 he made the most sweeping and fiercest attack upon paganism that had yet been known, and commanded that Christian observances should be established throughout the kingdom.

He had a sympathetic co-worker in Theophilus, the bishop of Alexandria, who was so forcible in his measures that a serious strife ensued between the Christians and Pagans, in the course of which the temple of Serapis was destroyed, together with the great library, numbering more than seven hundred thousand volumes.

The first great library of Alexandria had been destroyed in the time of Julius Cæsar; then Anthony presented to Cleopatra the library of Pergamus, containing two hundred thousand volumes, which had been increased to the size mentioned above, when this Christian zeal caused its destruction.

In 394, upon the death of Theodosius, the

Roman Empire was divided into the Eastern and Western Empires; Egypt was included in the eastern division, ruled by Arcadius, under whom no important changes occurred, and he was succeeded in 408 by his son, Theodosius.

As the last was but a child, Cyril was appointed governor, and under his rule another persecution of the Jews took place.

Theodosius II. reigned nearly forty-two years, and met his death by accident, being thrown from his horse while hunting near Constantinople, and receiving injuries from which he died. No glory, in truth no importance of any sort is associated with the time of this emperor. The story of his wife, the heathen Athenais, called Eudocia in Christian baptism, though not necessary to be related here, is of unusual interest.

CHAPTER IX.

FROM THE PERSIAN INVASION, A. D. 501, TO THE ARAB CONQUEST, A. D. 640.

Female playing on a guitar, from a box.

FROM the death of Theodosius II. to A. D. 501, the tenth year of the reign of the Emperor Anastasius, the history of Egypt is a mere story of petty civil and religious discords, of ups and downs, each year as it passed, leaving Egypt more unimportant than at its beginning, until (in 501) the Persians, after possessing themselves of a large portion of Syria entered Egypt at Pelusium, and laid everything waste as they passed on towards Alexandria. The capital, however, was not taken, and the Persians retired leaving starvation behind them. Then fierce riots took place, for the people, who were dying of disease and famine, rebelled against the officers of the government, and were with difficulty restrained from themselves destroying their city, which had escaped the pillage of the invaders.

The Persian inroad should have taught the Christians of Alexandria and Constantinople that their only safety was in union; but the lesson was unheeded, and they were so occupied with quarrels between Jacobites and Melchites, between rival bishops and rival forms of worship, that they were fatally unfitting themselves for any concerted action, fatally preparing to fall a prey to the worshippers of the sun. Worse than all the persecution of the Copts, and kindred measures, engendered in many Egyptians an envy of the Arabic subjects of Persia, who while under foreign dominion had, in a certain sense, more freedom than was accorded the people of Egypt.

That wise policy, which Augustus so well appreciated when he allowed the Egyptians to follow their own religion and customs, was forgotten, and exactly the opposite course pursued.

The Persians had obtained possession of the fortress of Petra, and in the year 527 Justinian, in order to protect the sole pass by which a Persian army could enter Egypt without a fleet, built a fortified monastery near Mount Sinai. This monastery is said to have been built upon the spot where

THE MONASTERY OF ST. CATHERINE.

Moses stood when God spoke to him. It is now called the monastery of St. Catherine.

After this convent was finished it was found that another peak commanded it, upon which the emperor beheaded the builder, and put another small fortress on the higher ground.

The monastery of St. Catherine is now visited by many travellers, and until recently all who went there were hoisted and lowered by a crane and windlass, as no outlet existed below an aperture high up in the wall. Now there is a gateway which is jealously guarded.

The idea of making a monastery a fortress seems to have been borrowed from the ancient Egyptians, for the old temples were always the strongholds of the cities. So the Roman emperors made the monks their protectors, not only in the monastery of St. Catherine, but also in those of St. Anthony and St. Paul, near the Red Sea.

Under the reign of Justinian the final blow was given to learning in Egypt, for among the Egyptians the priests alone had been scholars, and the extinction of their worship thus included that of learning. At Alexandria severe measures had been taken at times against the pagan philosophers, and their schools had been closed, yet the laws had rarely been strictly enforced, and the pagan teachers had fed the dying flame of Alexandrian scholarship and learning. But now the emperor commanded their perfect silence, and this city, famous for its erudition, was left to the ignorance of its last state, which was in certain ways worse than its first, since it is best that an ignorant people should be governed and held in check by those who are at unity, and hold one faith. But now in

WINDLASS AT THE CONVENT.

Egypt the doctors disagreed, and each point of belief was made a cause of unending quarrels and contentions.

Justinian was followed by the emperors Justin

II., Mauricius and Phocas, the latter being the murderer of his predecessor. On account of this murder Chosroes, of Persia, who had married the daughter of Mauricius, declared all his treaties with the Romans at an end, and immediately moved his army against Phocas. The reign of this emperor was a period of great disturbance in Egypt, and in the seventh year a rebellion occurred at Alexandria by which Heraclius, a son of a prefect of Cyrene, was placed in power. When Heraclius entered the port of Constantinople with his fleet, Phocas was murdered in his turn, and was little regretted, for during his short reign of eight years he had lost every province of the empire.

Chosroes of Persia commanded an immense army, and the early part of the reign of Heraclius was a period of continual warfare, for Chosroes attacked Jerusalem, Constantinople and Lower Egypt simultaneously. The latter was easily overcome, but the first two cost a longer and harder struggle. The conquest of Jerusalem, and the seizure of the True Cross by the Persian monarch, aroused Heraclius from an apathy which had apparently robbed him of all energy during the first years of his power.

Now Chosroes had conquered the whole territory, from the Euphrates to the Bosphorus; Chalcedon surrendered to him, and a Persian camp was maintained more than ten years in the immediate presence of Constantinople.

The provinces which had been taken from the Romans were hard to govern. The idea, if not the reality of a republic, had always been kept alive by both Greeks and Romans, and those who had always talked of liberty and law, submitted with poor grace to the absolute and insolent policy of an oriental monarch.

To the Christians of the East the worship of fire was an abomination and horror. Gibbon says that: "Conscious of their fear and hatred, the Persian monarch governed his new subjects with an iron sceptre; he exhausted their wealth by exorbitant tributes and by plunder; he despoiled or demolished their temples, and transported to his hereditary realms the gold, the silver, the precious marbles, the arts and the artists of the conquered cities."

At the time of the conquest of Jerusalem the Emperor Heraclius, in his capital of Constantinople, showed no sign of the noble courage which he later developed. Indeed, he made preparations to flee to Carthage, but the patriarch led him to the altar of St. Sophia, where he took a solemn oath to live and die with the people over whom God had placed him as a ruler.

Had we no other matter in hand, the Herculean labors of this emperor alone would furnish a most interesting study. Here it must be curtly said, that from the time when he aroused himself to his work, he undertook six arduous expeditions against the Persians before he stood forth as their conqueror. During that time he drilled and educated his army; he called them sons and brothers, and imposed no hardships that he did not share, until he came to be regarded with perfect confidence.

"Be not terrified," he said, " with the number of your foes. With the aid of Heaven one Roman may triumph over a thousand barbarians. But if we devote our lives for the salvation of our brethren we shall obtain the crown of martyrdom and our immortal reward will be liberally paid by God and by posterity."

Chosroes had at length exhausted his treasures, and his Arab troops, which had been of great use to him at Constantinople and in Egypt, rebelled against him, and thus took the first step towards the establishment of a new power, of which we shall soon speak. At length after many mishaps, the Romans advanced even upon Dastagerd, the favorite residence of the proud Persian, where he was surrounded by such wealth and magnificent state as has seldom been equalled by the world's rulers.

His parks were filled with unnumbered flocks and herds, while peacocks, ostriches and other game, and even lions and tigers were kept for the pleasures of the chase. He had nine hundred and sixty elephants to enhance his splendor; his tents and baggage were moved by a train of twelve thousand large and eight thousand smaller camels; and six thousand horses and mules were in his stables.

Six thousand guards were successively mounted before the palace; twelve thousand slaves served within, and three thousand virgins were in his harem. A hundred subterraneous chambers were scarcely sufficient to contain his supplies of gold, silver, gems, silks, and aromatics. It is said that thirty thousand rich hangings were on the walls, forty thousand pillars supported the roof, and one thousand gold globes were suspended from the dome to imitate the motions of the planets and constellations.

When Heraclius laid siege to this wondrous

palace, much of this wealth had been exhausted, but enough remained to satisfy the rapacity of the conquerors.

Chosroes fled to Ctesiphon, and one of his sons seized the throne; the wretched old monarch was thrown into a dungeon, where he died on the fifth day.

A treaty was made between Heraclius and the new king, by which the emperor recovered his power in Egypt.

During the years of the Persian invasion, Mohammed had come forth and declared himself a prophet, and his power began to arise, destined to control the Eastern World.

The revolt of the Arabs against Chosroes was the first stone laid in the foundation of the future mighty empire of the caliphs. The historians of Arabia reckon their time from the Hegira, or the flight of Mohammed from Mecca to Medina, which took place in the twelfth year of the reign of Heraclius.

The Moslems soon overpowered the Persians, and it was not long after the treaty made with the latter by Heraclius, before the Romans began to realize that a still more dangerous enemy opposed them. So great was the power of this sect, that in a short time Heraclius paid a tribute to the Prophet for the privilege of retaining his rights in Egypt. This continued eight years — then the emperor had no means of paying this tax. Now the Mohammedans began to force themselves and their religion upon Alexandria, which, in its miserable condition, easily yielded to any power, for so great had been the evil consequences of the factions in the so-called Christian church—the quarrels of the Jacobites and the Melchites — that the Egyptians saw the approach of a rival religion with little dread, feeling that no change could be for the worse.

At the time of the Mohammedan conquest, Omar, the second caliph, was in command, and his general, Amru, led the army which made an easy conquest of Egypt, since but two towns, Babylon and Alexandria, made anything worthy of being called resistance or attempted to defend themselves.

The story runs that just when Amru was about to enter Egypt, near Raphia, a sealed packet was given to him by a courier from the caliph Omar. Amru feared that it might contain his recall, and refused to receive it until he should have passed the boundary line and halted his troops upon Egyptian soil. Then he called his officers about him and

Omar's letter was read. It was as the wily general had suspected, and if he had not read it in Egypt he would have been compelled to relinquish the prey almost within his grasp.

When Amru reached the fortress of Babylon and saw that it would hold out against a siege, he sent to the caliph for more soldiers. The Greeks were brave and determined, and had not Makoukas, the governor of Memphis, proved a traitor, the victory would have been dear to the Moslems. But Makoukas pursuaded the Greeks that if they remained within the citadel they must be lost, and a large portion of the garrison retired with him to the island of Rodah in the Nile, and destroyed the bridge over which they passed. By this means the fortress was easily captured by Amru.

The Egyptians, through the medium of Makoukas, had basely agreed to pay tribute to the caliph, but the Greeks, less cowardly in spirit, and full of hatred for the Arabs, made a brave retreat to Alexandria, in the course of which they fought several desperate battles and lost many men. This retreat occupied three weeks time and covered a distance of one hundred and fifty miles.

When the Greeks who had made a part of the garrisons of Babylon and Memphis thus threw themselves into Alexandria, all began to make ready for a brave defence of that city, and the Arabs, on their part prepared for a long siege.

One incident of this conflict shows how great results often hang upon a look or word. The Greeks made daily sallies upon the Moslem camp, and on one occasion Amru, with a handful of men, followed rashly within the gates of the city, which were promptly closed behind them. The Greeks then demanded of the prisoners what they would choose for their fate, since they were wholly within the power of their enemies. Amru haughtily replied, "You must pay us a tribute, or become Mohammedans, or one of us must die." Then the Greeks guessed his rank, but a cunning Arab, who saw his general's mistake, boldly slapped his face and commanded him to keep silence before his betters, while he proceeded to convince the Greeks that the best course would be to allow the prisoners to act as messengers for them and thus arrange a peace with the Arab chief.

He gained his point, and a letter was written to Amru, and despatched by the prisoners to the camp. The joyous shouts with which they were received, and the cry of "God is great," soon convinced the Greeks of the value of the prize they had thus foolishly released.

After fourteen weary months the Moslems were victorious; the Greeks fled, some by land and some by sea, and Amru was so incautious as to pursue the former. Then those who were in the ships returned, and again possessed the city, putting to death the Arabs who were left as a garrison. But the weakened Greeks could not long hold out against the renewed attacks of the maddened Amru, and finally, on Friday, December twenty-second, in the year of our Lord six hundred and forty, Egypt became an Arabian province.

Sharpe, in his history of Egypt says, " Amrou, wrote word to the caliph Omar, boasting that he had taken a city which beggared all description, in which he found four thousand palaces, four thousand public baths, four hundred theatres, twelve thousand sellers of herbs; and, having a thievish eye for Jewish industry, he added that there were forty thousand Jews paying tribute. Such was the store of wheat which he sent on camels' backs to Medina, that the Arabic historian declares, in his usual style of eastern poetry, that the first of an unbroken line of camels entered the holy city before the last camel had left Egypt."

VIEW FROM THE CITADEL OF CAIRO.

The Greeks regarded Alexandria at this time as greatly fallen from its former estate, but to the Arabs it was even now of wondrous beauty. There were the Pharos; the Heptastadium; bridges uniting two harbors; the four beautiful gates of the Sun, and Moon, the Canobic gate, and that of the Necropolis; the magnificent Soma or Mausoleum of the great founder of the city; the Museum which had been rebuilt since the destruction of that of the Ptolemies; Cæsar's temple and several Christian churches; and more than all, the temple of Serapis, only exceeded in all the world by the capitol at Rome.

Besides these edifices and noble works which still remained, there were the ruins of the Hippodrome, the Bruchium, the aqueduct, and many other remnants of a still grander past.

Although the famous library of Alexandria had been twice destroyed, once in the time of Julius Cæsar, and again under Theodosius I., as has been already mentioned, yet at the time of the Arab conquest many books remained, for history relates that when Amru set his seal upon all the public property, John Philoponus begged that the books might be spared; accordingly, Amru asked the caliph for direction in the matter. Omar replied that if the books were the same as the Koran they were useless, and if not like the Koran they were worthless, therefore they should be burned in any case; history adds that they were used for heating the public baths, and were sufficient for that purpose during the space of six months.

EGYPTIAN GIRL.

CHAPTER X.

FROM THE ARAB CONQUEST, A.D. 640, TO THE FRENCH INVASION IN 1798.

AT the time of the subjugation of Egypt by Amru, the Mohammedan or Saracenic government was in an utterly unorganized condition. As far as Egypt was concerned no clear history of it under Moslem rule can be given before the end of the tenth century, when Cahira or Cairo became the chief city of the Fatimite caliphs. The eighth and ninth centuries were spent in settling the claims of the various descendants of the Prophet, for the three families of his uncle Abbas, his son-in-law Ali, and his daughter Fatima, expelled one another from the thrones of Damascus and Bagdad, and at times Egypt and other conquered provinces were able to add to the general confusion by declaring their independence. But at length the lineal descendants of the Prophet were in its midst and the Egyptians were hopelessly doomed to ages of Saracenic slavery.

The Arabic name of Cairo is Musr el Kaherah, and signifies "the victorious capital." It was founded in 969. The Fatimite caliphs removed the bones of their ancestors to this new city and its increase and adornment became their chief care.

The eleventh century brought many misfortunes to Egypt. The more eastern caliphs sent the Turks who were in their service to attack the Fatimite rulers; a famine, followed by pestilence and plague depopulated the land; and the crusaders threatened Cairo with destruction. The building of the city went on slowly until 1171, when the Mameluke Saladin usurped the power and laid the foundation of his remarkable dynasty, called that of the Ayubites.

Saladin, not being a lineal descendant of the Prophet, could not assume the title of caliph, as that implied a sacred office as well as a kingly one, therefore, he called himself a Sultan, and appointed a priest from among those who claimed to have the blood of the great Mohammed in their veins.

Saladin was not by any means allowed a peaceful enjoyment of his rule. Though acknowledged

EGYPTIAN WOMAN.

as the sovereign of Egypt by many smaller states, and though the caliph of Bagdad sanctioned his government, the king of Syria opposed him because he feared so powerful a neighbor, and the descendants of the Fatimites succeeded in bringing one hundred thousand men into the field against him. Next, the crusaders, under William of Sicily, laid siege to Alexandria, and though they ignominiously fled before meeting the Saracens, they gave Saladin much trouble in his warlike preparations. Finally, the Damascenes made war upon him, and it was not until these most jealous foes had been overcome that the new Sultan could sit firmly in his royal seat.

He now turned his attention to the fortification and improvement of Cairo; he encouraged schools and literature, and had the ambition to make his city excel the ancient Thebes or Memphis. Many of the magnificent works of Egypt were despoiled or entirely destroyed in order to furnish materials for the enriching and adornment of the new Mohammedan capital.

But the soldier spirit of Saladin could not long remain quiet, and he soon craved new conquests. A history of his Syrian campaigns, in course of which he carried his victorious arms even to Jerusalem, does not belong here, interesting as it is.

Saladin died in 1193, leaving behind him many works which still testify to the truth that though he was preëminently a soldier, he was also attentive to the welfare of his kingdom in many ways. The citadel of Cairo, the walls, canals, roads and dykes, and various other large labors, attest his intelligence in his home rule.

Saladin was chivalrous according to the highest standard of mediæval times; faithful to his promises; moderate in his judgments; brave to a fault; just, generous, and pious. These qualities were accorded him even by his enemies.

Saladin was succeeded by his son Alcamel, who made himself a great name by his victories over the crusaders.

Alcamel died in 1238, and was followed by Aladil, a younger son, whose death soon placed Nojmoddin, the eldest brother in power. This Sultan was, like his predecessors, much occupied with the crusaders, but the chief matter of Egyptian interest connected with his reign, was the rise of the power of the Mamelukes, who finally governed Egypt during more than five centuries.

The word Mameluke signifies "the possessed," or slaves, and this formidable class were indeed

Circassian slaves, brought to Egypt as body-guards to the Sultans, who feared to trust themselves entirely in the hands of the people they had conquered. Each Sultan unthinkingly added little by little to the power of these slaves, until at last, the occasion of a very young prince being left heir to the throne presenting itself, one of the Mamelukes called Ibeg or Moez was made regent; the young prince died; Moez married the queen-mother, and ascended the throne as Sultan. After a short reign he was assassinated by the order of his wife, but his son succeeded him, and though many rebellions had taken place, the Mamelukes retained the power.

The history of the Mamelukes is so much a history of wars, massacres and general horrors, that it is pleasant to turn to one of their number whose name is now principally associated with the arts of peace. Sultan Kalaon came to the throne in 1279, and though at first he devoted himself to the expulsion of the Franks from Syria, yet, that being done, he turned his attention to the fortification of Damascus, Aleppo, and other Syrian towns, and rebuilt the castles, walls and gates in so picturesque a style as to command the gratitude as well as the admiration of all beholders to the present day.

The son and grandson of Kalaon, Mohammed-el-Nasr and Hassan, maintained his reputation as an architect and a lover of beautiful things. In truth the fourteenth century was a golden period in the history of the Mameluke Sultans. Machiavelli says of this epoch, "The influence of a land full of delights was so modified by the vigor of the institutions, that Egypt produced most eminent men of every kind; and, if the long succession of ages had not extinguished their names, we should have seen how much more worthy of praise they were than Alexander the Great, and so many others whose renown still flourishes."

This sounds like very exaggerated praise, but it indicates that the Egyptians of the period commanded the respect of Europeans. The whole history of the Sultan Hassan seems to be told in that of his mosque, still one of the most beautiful and interesting monuments in Cairo. (It is seen on the right of the illustration of the view from the citadel of Cairo). This Sultan came to the throne when but thirteen years old, in 1347. He was very strict in his religion and conformed his life to the exact precepts of the Koran. When he was twenty-two years old he commenced the building of his mosque, and when his treasurer complained of his lavishness in the sums he spent upon it, and the low state of his purse, Hassan replied, " It is better that the Sultan should be poor, than that people should say that he began a mosque and could not finish it." This mosque is built of stone which formerly made the outer, highly polished covering of the pyramid of Cheops. It is a very imposing building, and it is said that when the architect who built it had completed his work, his hands were chopped off, that he might not build another more beautiful. The burial-place of Sultan Hassan, said to be on the spot where he was murdered, is entered from the court through a lofty archway, leading into the chamber which contains the tomb. Fairholt says of this mosque, " It abounds with the most enriched details of ornament within and without: not the least remarkable of its fittings being the rows of colored-glass lamps hanging from the walls, of Syrian manufacture, bearing the Sultan's name, amid colored decorations; they are some of the finest early glass-work of their kind, but many are broken, and others hanging unsafely from half corroded chains.

The dynasty of Saladin endured but about one hundred and twenty years. In 1382 the Barghite dynasty was founded by Barcok, who named it for the Barghites, a class of Mameluke garrison troops, thus called to distinguish them from the troops in active service. Barcok was a good Sultan, though an usurper, and proved himself a benefactor to his subjects.

The close of the fourteenth century was much disturbed in the Orient by the strife between Tamerlane, the chief of the Monguls and Tartars, and Bajazet, the leader of the Ottomans. For a time it seemed that Egypt must become an ally or perhaps a tributary to one of these warriors, but it retained its independence and continued under the Barghite dynasty until 1517, when the Turks conquered the Egyptians, and the country was once more a province of a foreign power. At first, the Turkish government, called the Porte, thus organized its service in Egypt. The Pasha or Viceroy was at its head; the Sheik or governor of Cairo was chosen from the Mameluke Beys, and presided over the affairs of the provinces of the country; the Janizary Aga was the commander of the Janizaries; the Defturdar was the accountant-general; the Emir el Hadgi was the conductor of the caravan; the Emir el Saïd was the governor of Upper Egypt, and the Sheik el Bekheri was the governor of the Sherifs.

This first, and well conceived organization, was gradually changed, and finally, twenty-four Beys superintended the districts into which the kingdom was divided, and each one collected the revenues of his own district; this gave these Beys an influence which rendered them formidable, and permitted their indulgence of an insolence not at all in harmony with the prejudices of their ruler. But the Pashas and military officials became tools in the hands of the Beys, on account of the reward given by the latter, and, in short, one set of officers after another yielded themselves as tools of the Beys, being governed by avarice or other sinister motives. In the beginning these governors or Beys had each a few slaves; this appeared to be a necessity in order that they might command the respect of the people over whom they were placed; but the slaves were materially increased until the force under each Bey made him truly independent, in an alarming degree, of the power which had created his office and chosen him to fill it.

Again, when a vacancy occurred in a province, a neighboring Bey frequently filled it with his favorite Mameluke, who, thereafter was but a tool in the hand of the master who had thus exalted him. These particulars will indicate the means by which it came about at last that the most capable and active Beys held great influence in the government, their Mamelukes being the most efficient and reliable soldiers and subordinate officials in the country.

The history of Egypt, from the establishment of the Ottoman power down to the time of the French invasion, is merely an account of the quarrels, more or less serious, between the Sultans, Pashas and Beys. There were many revolts, numberless murders, sometimes actions which could be dignified by the name of battles, always the most cruel and diabolical acts concealed by an appearance of fair dealing, and, in short, a sickening chapter of what can be done by ignorant and ambitious men when they are in power. Meanwhile, the common people were oppressed to the very dust; taxes were extorted by the koorbash from starving men; disease and pestilence swept through the land, and the ravages of these last were past belief, for, as the Mohammedan faith in predestination was absolute, no care was even used to prevent or remedy disease. Taken all in all, there was at this period in Egypt, a degradation for exceeding any that had come to her under any preceding foreign masters.

One cause of the extremely oppressive taxation was the enormous cost by which the Pasha maintained his position. It is said, upon good authority, to have cost each Pasha at least four hundred thousand crowns before he obtained his office from the Sultan, and was established in Cairo. The yearly demands of the Sultan were enormous; six hundred thousand crowns must be sent to Constantinople, besides supplies of sugar, rice, spices, coffee, and so on, for the Seraglio; then the Pasha of Egypt was compelled to pay the expenses of the annual caravans to Mecca from both Egypt and Damascus, and to send with them one hundred thousand crowns in specie for the costs upon the route; and it must be remembered that in addition to these the entire support of the Egyptian government and army was drawn from the Egyptian tributes.

One great source of income to the Pashas was the result of the pestilence, for all the lands owned by those who died from the plague reverted to the Pasha, who sold them to the highest bidder at public sale,— and as it often happened that one purchaser after another died in quick succession, the same lands were sold again and again, and at such prices that the purchasers were forced to farm them out at extortionate rates, in order to obtain any return upon their capital. Such a system must inevitably reduce any country to beggary, and the riches of ancient Egypt must have passed all power of telling, or the country would have come to naught much sooner than it did.

The above facts give an outline of the system followed by the officers of the Porte, but the details, the petty modes of increasing the revenue were almost numberless, and though many unlawful acts were perpetrated by the Beys and Janissaries which were made causes of complaint to the Sultan, no means were used for the reform of these abuses. The state of affairs was more desperate in Upper than Lower Egypt, since that country was subject to the inroads of the Arabs in addition to all other burdens.

The magnificence of the Pashas and Beys was almost unsurpassed. The Beys seldom appeared on their daily promenades except they rode superbly caparisoned horses, with trappings embroidered in gold and silver, followed by thirty or forty youths, all equally mounted and marching with that peculiarly grand and dignified carriage of the Turks. The chief Beys, such as the commander of the Mecca caravan, and those in the

WATCHING FIELDS IN EGYPT.

higher offices, seldom appeared with less than three hundred attendants, all of whom were fitted out in true oriental magnificence.

Under this government, architecture, and everything which may be included under the general term of art, fell into a despicable condition. The present city of Cairo was founded in 969, and four years later the walls and many buildings were completed. This could not have been done had not much material been stripped from the edifices and pyramids of ancient builders; even to this day paving stones are seen upon which are hieroglyphics and traces of antique sculptures. Cairo is situated about a mile from the river, on a sandy plain at the foot of a mountain, and has a much hotter climate than other places in the same latitude, indeed, in the summer season the heat is almost unendurable. Since the opening of the Suez Canal many streets have been widened, Ezbekieh Square has put on the appearance of a Parisian park, whole blocks of houses and shops are fac-similes of those most approved on the continent, and much that was characteristic has passed away forever. But in the old portions of Cairo the streets are little more than lanes in width, and the houses ugly and uncomfortable in the extreme, with few exceptions.

They are generally of stone in the lower part with the upper stories in wood, or unburnt bricks, or earth whitened with lime. They are built around a court with no windows on the street, and without ornament, besides lacking the airiness that one would naturally look for in such a climate.

The courts are sometimes made attractive by plashing fountains, shady palms, and the plants which grow and flower luxuriantly with little care; but the apartments, with perhaps the exception of a single *salon*, where guests are received, are bare and comfortless. Cairo is the city of mosques; those with minarets or towers are numbered by hundreds while there are many more humble ones, in reality chapels or oratories. Some of these mosques are very beautiful. One of the oldest is that of the Sultan Touloon, built in 879, before the walls of the city were laid. It is interesting to note that this mosque had pointed arches at least two centuries before they were introduced into England.

There is a legend that Abraham had sacrificed, upon the site of this mosque, that ram which appeared to him when he was about to slay his son Isaac. It is built around a large open court, with rows of pillars surrounding it. This is a very interesting building, though it has small claims to being called beautiful The mosque of Sultan Hassan has already been spoken of. That of

DISTANT VIEW OF CAIRO, WITH THE CITADEL AND THE PYRAMIDS OF GIZEH AND SAKKARA.

Mohammed Ali is the only one that is not falling into decay. Various reasons have been given for this, such as a decline in religious zeal, and a superstitious hesitation to touch the work of the builders who lived so long ago; but the truth probably is, that the Sultans have taken the riches of the mosques for other uses, and the government has now no money with which to repair the decaying city. The mosque of the great Mohammed Ali is on the same eminence with the citadel of Cairo, which is a sharp projection of the Mokattam hills. It is built of oriental alabaster from Tel el amarna, and is very beautiful. Without it is unfinished, but within it is gorgeous; the alabaster is in large panels and so highly polished as to be dazzling in effect. The floor is covered with Turkey rugs, and the tomb of Mohammed Ali is in a quiet corner, very near the scenes of some of the most important events of his life.

From the citadel the entire city may be seen; palaces, minarets, groves, gardens, cupolas, all are spread out; to the north and west are the fertile plains of the Nile valley, while to the south the river, separated into its branches, flows towards the Mediterranean. The so-called "Joseph's Well," is also on the citadel hill. It is in fact two wells, one below the other; the lower one is two hundred and sixty feet deep. A winding staircase leads to the bottom. Horses and oxen are used to turn the machinery which raises the water, and on

MOSQUE OF SAID.

account of the narrowness of the staircase they are taken down when small, and pass their lives there.

At the close of the eighteenth century the citadel of Cairo was the residence of the Pasha, and there was seen all his pomp and state. Its court-yard was the rendezvous for the magnificent Beys whose houses were in the town below, and there, with their attendants, their richly caparisoned steeds, and their splendid costumes and glittering arms, they made an imposing assemblage.

The highest and most intelligent class among the Arabs is that of the Ulema, or the hierarchy composed of the imans, or ministers of religion; the muftis, or the doctors of law; and the cadis, or the administrators of justice. The Ulema of Cairo, at the time of which we speak, managed the revenues of the mosques and the charitable institutions, which were then numerous and important. They governed themselves by the doctrines of the Koran, intelligently understood; they esteemed virtue and honor, and were governed by motives widely differing from those of the Mameluke Beys, and while they lived in a style befitting men of superiority and position they avoided the luxury and grand establishments of the Beys.

Trade was flourishing in Egypt, and merchants

held an honorable position; the bazaars of Cairo were filled with the products of the East; the Latakia tobacco, the dates of Nubia, the sweet-

MOSQUE OF MOHAMMED ALI IN THE CITADEL.

meats of Damascus, and the odors of the Fayoum were seen together; in another part the satins of Aleppo and the fabrics of India were mingled with the rich stuffs from the continent, brought by the Venetian merchants. All these things and many more were required for the Beys and their harems, but taken as a country, the commercial importance of Egypt was much diminished by the removal of the Levantine trade from Alexandria to Aleppo, and at the end of the eighteenth century Alexandria had little more than eight thousand inhabitants,

A ROADSIDE WELL.

and it was not until the revolution created by steam navigation that Egypt resumed a commercial consequence.

Siout, on the Upper Nile, was then an important

place, because there the caravans from Darfour arrived and departed, and the trade in gums, ivory, and other articles from the upper country was there transacted, the natives being the traders here; they also took the goods down to Rosetta or Alexandria, where the Frank traders received their supplies.

Such was the state of Egypt when Napoleon I., in 1797, addressed the squadron of Admiral Brueys as follows: "Comrades, as soon as we have pacified the continent, we shall unite ourselves to you, in order to conquer the liberty of the seas. Without you we can carry the glory of the French name only into a little corner of the continent; with you we will traverse the seas, and the national glory will see regions still more distant."

CHAPTER XI.

THE FRENCH INVASION, FROM 1798 TO 1801.

BEFORE entering upon the French Invasion of Egypt, led by Napoleon Bonaparte in 1798, it is well to understand that the plan was not original with that great general.

The same undertaking had been so seriously contemplated in the time of Louis XV. that plans had been projected for it, which were found by Talleyrand among the state papers and submitted by him to Bonaparte. All preparations were made for this expedition with great secrecy, in the ports of Genoa, Civita Vecchia, Corsica and Toulon, while troops were assembled in France and Italy.

Finally, in May 1798, Napoleon proceeded to Toulon, and took command of the expedition. When everything was in readiness he embarked with his staff in *L'Orient*, a three-decker, which carried one hundred and twenty guns; they were accompanied by twenty ships of different sizes, and more than three hundred transports, with Vice-Admiral Brueys in command of all. More than a hundred artists, scientists, and men of letters went with them, besides a corps of professional engineers.

The fleet arrived near Alexandria the first of July. The troops were disembarked, and the leader soon possessed himself of the city, and made an alliance with Mohammed Kerim, the chief magistrate of Alexandria, to whom the French leader represented that the object of the expedition was to re-establish in Egypt the authority of the Porte, which had been usurped by the Mamelukes. Napoleon proceeded to land his stores with great despatch, and to make Alexandria the base of his operations. He feared the arrival of the British fleet under Nelson, who, he had good reason to believe, as was indeed true, was already in pursuit of him. The energy with which preparations were made was simply miraculous; the men of science quickly organized their labors, the geographers commenced their plans and maps, the medical staff was efficiently constituted, and as soon as the

MONEY-CHANGER AT SIOUT.

printing press could be landed, Napoleon issued his famous proclamation, published in Arabic, as follows:—

"In the name of God the Merciful and Indulgent. There is no god but God. He has no Son, and reigns without a partner. On the part of the French Republic, established on the principles of liberty, and on the part of the General-in-chief, Bonaparte the Great, the Emir of the French Armies, we make known to all the inhabitants of Egypt, that for a long time back the Beys who govern this country overwhelm the French nation with contempt and opprobrium, and cause their merchants to experience weary exactions and injustice. But the hour of their chastisement is come.

"For a long time back, this troop of Mamelukes, drawn from Circassia and Georgia, tyrannizes over the fairest spot of the globe; but the Lord of the Worlds, whose power extends everywhere, has ordained the termination of their power. Egyptians! you will be told that I come here with the design to overthrow your religion, but this is a gross falsehood. Do not believe it. Answer the impostors that I have come to restore your rights, which have been invaded by usurpers—that I adore God more than the Mamelukes, and that I respect the Prophet Mohammed and the noble Koran. Tell them that all men are equal before God—that intelligence, virtue, and science, are the only distinctions between them. What intelligence then, what virtues, what sciences, distinguish them from other men, and render them worthy of possessing all that constitutes the happiness of life?

"Wherever there is a fertile land, it belongs to the Mamelukes; the most costly dresses, the handsomest slaves, the most agreeable houses belong to them. If Egypt is their farm, let them show the lease that God has given them for it. But God is merciful and just, and henceforth all will be able to arrive at the most elevated functions; henceforth the most intelligent, virtuous, and learned will direct public affairs, and in this way the people will be happy.

"Cadis, Sheikhs, Imans, Tchorbajis, tell the people we are friends of the true Mussulmans. Have we not destroyed the Pope, who says that war ought to be made upon the Mussulmans? Have we not discharged the Knights of Malta, because these bigots believed that God required them to raise their swords against the Mussulmans?

"Happy those, therefore, who will promptly

CAMEL-DRIVER.

unite with us, for they shall be exalted. Happy those who remain neutral in their dwellings, without troubling themselves about the two parties that dispute possession of the country. When they come to know us better they will proffer us a cordial union. But woe to those who join the Mamelukes. Every vestige of them shall disappear from the face of the earth."

Napoleon (leaving General Kleber in command at Alexandria) next moved his army upon Cairo. The march thither was one of great suffering to the French soldiers—hunger, thirst, heat, all were insupportable. They left Alexandria at evening, on the seventh of July, and arrived before the Pyramids, near Cairo, on the twenty-first of the same month. Cairo had been the scene of intense excitement since the landing of the French army had been known there, and all possible preparations had been made by Ibrahim Bey for the defence of the city against the invaders. But all in vain, the Battle of the Pyramids proved a signal defeat for the Egyptians, and the night following it was one of dreadful horror. Within the city of Cairo confusion prevailed; a panic of fear had seized upon all, and to flee was the one idea. Those who could command horses or other animals departed, bearing their treasures with them; others were on foot, and it seemed that Cairo would be deserted by all but those who were too poor and miserable to have any object in going. The terror was increased by the report that the French had burned Boulak and Djizeh, and the fear that the same fate would be visited upon Cairo. This report arose from the burning by the French of the boats which they had used between the island of Rodah and Djizeh.

Those who succeeded in leaving the city soon met new dangers outside. They were attacked by Arabs, their animals seized, the riches they had managed to bear away were stolen, and many were even stripped of their clothing and left naked by the way. "Never was there a more cruel night," says Abderrahman Gabarty, "the ear hears the recital of deeds, the sight of which could not be supported by the eye."

The following day the city formally submitted to Napoleon, and he represented to the people that he only desired "that the French should live in amity with the Egyptian people and the Ottoman Porte, and that the customs and the religious usages of the country should be scrupulously respected." That evening the French were installed in the citadel of Cairo, and the struggle here was ended. The passions of the excited populace now vented themselves upon the Mamelukes; their power was ended; their palaces and houses were plundered and burned, and large amounts of property were destroyed in spite of the efforts of the French to restrain them.

On the twenty-fifth of July, Napoleon entered Cairo, and established himself and his troops in such comfort as brought courage and good spirits to replace the weariness and discouragement which the hardships of their march from Alexandria had caused them to feel. "The civilians and the corps of *savans* were satisfied, and even gay; for after thirsty marches over scorching sands, and exposure to the sun in Nile-boats, with water-melons or indigestible cakes of half-pulverized and half-baked dates for food, they now enjoyed white bread and all the luxuries of the table."

A proclamation compelled all to wear the tri-colored cockade, which produced a novel effect upon the many oriental garbs of Cairo. European discipline soon established order, and for the moment Cairo was at ease, and amused, for the gay and charming manners of the French soon rendered them popular with the very people whom they had conquered. This overthrow of the Mamelukes may be said to have formed the beginning of the modern history of Egypt. A native Divan was formed, state and municipal governments were established, a police system inaugurated; and every practicable measure taken to bring about good order.

Tradesmen, artists and mechanics, who had accompanied the invaders, began to establish themselves, and even coinage was resumed, for Cairo had shared with Constantinople the privilege of making money. Bonaparte used the old dies bearing the name of Selim III., the ruling Sultan.

A great impression had been made on the minds of the Moslems, fatalists as they were, by the defeat of Murad Bey, whom they had believed invincible, and following that event, the utter discomfiture of Ibrahim Bey. But Napoleon was not yet content with what had been done, and resolved to drive Ibrahim Bey (who had made a halt at Bilbeis with his Mamelukes) into the desert. General Leclerc was sent with troops to attack this formidable enemy. The battles of Elhankeh and Salahieh were fought and no absolute victory was obtained by the French, but Ibrahim Bey retired to Acre and joined the Djezzar there, which act virtually surrendered Egypt to the French.

This Djezzar (or Butcher) was named Achmed Pasha, and received the above title on account of his cruelty—all along the way the Mamelukes were taunted with cowardice for having surrendered Egypt to the enemies of Islamism, and there is no doubt but that Ibrahim Bey did what he could to kindle the fearful hatred of the French in the heart of the Djezzar, which he poured out with such fury when Napoleon laid siege to Acre, in March 1799. It is said that this monster sat on the floor of his palace and paid for every French head that was brought to him, until he was surrounded by piles of these gory trophies.

The French had scarcely made themselves comfortable in Cairo, before news arrived of the appearance of the British fleet off the Bay of Aboukir, and soon that engagement took place which proved so disastrous to the French. Just before this battle Nelson declared, "By this time to-morrow I shall have gained a peerage, or Westminster Abbey."

It requires no great wisdom to see that from the day of the battle of Aboukir, the fate of the French expedition was sealed; the fleet destroyed, the army could not return to France; the British maintained such a watch that no reinforcements could reach their opponents, and though by a series of stratagems such as Bonaparte alone could have conceived and executed, they might for a time exist in Egypt, yet in the end only defeat could result.

This great general proceeded to assure himself that the rise of the Nile had been such that no famine would occur, and he then commanded the old ceremony of the cutting of the canal at Cairo to be carefully observed, and surrounded by his staff in brilliant holiday attire, as well as by the most prominent Moslems of the city, he witnessed the spectacle.

He even made it his care to provide money for the celebration of the birth-day of the Prophet, and by every possible means endeavored to induce

A SHADOOF.

the belief that he was a sincere convert to Mohammedanism.

Bonaparte had allowed Saïd Mohammed Kerim, who had held office under Murad Bey, to remain in a prominent position in the administration of affairs in Alexandria. It was soon discovered that he was in correspondence with the Mamelukes; he was arrested, sentenced to pay three hundred thousand francs, or lose his head. He refused to pay the fine, saying, with fatalist reasoning, "If I am to die now, nothing can save me, and I should be giving away my piastres uselessly; if I am not to die, why should I give them at all?"

After his execution his head was paraded through the streets, thus labelled, "Kerim, Sherif of Alexandria, condemned to death for having violated the oaths of fidelity he had taken to the French Republic, and for having maintained correspondence with the Mamelukes, to whom he was a spy. Thus shall be punished all traitors and perjurers."

The Mohammedans regarded Kerim as a martyr; discontents began to arise; curses were whispered, but they were deep; and an intense distrust of all the promises and pretensions of the French possessed every inhabitant of the land. The new regulations in all departments of the government were not comprehended by the Orientals, and such measures as were in fact most advantageous for them were regarded with suspicion; the new laws and usages concerning women were so abominable in their eyes that they could not submit to them; the sanitary regulations and the interference with intermural burials added fury to their already excited feelings, and, Paton says, "It was with their hearts filled with gall and bitterness that the Ulema and Delegates lent themselves to the deliberations of a council held under infidel auspices. The news of a Turkish army marching towards Egypt; the relaxation of manners which had resulted from the wives and daughters of Moslems going into the streets with their faces uncovered; the public sale of wine; the demolition of mosques and minarets; the levelling of cemeteries, to carry out works of improvement which were regarded as calamities and innovations; the removal of the internal gates of the streets; the active preparations made by General Cafarelli for covering the mounds round Cairo with forts, the completion of which would render a general rising more difficult; and, last of all, the letters from Achmed Pasha of Acre, containing positive assurances of support, combined to determine the people of Cairo to try their fortunes in a general rising." This revolt occurred on the twenty-second of October, and was of such proportions as to require three days of great activity on the part of the French to put it down, even with their discipline, their superior arms and other advantages. The Egyptians were at length subdued and again appeared to be submissive, but the French did not relax their vigilance; forts were built; the manufacture of powder was established; an armory was fitted up; a dromedary corps organized, and mills erected for the grinding of flour.

The French had tried their arts of pleasing without success; they even adopted oriental costumes and customs, but do what they would, they instinctively felt that might alone preserved their lives. The soldiers were often disheartened; they were cut off from all correspondence with their friends at home by the vigilance of the British fleet, and the monotony of their lives afforded them many hours for thought and regret.

Napoleon found a resource in the Institute of Egypt, which was founded at Cairo by the learned men whom he had brought with him. Among its members were such men as Monge, Fourier, Andreassi, Le Père, Nouet, Laucret, Desgenettes, Larrey, and many others.

However much is to be regretted in connection with the French invasion of Egypt, the formation of this Institute, and the studies and researches of its members, must ever throw a bright light upon its dark surroundings, and demand admiration of that trait in Napoleon Bonaparte which led him, in the midst of all his cares and anxieties, to remember and protect the interests of science and learning. The researches of the Institute were extended to every department of scholarly investigation, and these men seem to have forgotten, in their devotion to their pursuits, the manifold dangers which surrounded them.

Considerable attention was given to the consideration of a project for making a Suez Canal, and various surveys were made with this object in view; the antiquities of Egypt afforded a most fascinating field for scholarly research, and the vivacious writer and clever artist, Vivant Denon, drew the first outline, with brush and pen, of that which has since been so well finished and filled in by Rosellini, Champollion, Wilkinson, Lepsius, Brugsch, and many others.

While these peaceful pursuits occupied the

SAND-STORM IN THE DESERT.

French in Lower Egypt, Desaix, with his command, was in pursuit of Murad Bey, the Mameluke chieftain, in Upper Egypt. All the ups and downs of this expedition will not be recounted; in the end Desaix was successful and established such defences at Assouan as gave security to those who held it. The Mamelukes had been driven to the desert, and were pursued no farther.

When Napoleon went to Suez he obtained such information as led him to believe that the Porte was preparing to attack him on the Syrian border of Egypt, and thus undertake to reconquer the country.

He resolved to meet his enemies on Syrian rather than Egyptian soil, and his famous Syrian expedition was decided on. The Syrians were not Moslems, and Napoleon, who was by this time convinced of the impossibility of affiliating with the disciples of the Prophet, hoped to draw the mountain tribes of Syria into a genuine alliance with him against the Turks. These tribes held no common creed, and had never united themselves against the Ottoman power; neither were they ever submissive to it, as were the Copts of Egypt; they were sometimes in open revolt; always ready to enroll themselves under the banner of a successful general, and in them Bonaparte thought to find strong allies.

Another argument in favor of the occupation of Syria was founded upon the extent of sea-coast which would thus be available to the French, and by which they might hope to communicate with the continent, for while it was a simple matter for the British to blockade Alexandria, a more extended coast could not be easily kept under strict surveillance.

Therefore, after arranging the affairs of Egypt as best he could, Napoleon, in February, 1799, took the larger part of his army into Syria. They first encountered the hunger, thirst and heat of the desert, and suffered much before they reached El Arish, a fort which, though miserable in itself, was important as a boundary stronghold between Egypt and Syria: this was soon in possession of the French, who pushed on with all possible speed to Jaffa. The attack of that city, the hand to hand conflicts in its streets, the surrender of the four thousand Arnauts who had entrenched themselves in a strong khan, their subsequent butchery in cool blood by the unwilling soldiers at the command of Bonaparte; all this horrible story is well known. "The course pursued on this occasion was a summons to every place in Syria to unfurl the black banner of "no surrender;" and to this summons Acre responded, a few weeks later, with an energy that astonished all Europe. With the appalling fate of Jaffa before their eyes, no garrison was likely to surrender, so long as the crumbling corner of a wall remained erect; and there was no Moslem who could hold a pike who would not prefer death in the excitement of combat to a repetition of the despairing scenes on the sands of Jaffa.

Napoleon wrote to Cairo a full account of the taking of Jaffa, in which he said that more than four thousand soldiers had been killed in combat. He added, "The inhabitants of Jaffa did not know that arms were of no avail against the will of God," and then, "Egyptians! submit yourselves to his decrees, obey his commandments, and acknowledge that the world is his property, and that he gives it to whomsoever he pleases."

Bonaparte sent a letter to the Sheikhs of Jerusalem concerning the surrender of that city, and received the reply that "they were subjects of the Pasha of Acre, and when he had conquered that city Jerusalem should be delivered to him." The French army now proceeded to Acre, which was the home of that Djezzar, before spoken of, who was the Pasha of Sidon, and as such, in reality had made himself quite independent of the power of the Sultan. His cruelty was well known, and his subjects, many of whom went about with mutilated ears, noses and limbs, were a continual witness to his savage instincts. This man determined never to surrender, was well backed by Sir Sidney Smith with a British fleet, who not only did all in his power to harass the French by a constant fire from his ships, but also seized the gunboats which were bringing battering cannon and siege equipage to them.

The army of Bonaparte was before Acre from the eighteenth of March until the twentieth of May, when, with all possible secrecy of preparation, it was drawn off and a retreat to Jaffa commenced. The history of this Syrian campaign scarcely belongs to a history of Egypt, and yet, as it was undertaken to prevent a war in Egypt, it cannot be entirely disconnected from our subject, but must be passed with a very general and insufficient sketch. Before Acre the best officers of the French army were cut down by disease or the chances of war, and all sorts of maladies belonging to the country attacked them. Upon its retreat the army presented a soul-harrowing spectacle; there were sick men for whom no means of transport could be furnished, their wounds were alive with vermin, as is proved by the report of the surgeon-general, Larrey; to leave them meant a death by Turkish torture,

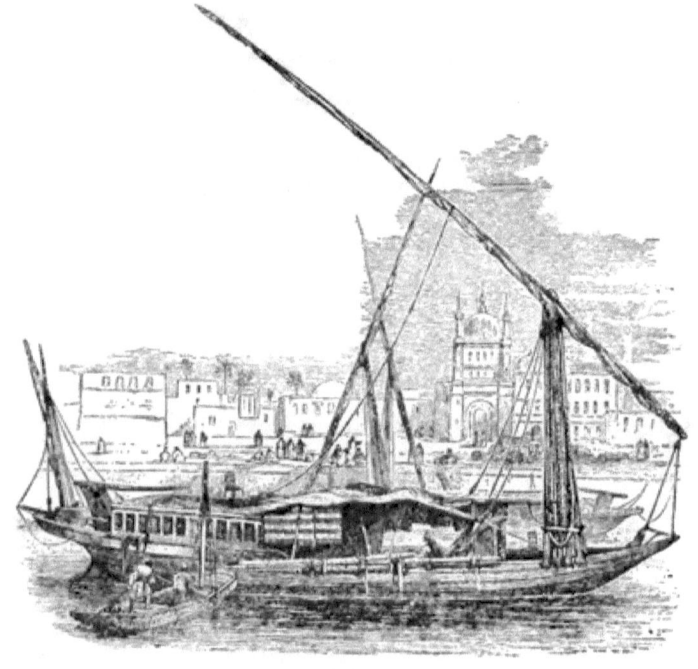

NILE BOAT.

and there is much reason for believing that many were poisoned.

At Jaffa the hospitals were full of plague-stricken wretches — here, again, poison was called in to finish the work of war and hardship, and at last, with a remnant of his army, Napoleon entered Cairo, which seemed to those who were left to tell the tale of this horrible campaign, like the "land flowing with milk and honey." Whoever has seen in the Louvre, that picture by Antoine Jean Gros, of "Napoleon visiting the sick at Jaffa," must have one scene of this Syrian tragedy stamped upon his memory. We are told that Bonaparte cried out there, "In a few hours the Turks will be here; let all those who have strength enough rise and come along with us; they shall be carried on litters and horses." Profound silence and the dead stupor of the sick men was the only answer.

The joy of the return to Cairo was too great to be entirely suppressed, even by the thought of the many who had been left behind, and the Egyptians, who had received full accounts of all that had occurred, were surprised to see this army come from the desert, and enter the city in full parade order, after four such months as it had passed through.

During the Syrian campaign the Mamelukes had again made themselves felt in Upper Egypt, and Napoleon had scarcely time to reorganize his demoralized troops before he saw signs which convinced him that Murad Bey had determined to reach the coast with his forces, to combine with the Turks, who counted on joining him there. Immediately the French attacked a large body of Mamelukes who were passing within a short distance of Cairo, and were so completely routed that in their flight they left enormous amounts of baggage and seven hundred camels behind. Their food was left cooking on the fire, and Osman Bey, their leader, escaped in his shirt, forgetting letters from Ibrahim Bey which disclosed to the enemy their plans for joining forces. The Mamelukes were pursued in various directions, and Bonaparte himself led an attack on Murad Bey when he encamped near the Pyramids of Gizeh, and routed him completely. In the midst of all this, on July fifteenth, news came that the Turks had landed at Aboukir four days before. Hasty preparations were made and in ten days, on July twenty-fifth, that great battle of the French and the combined Turks and British was fought. The victory was with the French, but in the hour of triumph the strange mind of Napoleon thought not of that, a new resolve was made — he would return to France!

Scarcely a month passed before he had made his plans secretly, and succeeded in carrying out his design, for on August twenty-third he sailed from

Rosetta, taking with him but a handful of officers and *savans*.

"Thus ended the residence of Bonaparte in Egypt, leaving no foe unconquered from the Cataracts to the Mediterranean, from the Red Sea to the sands of Libya; but at the same time leaving, for the interests of France, nothing permanent, nothing consolidated. The colonization of Egypt was a failure, in spite of the vast genius of the conqueror. But the name of Bonaparte, like those of the heroes of Greece, Rome, and Arabia, will ever be associated with one of the great landmarks of Egyptian history."

One important fact had certainly been established by Napoleon — the Mameluke power, which had ruled Egypt since its establishment by Saladin, was at an end, and to fill the space thus left vacant, an organization gradually arose, which was liberal and far-seeing enough to unite with the enterprise and genius of Europe in restoring to Egypt the transit between the Mediterranean Sea and India.

Bonaparte had left General Kleber as commander-in-chief, and the rage of this brave man when he realized how he had been duped and deserted by the wily Bonaparte, can be better imagined than described.

In the dispatch left for Kleber, Bonaparte said, that he left Egypt on account of the news he had received from Italy; he promised to send recruits and military supplies to him; he permitted him to make peace with the Porte (even though the evacuation of Egypt should be a stipulation of the treaty) if he should lose fifteen hundred more men, or if he did not receive aid from France before the following May.

Kleber first drew up a statement of the circumstances under which Napoleon had left him, the other officers, and the soldiers whom he had led into Egypt. It was a calmly bitter recital of the facts, which were bad enough. A portion of it follows:

"General Bonaparte departed for France on the Sixth Fructidor, without informing anybody; and besides sending me a letter, addressed another to the Grand Vizier at Constantinople, although he knew perfectly well that he had arrived already at Damascus.

"The armed force has been reduced to one-half since his arrival in Egypt, occupying the principal points from El Arish and Alexandria to the Cataracts.

"Our enemies are no longer merely the Mamelukes, but three great powers—the Porte, the English and the Russians. The deficiency in arms and ammunition is as alarming as the diminution in men. The manufactories of arms and powder are unproductive; while the troops, from want of clothing, are subject to the severe diseases of the country. With a deficit of almost twelve millions of francs, the resource of extraordinary taxes has been forestalled by my predecessor.

"The Mamelukes are dispersed, but not destroyed; Murad Bey is always in Upper Egypt, with a sufficient number of men to incessantly occupy a part of our forces. The Grand Vizier, with his army, has advanced from Damascus to Acre; and Bonaparte's allusion to the French army is sufficiently indicative of the critical position in which I find myself.

"El Arish is a miserable fort. exposed to any invading army; and Alexandria is not a fortified town, but an intrenched camp, partly denuded of artillery to fit out the frigates. In this state of things, the best measure that I can take is to negotiate with the Sultan; and I have just learned that a Turkish naval force has appeared before Damietta."

Kleber was a strong man in field and council, and he summoned all his powers to aid him to make the most of his discouraging position. He took his command in September, and after much discussion and many negotiations, an agreement was made with Sir Sidney Smith, in January, 1800, to the effect that the French should evacuate Egypt, and should retire with arms and baggage to Alexandria, Rosetta and Aboukir, from which ports they should embark for France.

Unhappily this agreement was cancelled by a command from Admiral Lord Keith to Sir Sidney Smith, forbidding him to allow the French to leave Egypt, except as prisoners of war, first surrendering all their ships and stores and laying down their arms.

This the French refused to do, and hostilities were resumed. Kleber, through many difficulties, again established his power at Boulak and Cairo, and through dreadful scenes of butchery and horror had, early in June, placed himself in comparative safety, and made a league with his old opponent, Murad Bey, who feared and did not desire to be placed again under Turkish rule.

Just then, when so much had been accomplished, when Egypt was freed from Ottoman troops, when the Cairenes had been suppressed, when an advantageous ally had been gained, and his own army had regained its spirit and courage, Kleber was assassinated by a young scribe, urged on to the deed by an Aga of the Janissaries.

Kleber's successor was General Menou, a man as ill suited to the position as could well have been found. He had adopted the religion and manners of the Orientals, and had rendered himself extremely obnoxious to all his countrymen. As soon as he obtained the leadership he endeavored to carry out a project of establishing a permanent residence in Egypt, and making the country a colony of France.

His plans were not successful with the Moslems any more than with the French, for no manner of flattery or professions of their religion could ever reconcile Orientals to Franks, and all his calling himself Abdallah, all his wordy proclamations affirming the wisdom and truth of the Koran, all his ardent love of their institutions, failed to gain for him either their confidence or their respect.

With the beginning of the year 1801, the British government determined to take more active measures by which to compel the French to evacuate Egypt, and an expedition was fitted out under the command of Sir Ralph Abercrombie.

Marmarice Bay was chosen by Lord Keith as a rendezvous for the British fleets. There all the troops were landed and systematic preparations made for the arduous undertaking which awaited them. When all was in order they made sail for the Bay of Aboukir, which they entered on the first of March. General Abercrombie immediately made a reconnoisance, and in a week had possessed himself of the eminences which commanded the shore, and this he accomplished under full fire from the French. On the thirteenth he had driven his enemies within the city of Alexandria.

On the twenty-first General Menou thought to surprise the British, but was himself amazed at the mode of his reception; a great battle ensued, and the brave Abercrombie received a wound from which he died a month later; but he did not yield to his sufferings or leave the field until he saw that the British were victorious.

From this moment the result was inevitable; the beginning of the end of the French Invasion of Egypt had come. On the twenty-fifth of March the British were joined by six thousand Turkish allies, among whom was the far-famed Mohammed Ali, then but a captain of Albanian mercenary troops.

We will not follow, step by step, the actions of the allies against the French. By the twenty-fifth of July all was over; a capitulation was signed; the evacuation was agreed upon, and the French were to be conveyed to a port of France. The British allowed the *savans* to retain their instruments of art and science, and, upon special request, also left to them the various collections which they had made.

The first of September, General Baird (famous for his part in extending the British power in India) arrived at Cairo with his army of Sepoys, which he had led across the desert to the Nile, and thus joined his countrymen in Egypt.

"Since the days of the dynasty of Saladin, when the mailed horsemen of Europe encountered the Turk, the Kurd, and the Circassian, no such assembly of various nations had encamped on the banks of this historic stream. But now the Arab had sunk to be the slave, or torpid citizen. The high-cheeked Tartar Bournau from the plains of Asia, muttering his coarse Ouighour, was no longer recognizable in the indolent, dignified, modern Turk, whose breed was crossed with the blood of

Greece and of Circassia, and who spoke a language strengthened with the vocabulary of the Koran, and refined by the elegance of Persian song.

FRENCH ARMY PASSING THE GREAT SPHINX AFTER THE BATTLE OF THE PYRAMIDS.

There was no Mansourah for the modern Mamelukes. Their battles with Bonaparte were battles of spurs — not pitched contests, but races for existence. As for the eastern enemies of the Mamelukes, they had disappeared. The great so-called Mogul Monarchy, that had shaken to its centre the political fabric raised by Saladin, had sunk into insignificance, and the heirs of Tamerlane were now the protégés of the kings of Britain."

No time was lost in carrying out the terms of the capitulation; on the third of September the

English Grenadiers marched into Alexandria, and fifteen days later, General Menou and the French who wished to go, sailed for home, but several hundred converts to Islamism remained behind.

CHAPTER XII.

FROM THE TIME OF MOHAMMED ALI TO THAT OF ISMAIL KHEDIVE.

FROM the time of the departure of the French from Egypt, the great interest in the history of the country centres in the career of Mohammed Ali, a man destined to give the last, most fatal blow to the Mameluke power, and to bring much good to Egypt by a course of action in which right and wrong were singularly mingled.

Mohammed Ali was born in 1769, at Cavala, in Macedonia, in Turkey, (now Rumelia). He early entered the Turkish army, and at the same time was engaged in the tobacco trade in Rumelia. He thus showed in his youth a love of the soldier's life together with great courage—and a hankering after trade and its profits. He went to Egypt as the commander of three hundred soldiers, but his qualifications for military service soon showed themselves, and he was rapidly advanced to the command of the Albanian corps, in Egypt.

The Mamelukes hastened as soon as the French had gone, even before the departure of the British, to re-assert themselves. They fancied that they had only to deal with the Turks as of old, while the Turks, on their part, had determined never to allow the Mamelukes to resume their rank, and would hesitate at nothing in order to make good their resolution.

The first act of the Porte was characteristic of Turkish policy. The Capitan Pasha invited the principal Mameluke Beys to a conference at Aboukir; there they were magnificently entertained, and were then prevailed upon to embark upon a large barge, under pretext of holding a consultation with the officers of the British fleet. When far enough from shore the barge was surrounded by armed boats, into one of which the Capitan Pasha entered, while the Mamelukes were killed or wounded. Capitan Pasha represented to the Mamelukes that General Hutchinson was in some way connected with this villanous affair. That officer was full of indignant wrath, and did all in his power to prove the falsity of the accusation;

THE DOUM PALM IN NUBIA.

he buried the dead Beys with great care, and faithfully nursed the wounded.

At the same time a similar affair took place at Cairo. Yousouff Pasha had pretended friendship for the Mamelukes, but he suddenly dispatched his emissaries to attack them near Gizeh, and a wholesale slaughter ensued; in this case, too, the British succored the Mamelukes as well as they were able.

It soon appeared that Yousouff Pasha, the new Grand Vizier, and Capitan Pasha could not agree, and by the efforts of the latter the famous Khousreff Pasha was appointed Governor of Egypt. In his service, while fighting the Mamelukes, Mohammed Ali first made himself a name, both in Egypt, and on the continent of Europe.

The celerity with which the Mamelukes moved was surprising. They were now led by Osman Bey-el-Bardissy and Mohammed Bey-el-Elfy, the first of whom succeeded in establishing his power over a large portion of Egypt before the British left Alexandria.

The Mamelukes had profited greatly by their observations of the Continental troops, and their mode of warfare was now far superior to that of the Turks; they were also more at home in Egypt than the soldiers of the Porte; the Egyptians had more confidence in them than in the Turks, because they knew them better, and all the preliminary circumstances of the struggle about to begin were in their favor.

Alexandria, Cairo, and other large towns remained under the control of Khousreff Pasha, but

BRINGING WATER FROM THE NILE.

his inability to pay the troops induced a revolt;—he was driven from the capital, and as a *finale* to this movement, Mohammed Ali became master of Cairo, and made an alliance with the Mamelukes, in order to overcome the Governor Khousreff, who had established himself at Damietta. By a ruse, Mohammed obtained possession of this place, and Khousreff retired to Lesbeh, at the mouth of the Nile, where he was finally obliged to capitulate.

The foregoing is a good type of the events of several months. The Porte sent new officers to maintain its authority in Egypt; Mohammed Ali and the Mamelukes, separately, and in concert, worked against the Porte, and sometimes against each other, until in March 1804, Mohammed Ali had so woven his net and set his snares, that Bardissy Bey fell into it, and Khurschid Pasha was placed at the head of the government. This man only appeared to disappear, like those who had preceded him in his authority.

Mohammed Ali, constantly working himself into favor, by one means or another, received from the Porte the appointment of Pasha of Djiddah, and finally, in May, 1805, another serious revolt occurring, a deputation of Sheikhs begged Mohammed Ali to assume the government. At first he made a feint of declining, but being again persuaded, he consented with apparent unwillingness to occupy the position which he had so cunningly prepared for himself. The deposed Kurschid made a resistance, but the friends of Mohammed obtained from Constantinople an order giving the governorship to him, and on the third of August, this remarkable man received command of the citadel of Cairo.

Having won his way to the favor of the Porte, Mohammed Ali now gave his attention to the Mamelukes, by no means an unimportant foe. Their improvement in discipline has been mentioned; they were also in close alliance with the nomadic Arab tribes, and Mohammed Ali knew well that he stood little chance of success with them in open and fair combat; so strategy and murder were called to his aid, and the unvarnished truth is, that two of the most revolting treacheries and butcheries of all those that stain the pages of Oriental history, were the means by which Mohammed Ali secured himself in the place which he was determined to hold.

His first step was to send his emissaries to the Mamelukes and offer them an entrance into Cairo, on the occasion of the festivities upon the day of the opening of the sluices of the Nile, when, with his officers, he would be outside the city. The wily Mamelukes fell into the trap, and when they had ridden into the town, and reached the tortuous bazaars, the Albanians, who were concealed in the houses, cut off their retreat, murdered many, and took others prisoners, only to kill them on the following day. Thus ended the first massacre.

The power of the Mamelukes now being essentially lessened, Mohammed Ali was beginning to feel comparatively safe, when the Porte, with its accustomed jealousy of the capable officials, sent to remove him to the chief office at Saloniki, while Moussa Pasha was sent to assume the post of governor of Egypt.

But again Mohammed Ali was equal to the management of the Porte. His Albanians swore to support him; he sent memorials from the Ulema, or higher class of citizens, to Constantinople begging, for their part, that he should be left in his position. Just at this time a war broke out between Russia and the Porte, and the firman was despatched which made him Pasha of Egypt; this reached Cairo in November 1806.

During the next year, 1807, a second expedition was sent from England to Egypt, which was met with such efficient opposition by Mohammed Ali, that no disastrous results were suffered by him or his people. Being now left to act upon his own policy, the new Pasha set about strengthening himself in his position so as to insure a permanent hold upon the government of Egypt for himself and his family. First, he saw that he must exact a large revenue from his subjects, in order to send such sums of tribute to Constantinople as would propitiate the Sultan, and make it clearly for his interest to sustain the power of the Egyptian governor. Acting upon this principle he used many unjust means to obtain possession of large estates; he denied the legitimacy of many successions; he burned title deeds, and seized properties; in short, he set at defiance all universally acknowledged rights of landholders. Great disturbances followed, but Mohammed Ali was prepared for these, and, by his wonderful firmness he made it appear that the bare assertion of claims was an aggression on the part of the Sheikhs.

The taxes were constantly increased, and their collection put into the hands of the military governors; by this means the peasantry were ground to the very lowest point, and there is no doubt that their numbers were greatly diminished by the extreme policy of Mohammed Ali.

Early in the present century, the Wahabis, a sect of Mohammedan Reformers or Moslem Puritans, had taken possession of Arabia, and even forbade the yearly caravans to enter Mecca. At length the Sultan commanded Mohammed Ali to proceed against the fanatics, and to re-establish his rights at Mecca and Medina. Toussoun Pasha, the son of the great Ali, was selected to be the commander of this expedition. When the army was in readiness and encamped on the desert, near Cairo, the great Pasha made an occasion for the second massacre, which utterly destroyed the remnant of the Mamelukes.

All the civil and military authorities were invited to assist in the ceremony of investing Toussoun Pasha with the pelisse of his office, and on the evening preceding the fatal day, the Mamelukes were also asked to take part in the pageant. As a sort of peace had been made between Mohammed Ali and the remaining Mamelukes, they accepted his invitation with little suspicion of treachery. Then, when the procession was arranged, these fated men were placed between the Albanians and other troops devoted to the Pasha; when the citadel was reached a terrible fire was poured into them, and all were killed—none were permitted to escape, and orders had been sent into the different provinces commanding the pursuit and murder of every Mameluke. In all more than a thousand men were killed, and only one Mameluke remained to mourn—he could not hope to avenge—the extinction of his race. This man was Amyn Bey. By some accident he was late in joining his brethren at Cairo, and when hastening towards the citadel, he heard the firing, and took the alarm, and by almost miraculous courage escaped into Syria. After this slaughter, the houses of the Mamelukes were pillaged; their women were violated, and all possible atrocities were committed. It is only just to add that the men were decapitated who indulged in these excesses which were perpetrated against the command of Mohammed Ali.

In 1811, the Wahaby war was thus inaugurated, and it was characterized, throughout its duration, by the most sanguinary deeds. These people believed in nothing that was not taught in the law of the Prophet; they only insisted that the law should be followed letter by letter. They judged the Turks and other Moslems to be recreant to the pure faith of Mohammed, and were fighting for their soul's salvation, just as the Christian martyrs died for theirs.

The name of Wahaby was derived from that of their leader, Abd-el-Wahab. The contest between the army of Toussoun Pasha and these people was arduous, and at length Mohammed Ali went him-

IN THE SUBURBS OF CAIRO.

self to the scene of war, to Mecca, and when his prowess was joined to that of his son, the insurrection was so far put down that the yearly pilgrimages could be resumed, and all hindrances to trade were removed. The troublesome Wahabis were driven into the Hedjaz, and the keys of Medina were sent to the Sultan, at Constantinople, together with some dusky heads of the fanatics, with which he ornamented the entrance to his palace.

Mohammed Ali, on his return from this war, reached Cairo in June, 1815, and immediately proceeded to the execution of a grand project which he had entertained for sometime, namely, the introduction into Egypt of European military organization and tactics. The announcement of this plan created great excitement, and a conspiracy was planned which endangered the life of Mohammed Ali. Hearing of this, and fearing that ill might befall his father, Toussoun Pasha returned to Egypt, where he soon after died from the consequences of his indulgences as a voluptuary.

This was a bitter grief to his father, for Toussoun was his favorite son, and though his dissipations had been censured by the old Pasha, yet the heart of Toussoun was more affectionate than that of the iron-cold Ibrahim. When Mohammed was told of the death, he threw himself on the ground in a paroxysm of grief, and kept silence during three days.

Although Toussoun Pasha had left the Wahabis in a position favorable to the Egyptians, yet Mohammed Ali could be satisfied with nothing less than their utter conquest. Therefore, in September, 1816, his son, Ibrahim Pasha, was dispatched with an army to resume the contest in Arabia. After two more years he succeeded in exterminating the sect; the chief was sent to Cairo, where he was hospitably entertained as a mockery of his state; then sent to Constantinople, where he was beheaded. The capital city of the Wahabis, Derayeh, was levelled with the ground; the date trees were cut down, and the small remnant of these devotees fled in various directions.

Mohammed Ali had by no means relinquished his determination to reorganize his army, but the time had not yet come for a decisive action in the matter. Meanwhile, he gave his attention to the conquest of the country of the Upper Nile.

Heretofore he had done little towards the increase of the resources of his government. Arabia had given him no spoils, and the gold-dust, feathers, gums, and other productions of the upper country, presented great attractions to the merchants of Lower Egypt. The Pasha not only sent an army, but with them numbers of the Ulema, who, being learned men, could preach Islamism, and understanding political science, could also instruct the savages in their duty to the successor of the Caliphs.

A vast force left Cairo in June, 1820, for Assouan, which was to be the rendezvous for the three thousand boats with their burdens, and for the cavalry troops who made the journey by land. This expedition was commanded by Ismail Pasha, another son of Mohammed Ali. No great opposition was made to the army as it advanced, and it may be said that the Upper Nile was subjugated at this time; nevertheless, it was many years before discipline and peace were established there, and the murder of Ismail Pasha, just when his work was done, extinguished the satisfaction that his father might otherwise have felt in the success of his plan; this was the second son of the great Pasha who had died just as he had accomplished a task given him by his father. Ismail Pasha was literally burned to death by a barbarian whom he had exasperated; this savage drove Ismail Pasha and his men into the house which they occupied, surrounded it with savages, spread straw about and set it on fire; those who escaped the flames were

BEDOUIN WOMEN GRINDING CORN.

butchered. Thus the sins of Mohammed Ali seemed to be visited upon his child.

Although in 1815 the proposition to reorganize the Egyptian army had created an insurrection, before 1829 the skilful manœuvering of Mohammed

Ali had accomplished the change. A French officer, named Sèves, and now called Soliman Bey, had trained the soldiers; a Spanish colonel, Seguera, had organized the military school; the palace of Murad Bey was now a cavalry school, under the instruction of Monsieur Varin; and the citadel of Cairo an arsenal, where the native Egyptians, under the direction of European workmen, cast cannon, and manufactured arms and accoutrements.

The army being thus brought into a satisfactory condition, Mohammed Ali determined to build up an Egyptian navy, and to make Alexandria its chief station. That city had resumed much of its old commercial importance, and by means of all the schemes which the Pasha had carried on, he had realized such a revenue as made it possible to him to follow the usages of sovereigns; to reward those who served him; to dispense honors at his pleasure, and, more important than all, to command the skilled labor of other countries. He ordered frigates to be constructed in Marseilles, and other ports of Europe; he sent young men abroad to study in naval schools; he employed foreign engineers, and by these and other equally intelligent means, Mohammed Ali laid firm and broad foundations for his present power and future glory.

Nor did these important affairs demand all the thought of this ruler, for he also found time to introduce the culture of the cotton plant, and of opium; to plant trees and to make gardens which are still admired by travellers in Egypt, as well as to restore the canal between Alexandria and the Nile, called by the name of the Sultan Mahmoud.

So far everything seemed to prosper under the hand of Mohammed Ali, but when he undertook to establish various manufacturing interests, he made a sad failure. This might have been foreseen by a European, but how could this wonderful Roumelian know that his people were not suited to such labors? or how realize that a country without coal or iron, can never compete with Great Britain and other northern lands? The wonder is, not that he failed in this, but that he succeeded in so much else.

The educational system established by Mohammed Ali is the noblest monument which remains to his memory. The medical schools and hospitals which he founded under Dr. Clot or Clot Bey, were an inestimable benefit to Egypt, and the surgeons educated in them are much better suited to the people and army of their country than any foreigners, of whatever skill or education, could ever be.

Many other schools were founded; many text-books were translated, and, in short, a complete governmental and educational revolution took place under the guidance of this wise ruler. A good police system was inaugurated; Franks were protected where they had previously been robbed; the roads were made secure; system everywhere replaced anarchy, and foreigners were invited to settle in Egypt, rather than robbed, insulted and murdered as they had been hitherto. Handsome residences were built by Europeans, and many customs of advanced civilization introduced among the upper classes, which in time influenced those beneath them, and thus had a broader effect than at first appeared.

This new rule of order, together with the development of steam navigation, induced the resumption of overland communication and commerce with India; and soon the mails were as regular and reliable through Egypt to India and back, as from America to England.

In private life Mohammed Ali was a gentleman of good taste, easy manners, and an adaptability to people and circumstances such as is rarely seen.

He had fine palaces at Alexandria and Cairo, and at the latter place he spent much time at his pleasure-garden of Shoubra, which was connected with the city by an avenue of trees.

He said of himself: "I had not the benefits of early education. I was forty-seven years old when I learned to read and write. I have never seen countries more civilized than my own; so I do not expect to do what you are able to do, and to reach the height at which you have arrived. The difficulty is to begin; I had to begin by scratching the soil of Egypt with a pin; I have now got to cultivate it with a spade; but I mean to have all the benefit of a plough."

As far as the relations of Mohammed Ali to Egypt are concerned, he was a benefactor worthy of much praise, and alas! of heavy blame at the same moment. But no true estimate can be made of his character without considering his course towards the Porte, and its representative, Sultan Mahmoud, which was nothing less than inhuman, traitorous, and detestable.

Having wrung from the Sultan the control of Egypt, having exterminated the Mamelukes, and welded his power in every manner possible, he conceived the idea of founding an empire, of which

Egypt should be the centre, and which should embrace Arabia, Syria and Palestine, leaving to the Ottomans only those who spoke the Turkish tongue.

Ibrahim Pasha, his son, was made general-in-chief of the army which was to further this undertaking. He led his soldiers triumphantly through Syria; he occupied Acre, Damascus, Homs, and, at last, the sacred Konieh in Asia Minor. Consternation reigned even at Constantinople, and only the intervention of the European powers, excepting France, with the most decided action on their part, and the presence of an English fleet in the harbor of Alexandria, brought the great Pasha to consent to the stipulations which had been agreed upon by Great Britain, Russia, Austria, Prussia, and the Porte. By this treaty, called the quadruple alliance, Mohammed Ali evacuated Syria, Arabia, and Candia; surrendered the fleet, and submitted himself to the authority of the Porte. For all this, he received, on the fourth of February, 1841, the pardon of the Sultan for himself and his family, and the Pashalic of Egypt hereditarily.

Mohammed Ali, realizing that his limits had been fixed for him, and in spite of him, turned his energies to the improvement of what was now an assured heirloom to his descendants. He employed a large portion of his army in agricultural labors, but retained suitable garrisons at Cairo and Alexandria; the latter city was fortified; many improvements were made which beautified his chief cities; a telegraph was laid to Suez; the route to India was improved, and luxury increased in the large towns.

Throughout the country districts there was great distress: the cattle murrain brought dreadful consequences; the peasants could not pay their taxes; everything was as bad as it could be, and yet Mohammed Ali was blind to the pecuniary destruction into which his course was sure to lead his country. Ibrahim Pasha determined that his father should know the whole truth. When the old man heard all, he refused belief; he fancied that he was surrounded by traitors and would see no member of his family. After the first excitement was over, a reconciliation was brought about, and such measures taken as were practicable for the pecuniary relief of Egypt.

In 1845, Ibrahim Pasha, on account of failing health, went to Europe, where he received the most flattering attentions, in all the countries which he visited. In the summer of 1846 Mohammed Ali accepted the Sultan's invitation to go to Constantinople, and upon his homeward journey visited Cavala, his birthplace. Upon his arrival at Alexandria he was received with every possible mark of respect, and congratulated upon his safe return.

In April 1847, the long-talked of project known as the " Barrage du Nil" was inaugurated, the old Pasha himself laying the corner-stone. The purpose of this great work was to force back the water of the Nile at the season of the low water, in order to create an artificial irrigation, by filling arterial canals.

During the year 1847 both Mohammed Ali and Ibrahim Pasha suffered much from failing health; the latter went a second time to Italy, and his father passed a few weeks at Malta, but the knowledge of the troubles in Europe, so increased Mohammed Ali's maladies, that his mental faculties succumbed, and he was incapable of exercising any authority whatever. Thus Ibrahim Pasha was forced, in spite of his own feebleness, to assume the government of Egypt, which he did in June, 1848.

He went to Constantinople, where the Sultan Abdul-Medjid installed him as Pasha of Egypt, and decorated him with his own hand, and thus the great Mohammed Ali was buried, while still alive, for he lived on, until the second of August, 1849, when he ceased to breathe, and was buried in the beautiful mosque, which bears his name, within the ancient castle of Saladin, on the finest and most remarkable spot in all Cairo, which had been to him the City of Victory, indeed!

Mohammed Ali found the Egypt of the Mamelukes a country governed by the whims of a half-savage race, and as far as the modern Egypt is concerned, he may be called the founder of its government. He has been so often likened to Napoleon that the idea of the resemblance is weary with being constantly presented, and yet, it is too striking to be passed over. Both of these men were strangers to the countries they ruled—statesmen by nature rather than by training for the part,—unprincipled in gaining their ends, and ambitious of forming an empire for their families; and both lived while others occupied their thrones, and died in solitary sadness.

Mohammed Ali excelled Napoleon, in that he secured his place to his descendants, and thus his work endured longer than that of the European usurper. He failed to add to his territory as he wished, but he created an Egyptian empire, made up of the many differing tribes and peoples, which existed as separate powers in the Egypt which he found.

He should not be judged from his great sins alone—they cannot be forgotten or concealed, but they may be shaded by the good he did. His organization of his state and army, his system of education, his great improvements and the adornments of his chief cities, his increase of comfort and civilized life in Egypt, these should and do live after him, and make his memory dear to his people; and at this day it is a question whether the plan of Mohammed Ali, if carried out, would not be a world-wide blessing.

That intelligent writer, DeLeon, says, "An Arab empire, with Egypt at its head, embracing Syria and Palestine on the one side, and Arabia on the other, under a protectorate of two or more of the Great Powers, would oppose a breakwater to Russian aggression on the one hand, and relieve that alien race from the exactions and misgovernment of the Porte, which has amply proved its unfitness to govern, and which in fact does not govern them: the limits of its authority being those of its garrisoned towns, outside of which protection from native sheikhs is essential for the traveller's safety, and of whose nominal rule the tax-gatherer is the only representative. Among the various propositions made as to the partition of the Turkish Empire, it strikes me as surprising that British statesmen have not, as in the case of the Suez Canal, reconsidered and reversed the policy of their predecessors, and made the dream of old Mohammed Ali, which they so rudely dissipated, a reality in the hands of his successors."

The reign of Ibrahim Pasha lasted but seventy days: long enough to show his cold heart, his avarice and sagacity, and long enough to confirm his unpopularity.

Paton, in his "History of the Egyptian Revolution," goes so far as to declare that he had not a single sincere friend. He died nine months before the death of his demented old father, at the age of fifty-nine, and was buried in the family tomb, under Mount Mokattam, eleven hours after he ceased to live.

Ibrahim Pasha was succeeded by his nephew, Abbas Pasha, son of Toussoun Pasha, the conqueror of the Wahabis. He bore no resemblance to his grandfather; dark in complexion, short, stout, with a bloated and sensual face, and cruel eyes, he was more a Turk than an Egyptian, and hated and feared the Europeans and their habits as much as Mohammed Ali had admired and copied them. He spoke no foreign language, and lived apart from the world as much as possible. He was too narrow-minded to increase materially the commerce of his country; nevertheless he demanded a large revenue, for he sent much money to the Sultan, hoping to buy his favor, and to obtain the succession for his son, El-Hami.

The Crimean war broke out during the reign of Abbas Pasha, and he spared nothing that could prove his loyalty to the Porte; money and men were sent forward with dispatch, and in liberal supplies. When the Sultan ordered him to expel from Egypt all Greeks not enrolled as Christian subjects of the Porte, Abbas Pasha showed some good feeling—at least, he so delayed his obedience that it was at length arranged that the Greeks should remain in Egypt under the protection of foreign consuls.

The reign of Abbas Pasha endured but six years, and was, in some points, well conducted. He contracted no debts; railroads were first built in Egypt at this time; and he advanced the agricultural interests of his country. Though he hated foreigners, he well appreciated the advantages to be derived from them, and threw no obstacles in the way of profiting by these.

Under Abbas Pasha the fellaheen were much oppressed—no projects for their advantage met with his approval; for him they were but slaves.

Like his father, Abbas Pasha met a violent death. The motives for his murder have never transpired; it was committed in 1854, at the Benha palace, about twenty miles from Cairo, by two young slaves, who had been sent him as a gift from Constantinople, by one of his female relatives. The Governor of Cairo, Elfy Bey, was hastily summoned; he gave orders that the death of the Pasha should be concealed, and placing the dead body in the state carriage, and sitting opposite to it in his accustomed place, he drove to the citadel of Cairo. Elfy Bey then ordered the guns of the fortress to be pointed on the town, and every preparation to be made for placing El-Hami in power, in accordance with the desire of Abbas Pasha, and to the exclusion of the heir, Saïd Pasha.

However, through the influence of the foreign consuls, especially Sir Frederick Bruce, Elfy Bey was persuaded to relinquish his designs, which, to

EGYPTIAN FELLAHEEN.

say the least, were treasonable, and Saïd Pasha was installed as Viceroy without delay.

Saïd Pasha was the younger son of Mohammed Ali, and as attractive and frank as his predecessor had been the reverse of these. He had been carefully educated by an accomplished tutor, Kœnig Bey, and spoke French perfectly. He loved the society of Europeans and kept open house in a style that made everybody comfortable; his table was always well furnished and served, and his wines were of the best.

His mother was a Georgian, and Saïd was fair in complexion and had a large and powerful figure, while his eyes were wide open, and his expression was earnest and candid. His views of life were broad and liberal, and his morals not of the Eastern type, for he shared his love and his throne with one wife, the princess Ingee Khanum, a charming and accomplished lady, who survived her husband, and lived under Ismail Pasha in the state that became the widow of a Viceroy.

Saïd Pasha, like Mohammed Ali, loved to be seen by the people, and gave many *fetes* and balls, which were largely attended by strangers, as all were made welcome, even without invitations. In his day the European costume had not been so generally adopted in Egypt as at the present time, and his palace-grounds, illuminated with variegated lamps, and filled with promenaders in the Oriental costumes, afforded a good reproduction of the *fêtes* of the "Arabian Nights Entertainments."

Saïd Pasha was also a soldier, and during his reign great attention was given to the discipline and equipment of the army, which numbered fifty thousand men. He replaced the Oriental dress which had been discarded by Abbas Pasha; he provided suits of armor for several squadrons of horse, among which was a troop of Nubians, who, mounted upon black steeds, and wearing the chain armor of olden times, made an effective appearance.

Saïd Pasha was ambitious to do some great work which should immortalize his name. He sent for Stephenson and other engineers to construct railroads; for Mougel Bey to proceed with the "*Barrage du Nil*" commenced by his father; he made model villages for the fellaheen, whose condition he sought to improve; he endeavored to raise the standard of agriculture by the introduction of steam-pumps and other machinery, "and kept Father Nile within his bed, out of which, as now, he annually at a given time roused him, to make a run over the country, instead of allowing him to

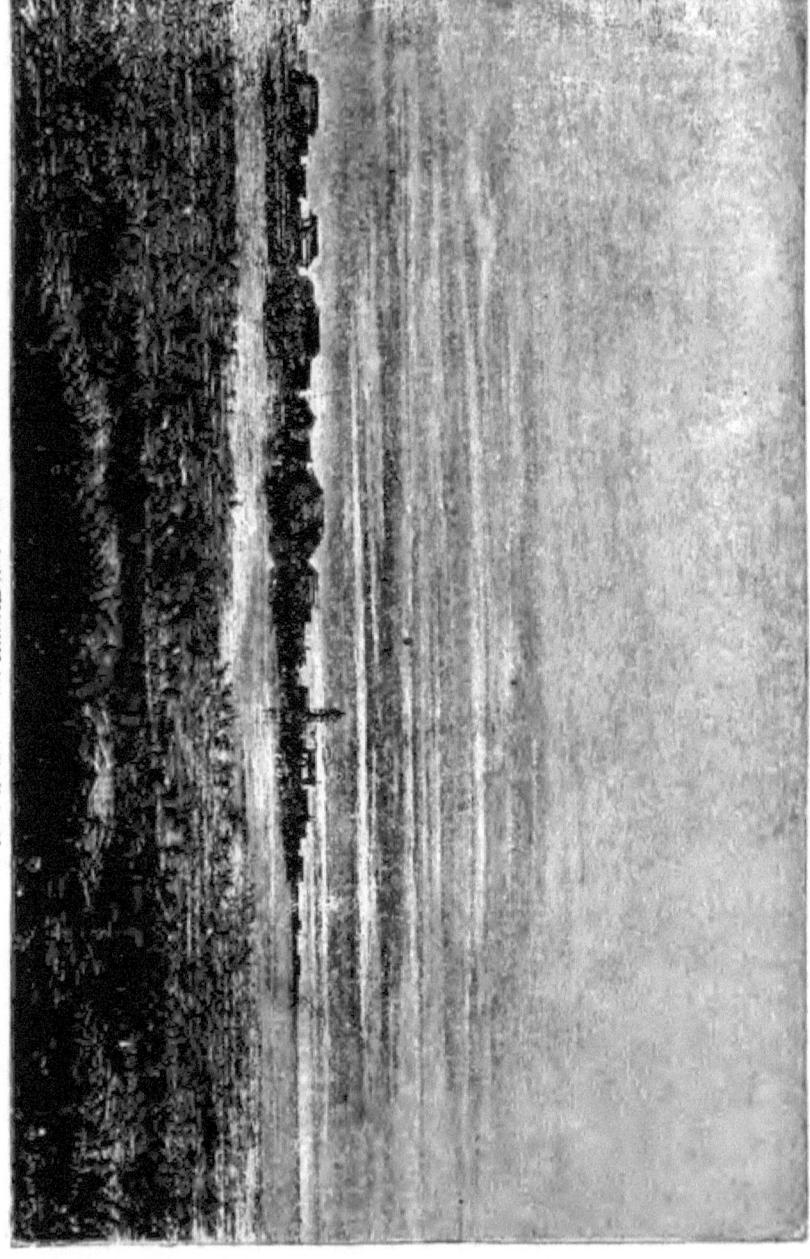

PORT SAID AND THE NORTHERN END OF THE CANAL.

tumble out himself in primitive fashion;" and finally, he gave to De Lesseps the concession for the Suez Canal, which of course made the fame and fortune of that great engineer. In recognition of this, Port Saïd and the northern mouth of the canal bear his name.

The American Civil War caused the revenues

CROSSING THE RIVER IN NUBIA.

of Egypt to be largely increased by the rise in the price of cotton; they reached the enormous sum of six millions of pounds, and yet, when Saïd Pasha died, after a reign of nine years, Egypt was in debt, and his own fortune was gone. When ill health and misfortune came his friends forsook him, and death was a release from pain of soul and physical agony. He was buried beside his mother in the burial-ground of a small mosque at Alexandria.

Saïd Pasha left an only son, Toussoun Pasha, who married a daughter of Ismail Pasha, the late Khedive; he was made the minister of education, but did not survive his father many years, and left his mother a widow and childless, surrounded with the burdensome ceremonies of Eastern etiquette, in the midst of all the bitter humiliations and misfortunes which came so rapidly upon Egypt under the rule of the successor of her husband.

CHAPTER XIII.

EGYPT UNDER ISMAIL KHEDIVE.

CAIRENE WATER-SELLER.

THE legitimate successor of Saïd Pasha was Achmet, eldest son of Ibrahim Pasha, but he having been killed by an accident, his brother, Ismail Pasha, came to the throne, and later received the title of Khedive, by which he is now known. After the death of Achmet Pasha, and during the life of Saïd Pasha, Ismail Pasha kept himself much aloof from the court, and gave his time largely to the acquisition of real estate, which was his chief passion, and to the culture of his lands.

This man became Viceroy with the new year of 1863, and he soon astonished the world by the revelation of the grasping ambition and boundless energy which he had so perfectly held in check so long as Saïd Pasha lived.

Early in life Ismail Pasha had been sent to France to be educated; he had visited Constantinople, and in 1855 had gone the second time to France, and from there to Italy, where he waited upon the Pope and made him magnificent presents. Later, when Saïd Pasha was absent from Egypt, on the continent, Ismail had borne an important part in the government. In 1861 he had led an army into Soudan to check an insurrection, in which undertaking he was successful. Thus, his experience had afforded him a certain knowledge of the affairs of the government he was to wield, and a good preparation for his duties. Two days after his accession the new Pasha received the members of the consular service in Egypt, and declared his intention of following the policy of Saïd Pasha.

M. Benoit Brunswick drew this striking picture of the Egypt ruled by Ismail Pasha: "In Egypt there are twenty thousand Frenchmen, ten thousand Englishmen, twenty thousand Italians, twenty-five

FELLAHEEN AT WORK ON THE CANAL.

thousand Greeks, two thousand Turks. There are no Egyptians, or rather the two millions of Egyptians count for no more than the agricultural population in the rest of the empire. In Egypt, the foreigner addicts himself to commerce and manufactures; the Egyptian labors and pays the taxes; the Turk governs. There is no national tradition in Egypt, because there is no Egyptian nation; there is but one tradition—one which reaches far away into antiquity: it is that of unrequited labor."

In the arrangement of his government Ismail Pasha made Prince Halim, the younger and last surviving son of Mohammed Ali, his President of the Council of Ministers. This prince was born in 1829, and at thirteen years of age was sent to Paris for his education. He remained seven years on the continent, and returned home at the death of his father to live upon the estate, thirty thousand feddans of land, which Mohammed Ali gave to each of his sons. While Abbas Pasha reigned, Prince Halim was scarcely heard of, but Saïd Pasha made him first Governor-general of the Soudan, and later, Minister of War.

He soon earned the reputation of a proud and haughty man among his equals—and of a merciful and gentle master of the fellaheen. Lord Derby said of him (when he sent a large subscription to England for the English operatives in 1862): "Unlike the Eastern princes of old, Halim Pasha is an active and enlightened agriculturist. He has spent vast sums on the improvement of his property and the introduction of machinery. His energy and administrative abilities are only equalled by his kindness and consideration."

The nephew and uncle did not long agree, for when, in 1864, Ismail proposed to appropriate certain lands unlawfully, Prince Halim took such a stand as rendered it necessary for him to leave the cabinet of the Viceroy; he retired to his palace at Shoubra, and gave himself up to his private cares, but so distasteful was he to Ismail, that at last, in 1868, after a series of steps pointing towards this climax, **Prince Halim** was banished from Egypt, and went to Constantinople, where he was received with much honor.

The first principal care of Ismail Pasha, after the formation of his cabinet, and the usual routine of business attendant upon the accession of a Viceroy, was to make himself the Merchant Prince of Egypt. He was already an immense landholder; he soon became the great producer and exporter of the country. He had extensive cotton and sugar plantations, and assumed the monopoly of all which he undertook. It was not an unusual circumstance for all the means of transportation to be employed by him, while other merchants were forced to wait until the produce of the Viceroy had been moved before they could ship a pound of their merchandise.

Another advantage of which he availed himself was labor by *corvée*, or unpaid labor. It was a custom to command the *corvée* for public works, but Ismail Pasha enforced it for his private gain. By these unprincely acts this Viceroy was a more literal realization of the Merchant Prince than is often seen—he seemed not to appreciate the unfitting position in which he placed himself, and was at no pains to veil the commercial phase of his life.

He early gained an undesirable reputation by calling off the *corvée* from the work upon the Suez Canal, and employing it in his private service. This created so much difficulty that Nubar Pasha was sent to France on account of it, and after much negotiation, the offices of the emperor being called in, mutual concessions were made by the Viceroy and the officers of the Canal Company, and peace was restored between them, in July, 1864, from which time the work upon this great undertaking went forward without interruption.

There is no doubt that from the moment of his accession to power the most cherished wish in the heart of Ismail Pasha, was that of obtaining from the Sultan a firman, which should change the succession of the Pashalic of Egypt, and give it to his own immediate family, in place of its descent by the Mohammedan law of inheritance—the same by which he had himself become Viceroy.

All his lavish gifts to the Sultan, all his humility before Abdul Aziz were but stepping stones to this end, and finally, in May, 1866, it was *un fait accompli*, the coveted decree was his, but at what cost? It is said that the Sultan received six hundred and fifty thousand Turkish livres, besides costly gifts to his wives, his mother and his ministers.

The following year, by another firman, Ismail Pasha received from the Sultan far greater absolute power than any other Viceroy of Egypt had ever held; he could regulate the customs, the post, the laws concerning foreigners, and various other like matters, without reference to the Porte; the only condition put upon him being that he should not violate the treaties already in force with other powers.

At the same time his title was changed from that of Viceroy or Pasha to Khedive, which, to Moslems, implies a higher authority in a religious sense, while it is no more kingly than that of Viceroy.

Following the gift of these new privileges, Ismail Khedive attempted to establish a constitution and a mode of government in Egypt, which should have an appearance of being more in keeping with those of other countries than that which had existed heretofore. He called together an Egyptian Parliament, which he opened in person, and he attempted to inaugurate a municipal government in Alexandria.

Under his influence, largely seconded by Nubar Pasha, the famous Minister of Commerce, many European manners and customs were brought out in Egypt, such as Parisian costumes, theatres, operas, and modes of arranging and refurnishing old houses, while an entirely different plan was followed in the erection of new ones.

Jerrold says in his "Egypt under Ismail Pasha": "His first care was to secure the vice-regal throne to his own family by order of primogeniture, to rid himself of the princes of his house who might thwart this dishonest design, and to buy up their estates, so that they should have no root in the country.

"His second care was to develop the material resources of the country, which he had secured to his family, so that the main stream of the wealth should flow into his own lap. In pursuit of this design he has performed many notable works, connected his name with many remarkable undertakings, enormously increased the exports from his kingdom, embellished Cairo and Alexandria, improved the system of agriculture, and extended the influence and area of Egypt until it has become, as he has boastfully remarked, almost a European power.

"All these labors, the direction of which he had monopolized, choosing passive instruments (as his own sons) for ministers, have left their marks upon him. He is not yet fifty, (1879), but his face is already marked with the deep lines of anxious thought; he has an aspect of weariness and fatigue. His score of palaces, his leagues of fertile land — tilled gratis — his gardens laden with the perfumes of every clime, his sumptuous harem, and his irresponsible power over millions of men, all settled on his children by the force of his own genius, have been bought at a heavy price.

"A prince of extraordinary astuteness and diplomatic *finesse*; capable of double the work an ordinary mortal can endure; with distinguished administrative faculties; keenly alive to all the material interests of his realm; a persevering and intelligent student of Western ideas, modes of government, and methods of production and manufacture; eager to seize upon any new invention, process of manufacture, and principle of agriculture; an unflagging man of business, with an eye for the smallest details; this remarkable descendant of Mehemet Ali (who gave few signs of the mental energy he possesses until he was called to rule) bears upon every passage of his life, as a ruler, the impress of his illustrious parentage. If his undoubted powers had been swayed and directed by lofty motives; if he had been solicitous solely for the welfare of the patient and long-suffering tillers of the soil, committed by the powers of Europe to the care of his family; if he had taken care that, in developing the unmeasured natural resources of the lands which the beautiful Nile fertilizes, at least a part of the new fruits should pass into the hands of the fellaheen; if he had really abolished the *corvée*, instead of perpetuating compulsory service, in order to fill his own coffers; if he had been, in truth, the earnest friend of the slave, he would have deserved more than the fame and praise which his creatures claim for him."

Much as one must now, in the light of all that has occurred, censure the Khedive, there are also many good works to be ascribed to him. His interest in public education stands first and foremost. In this way he has done more for Egypt than can be estimated, and has even inaugurated the public education of women; a decade before his time this would have been counted an impossible task by all the world, more especially by the Egyptians themselves. But this was easily done through the aid of a wife of the Khedive, who gave her royal patronage and countenance to the plan, and though at first there was a suspicious hesitation in profiting by so startling an innovation, a few months sufficed to fill the palace which had been arranged for the accommodation of three hundred girls. From this beginning the Egyptian mind has become accustomed to the idea of female education, and it will go on to do a great work in the future, as superstitions shall, one after another, be more fully overcome.

The Khedive summoned from Switzerland an able helper, Dor Bey, whom he made chief inspector of the public schools, and he, in his turn, has been ably seconded by Mr. Rogers. The public schools are divided into two classes, the primary, and government schools. The first are equivalent to the American common schools in the work they do—not yet, of course, equal to them in scope. The second class are of a special character, such as schools of medicine, mechanical and polytechnic schools.

The primary schools embrace paying and non-paying pupils, and the latter are subject to the call of the state, thus furnishing material from which are drawn teachers, doctors, engineers, and so forth for government service. There are, in addition to these, a few preparatory schools which stand between the primary and the government schools.

It may be said to the praise of the Khedive that he has shown himself far superior to any superstition or prejudice of race. In order to introduce into Egypt the leading features of Western civilization, he has employed men of all nations, who, he had the judgment to see, could advance his ideas much better than could be done by any other means; his army has been remodeled and controlled by Americans; his religious toleration has given peace and encouragement to the missionaries, who have certainly accomplished much in the larger towns; and until his financial embarrassments brought him into disgrace, he was much praised as a great reformer, and a light in the East, which would lead his people forth from the dense darkness of past centuries.

The true estimate of the influence of the Khedive cannot be made for years to come; certainly not now when he receives, and seems to merit only blame. DeLeon says: "But the financial embarrassments of Egypt have come up like a cloud to eclipse these glories, and he is now denounced in more unmeasured terms than he was lauded before, and even his good deeds and good works doubted and denied. My task is neither 'to bury Cæsar' nor 'to praise him.' I propose simply to depict the man and the monarch as I have seen and known him, and to do justice at the same time to the ruler, and to his people, not sparing the recital of his sins of omission and commission, while giving a catalogue of the benefits he has conferred on his country and his people, heavy as may be the price which both he and they may have to pay for them. This eastern prince is by no means 'that faultless monster the world ne'er saw,' but a mere man, like the rest of us, and as such made up out of a mingled yarn of vices and virtues. That he possesses that sin by which fell the angels—ambition, to which a moralist might add vain glory and rapacity, cannot be denied; that, in his zeal for rapidly reforming his cities and his people on the European model, he has gone too far and too fast for his own comfort and that of his subjects; that in annexing, and seeking to annex, Equatorial Africa to Egypt he has embarked on a dubious enterprise; that, in looking solely to the ends in view, he has often forgotten the means; and in the treatment of the fellahs left much to be desired; and, finally, that his expenditure has been greater than his means—all these charges cannot be disputed."

But in spite of all speculation, turn the picture as one will, some things must be told by the historian of Egypt that place the Khedive in a most unworthy aspect.

Mohammed Ali was the first Pasha who seized, to any great extent, the land of the fellahs, and gave it to his favorites or enriched his private property by its possession. Abbas Pasha, with all his other sins, had not that of unduly robbing the peasantry. Saïd Pasha, however, laid no claim to virtues of this sort, his policy was the reverse of that of his predecessor, and he increased largely what he chose to call the public lands, excusing himself for his robberies by the plea that the peasants could not improve them, while he took good care to render it impossible to them by the additional taxes which he imposed.

Ismail Khedive had still another mode of oppression. He not only exacted treble the amount of revenues paid to Saïd, but he secured to himself and his family, as private estates, a fifth of the best cultivable land in the whole country. When he came to the throne he was already a large landholder, having, as he himself has said, a mania for real estate. He then bought out all the properties of his relatives, Mustafa and Halim, in order to pay for which he made Egyptian loans; and in various lawful and unlawful ways, he so increased his own estates and those of his favorites that of the five million feddans of cultivable lands but three million five hundred thousand remain for the fellaheen, from whom the revenues must so largely come.

The taxes were so enormous that the peasants

only hoped to escape starvation, they could count on nothing more, and as the taxes were collected in kind, not in money, and the tax-collector had almost absolute power in valuation, the greatest oppression resulted in this direction, for the tax-collectors did not forget to take the full amount, usually a little more than was just. Then the *octroi* was added to the other taxes, and this so disheartened the fellaheen that they almost gave up all attempts to sell their produce. Then the date-bearing trees were taxed, and the trees too young to bear were taxed; all trades were taxed, even the donkey boys!

But more than all these taxes was the *corvée*, or unpaid labor for public works, which, shame to say, has been largely employed for the cultivation of private estates of the Khedive, especially for his enormous cotton and sugar-raising plantations. The wretched fellaheen are taken away from their own lands in gangs, and retained for months at a time, receiving neither pay nor food for themselves or their beasts; their wives must bring them bread, and God only knows where they obtained that, or the food for their half-starved camels and oxen. Besides these taxes upon crops and lands, there were the tax on tobacco, a commission on sales of cattle, a tax on mutton, and slaughter-house dues, dues to the public weigher, taxes on ferries, tolls over bridges, fees for marriages and burials, payments to be free from military service, and all sorts of fines, in order to escape punishment for crime—the last sort of revenue being carried beyond anything ever known in any European country.

To read all this calls up the indignation of any freeman, and yet how patiently were these burdens borne by the fellaheen of Egypt. The slave trade, against which Gordon Pasha labors, is a horror in Egypt, and has aroused the indignation and called out the protests of all countries; but in certain views the *corvée* is worse, for when the exhausted fellah and his family were starving no man owned them, and would not therefore feed them.

Happily the fatal policy of the Khedive put an end to many of its own evils, for when he was forced to resign his affairs to his creditors, no excuse existed for the continuance of such fearful oppressions, and a better future may be hoped for in the case of the Egyptian fellah.

It would be difficult to over-estimate the extravagance of the Khedive. One can fancy what sums it must cost to build a theatre, commission

Verdi to write an opera, import the most famous actors, dancers, singers and *artists* of every sort, as well as journalists to write up praises of Egypt and its ruler. Yet these were but a small part of the expenses to which he devoted the piastres wrung from the fellaheen.

To look back from this time to that of the opening of the Suez Canal, and recall the state and magnificence of the Khedive of Egypt at that time and to see him now, dethroned, exiled, affords one of those striking examples of the falls from greatness which attend all ages.

MAP OF THE CANAL.

Upon the completion of that great enterprise, Egypt and her ruler appeared to be upon the heights of prosperity. The Khedive had gone in person to invite the sovereigns of the world to attend his *fêtes*, and accept his hospitalities, and the Sultan allowed his ambitious subject to occupy what seemed to be the rightful place of the Suzerain upon this august occasion.

The making of this canal — a project which had disturbed the dreams of men for at least thirty centuries — was now realized, and the Mediterranean and Red Seas were united.

The canal is one hundred miles long and passes through lakes Menzaleh, Ballah, Timsah and the Bitter Lakes. Suez and Port Saïd are the terminal towns, and Ismaïla is the central station. This new city has many sanitary advantages. Its gardens are luxuriant and its boulevards, squares and promenades laid out in a manner that satisfied even the French engineers.

The Khedive had a palace here, and M. de Lesseps and others, have lovely homes. The shops are kept by French people, and their language is heard everywhere. Ismaïla is directly connected with Cairo by the Fresh-water Canal, and though in the midst of the Orient, is a French city—a complete outgrowth from the Canal and the French element which made that great work a success.

Port Saïd, too, is one of the consequences of the Canal, and is decidedly like a French town also, but scarcely an attractive one—being not too clean,

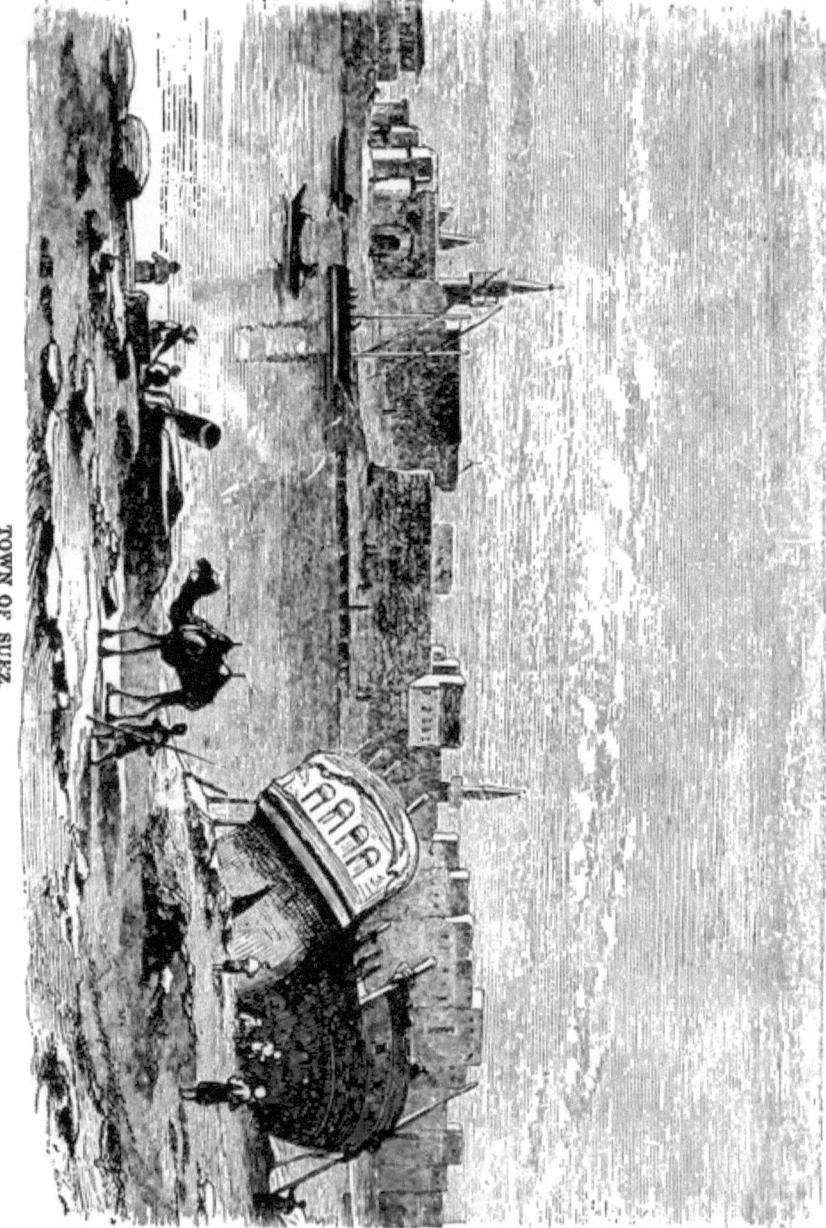
TOWN OF SUEZ.

and in some portions badly drained. It has, however, many fine residences and some good business blocks; its public garden is in the centre of the town, and the shops are good and in large numbers.

Suez is of course improved by the opening of the Canal, but the change here is not so great as in the localities just mentioned. There are many foreigners here—mostly men. One writer calls it "a kind of Eastern bachelor's hall," and it certainly has no attractions as a place of residence.

The cost of the Suez canal amounted to £19,-000,000, and it has been leased to the Suez Canal Company for ninety-nine years, at the expiration of which time the Government of Egypt has the right to redeem it by paying a certain sum. For all commercial vessels it is a neutral way, but for vessels of war a question may be raised. To the friendly powers the privilege for war vessels has been granted, but the vessels of Russia were not allowed to pass.

Since the doubts which for so many years existed as to the practicability of making the Canal have been answered, a new question—a financial one—has arisen, and that, will the Canal pay? can only be solved by time, as was the other.

There is little to reward the traveller for a

journey through the Canal, and it is tiresome and monotonous in the extreme. The great sea-walls at Port Saïd are a wonder of engineering, and bear testimony to the skill and science which have presided over all this work. It was the writer's good fortune to witness the works here, when they were in progress, in 1868, and that was a much more interesting and instructive sight than the finished Canal affords. The water was so shallow at Port Saïd that the vessels which would pass the Canal could not float within a mile and a half of the shore. To overcome this difficulty two enormous breakwaters were constructed; one is two thousand and seventy and the other two thousand seven hundred and thirty yards long; they are made of artificial stones, manufactured at Port Saïd from the sand found there, and lime brought from Europe. Each block weighed twenty tons, and twenty-five thousand were used. After they had been pressed and dried they were taken out and tumbled into the water, one after the other, until the two walls were made, after which the passage between them was dredged to a depth sufficient for floating large vessels. The constant deposit of sand along the Canal and at the mouth, has necessitated continual dredging, which is so large an expense as to require the passage of many vessels to pay even this charge, and this one difficulty has made it doubtful if the Suez Canal could ever be a success financially.

It is necessary, in giving any account of Ismail Khedive, to speak of four important men who have been his advisers and servants.

Nubar Pasha is an Armenian Christian, and was born at Smyrna, in 1825. When quite young he was sent to the continent to be educated, and went to Egypt in 1842, where he was the secretary of Boghos Bey, a relative of his, and a famous councillor to Mohammed Ali.

Nubar Pasha was next made interpreter to the Viceroy, and later to Ibrahim Pasha, whom he accompanied in his journey to Europe. He also held the same office under Abbas Pasha who made him a Bey. In 1850 Nubar Pasha was sent to London upon a diplomatic mission, and since that time has been honored with several similar affairs. At the time of the death of Abbas Pasha he was Egyptian Minister at Vienna.

At first Saïd Pasha believed that he required no service from Nubar Pasha, but he soon called on him for the delicate work of organizing the affairs of the transit to India. This office brought him into connection with the French and English transit companies, and through his untiring zeal the railroad from Cairo to Suez was completed.

Again Saïd Pasha endeavored to get on independently of Nubar, but he soon recalled him and sent him on a mission to Vienna, after which time he was retained near the Viceroy as long as he lived.

Ismail Pasha, after his accession, found immediate occupation for Nubar Pasha; he sent him to Constantinople to conduct the arrangements for the completion of the Suez Canal, and other important matters. Upon this occasion he so commended himself to the Sultan that when that sovereign visited Egypt he made Nubar a Pasha—a very unusual honor to be conferred upon a Christian.

Ismail Pasha next required his offices in France, to reconcile the difficulties which arose on account of the Viceroy's taking the fellahs from the work on the Canal and employing them for his private purposes. This troublesome mission being satisfactorily arranged, Nubar Pasha was made Minister of Public Works, in which position he manifested unusual energy, and was just beginning to make himself felt when the Viceroy called him to

CARAVAN STARTING FROM SUEZ.

go again as Envoy Extraordinary to Constantinople. It was Nubar Pasha who now obtained from the Sultan the firman which made the succession direct, enlarged and consolidated the power of the Viceroy, and placed Ismail Pasha where, if only he had been wise, he might have now the most enviable fame of his age.

Nubar Pasha, with the consent of the Porte, went again to Europe and visited several courts for the purpose of reforming the consular service between Egypt and European powers. He also represented Egypt in the Monetary Congress at Paris in 1867.

This accomplished man speaks the French, English, Italian, Armenian, Greek, Turkish, and Egyptian languages, and it has been said of him, that when he learns the language of a people, he also seems to imbibe the spirit and to understand the character of that people. It is certainly true that he has been of great use to Egypt, and to Europe as well. In recognition of his services he has been decorated with many orders, and otherwise rewarded.

In spite of all the important services of Nubar Pasha, he fell under the displeasure of the Khedive, and spent his time in foreign travel until recently, when, after the pecuniary downfall of the Khedive, he made one of the new Ministry.

In person, Nubar Pasha is striking and attractive. His complexion is dark, his features regular, and his smile prepossessing; he is of medium height and has such an address, and so fine a talent for conversation, that he only requires a few moments in which to commend himself, whenever he desires to do so.

With all this he is singularly independent; not in the remotest degree fawning in his intercourse, even with the loftiest and most exacting sovereigns. This pride, which renders him frank always, rude at times, has made it all the more remarkable that he has been able to hold his position, at home and abroad, under the chances and changes of the governments of three Viceroys.

Perhaps his greatest work was that which made him obnoxious to the Khedive, the establishment of the mixed tribunals, which checked the absolutism of his master and the power of the consuls. This was his favorite scheme for more than twenty years, and any benefits which may arise from the new system are certainly the result of the foresight and perseverance of Nubar Pasha.

The old rule in Egypt was, in the main, simply

this: the Khedive and the Egyptian courts had no control over the affairs of foreigners, which were settled by the consuls entirely; the Khedive, on the other hand, had absolute power over the natives, in both civil and criminal cases, where the interest of no European was involved. The mixed tribunals were intended to give the Egyptians some voice in the doings of foreigners in their midst, and to take from the Khedive his absolute power in all cases. The full intent was not accomplished by Nubar Pasha: this could not have been expected, but as much as was done was his work.

Cherif Pasha, Minister of Foreign Affairs, has somewhat divided the honors with Nubar Pasha, for, when one was in disgrace the other was in favor. Cherif Pasha was born at Constantinople, about 1819, and was of an old and noble Moslem family. He was educated in Europe, and was a distinguished scholar in the military school of St. Cyr.

Upon his return to Egypt, in 1844, he made one of the suite of Halim Pasha; when Saïd Pasha became Viceroy, he placed Cherif (who had been his schoolmate in France) in the army, and gave him rapid promotion, until, at last, he was made a Pasha. In 1857 he was changed from military to civil service, and was made Minister of Foreign Affairs, for the first time.

Upon the accession of Ismail Khedive, Cherif Pasha received one portfolio after another, and was made regent of the country upon three separate occasions when the Viceroy left Egypt. Cherif Pasha has received many honors in foreign nations, has numerous decorations, and is a member of the Institute of Egypt. He married the daughter of Colonel Sèves, or Soliman Pasha, and thus has many French interests and attachments.

In person, Cherif Pasha might be readily mistaken for a Frenchman; he is fair and florid, with gray eyes. He is so frank and soldier-like in his manner that he inspires perfect confidence; he is extremely popular, and has a passion for the chase.

Riaz Pasha, the Minister of Justice, is a younger man, a pupil of Nubar Pasha, and is a man of the future rather than of the past.

But the most marvellous man in the service of the Khedive was Ismail Sadyk Pasha, the Minister of Finance, or the Mouffetich of the late *régime*. No story of fiction could be more marvellous than are the facts of this man's history—when writing the sober truth about him one feels as if it were a Munchausen.

He was a fellah—an ignorant creature—speaking to his latest day no language but that of his own class, and yet he may be said to have ruled Egypt, from the Khedive himself, down to the lowest of his own caste, for the space of ten years. In person Sadyk Pasha was slight and stooping, sharp featured, dark skinned, with a cunning eye; with his superiors and equals he assumed a fawning manner, at other times he was a brute. To a stranger he was simply disgusting and repellant, but he must have possessed some remarkable quality which enabled him to gain and to hold his strange influence over Ismail Khedive; let us hope that it was not solely because he was an unmitigated rascal and would serve for purposes which other Moslems would scorn.

He was first employed by the Khedive as an overseer of a small estate, in which capacity he so gained the confidence of his sovereign that he was gradually promoted to the prominent position of Minister of Finance. His cruelty to those beneath him was so extreme that one could not frame in decent language the story of his crimes. He permitted the free use of the koorbash to his agents, "until a cry went up to earth and heaven against his oppressions, perpetrated in the name, if not by the authority, of his master, who has ever borne the character of a humane man, constitutionally averse to cruelty."

It is but fair to say that these things were largely unknown to the Khedive; in Egypt it is possible to conceal much from one high in power. It would be charitable to believe that Ismail Sadyk Pasha was a madman — made such by his great power — by his excesses and by the benefits conferred upon him by the same hand that finally cut him down.

As Minister of Finance he made loan after loan, paid any exorbitant rate of interest that might be asked, and plunged his master and his country into a pit so deep that no exit can be hoped for in years and years to come. When at last the Khedive became convinced of the real character of this wretch, he did not hesitate to turn upon him, and his benefactor was threatened by him with disgrace and humiliation which should come from the lips and hand of his fellah-minister. In this he went too far; the Khedive invited him to drive, and from that time he was lost to the sight and knowledge of man.

It was said that he was sent a prisoner to Dongola; it was said that he died there, and a circular signed by the officials of that place, certifying his death, was sent to the consuls in Egypt, but no one feels that he knows the manner of the death of Ismail Sadyk Pasha, or the place of his burial, if, indeed, any was accorded him.

In the new quarter of Cairo, called Ismaïlieh, this wretch had three vast palaces, profusely decorated and furnished with the rarest and choicest *articles de luxe* that money can buy. His plate cost the fortune of a prince, and the jewels belonging to his thirty-six wives embraced every possible ornament, from a *ceinture* of diamonds, valued at £7,000, to a six-penny buckle!

Here this low fellah lived, in the midst of surroundings which would have made the heaven of a Sybarite; even the ewers and basins used for his hands were of solid silver, of artistic form, the *portiéres* and hangings of his rooms were in exquisite taste, and it is impossible to imagine this low creature squatted down amongst his companions in such apartments.

These palaces were confiscated, and their entire contents sold at public auction. DeLeon attended the sale, and says, "'Wolsey, with his Hampton Court, that bluff king Hal considered too great for a subject!' dwindles into insignificance when compared with this more regal robber, who sprang from a mud-hut on the Nile, in less than ten years, into the possession of more palaces, jewels, women, and slaves, than Solomon in all his glory could boast of.

"Such mushroom growths are possible only in the soil where Jonah's gourd attained its wonderful growth in the shortest possible space of time; but his rise and fall, and the relics of his luxury, must recall more the romances of the 'Thousand and One Nights,' than the sober experiences of modern Egypt in the nineteenth century."

To return to the history of Ismail Khedive, his financial embarrassments reached such a point in November, 1875, that his cunning minister declared himself unable to supply the needs of His Highness longer. The Khedive then turned to England, and begged to be saved from total ruin. (Only an outline statement can be given here, of what followed, and gradually led on to the exile of the Khedive.)

Then began a series of investigations of the Finances of Egypt, conducted by Mr. Cave, Mr. Goschen, Mr. Romaine, and by a Commission of Inquiry. All these investigators were unable to come at the exact truth, for they were met at each and every point with deceit and falsehood, so that the results shown by their figures are probably but an approach to the whole truth of the rottenness of the Khedive's government.

Jerrold says: "It is now patent to the world that since that crisis at the end of 1875, which brought about the fall of Ismail's powerful minister and accomplice, his Highness has never ceased from endeavors to abstract his possessions from the power of his creditors, by making them over to his family, by setting up fictitious charges upon them, and by intercepting sums on their way from his estates or his provincial treasuries to the Public Debt Office. It was his wholesale dishonesty, indeed, that upset the Goschen-Joubert arrangement of November, 1876, and, by a series of scandalous revelations and contentions, so stirred public opinion, that a violent and sweeping remedy was at length insisted upon, in the shape of a semi-European Ministry, with Nubar Pasha at its head, and an English and French Minister at his elbow to guard the interests of Egyptian bond-holders."

The Goschen-Joubert arrangement left too much power in the hands of the Khedive, who always insisted that the nomination of the tax-gatherers should be left with himself. He employed only such men as knew no master save the Khedive, and the consequences of this system soon appeared.

All through the year 1877, things went badly in Egypt; a bad Nile was added to the other difficulties, and the total lack of honor on the part of the Khedive was more and more plainly seen. During all this time he seemed to think only of the best mode by which his creditors could still be cheated, and of how to spend all the money possible upon himself. He relinquished no luxurious expenditure. His palace of Abdin was a scene of constant excitement and gayety, and he still went on with the erection of new palaces.

If any creditor attempted to communicate with him, he coolly replied that all his affairs were now administered by his European Bankers. "Hundreds of his subjects, to say nothing of Europeans, are starving only a few yards from his doors; but nevertheless the construction of three stately palaces, between Ghezireh and the Pyramids, is being proceeded with as before. Such being the case, it can scarcely be wondered at if his Highness's popularity is not on the increase, or if his creditors refuse to acquiesce in any reduction in the interest stipulated for." The above extract from a letter read by Mr. Cobb before the Society of Arts, shows the personal feeling which ran high against the Khedive.

This dislike was increased by the fact that Ismail Khedive made the bad Nile, and the alleged dishonesty of those who handled the revenues, an excuse for the repudiation of a portion of his indebtedness. In this he was checked summarily, and made to understand that the action of the Sultan could not be repeated by the Khedive.

At this point, Prince Halim Pasha (the lawful heir whom the new law of succession had set aside, and the only surviving son of the Great Mohammed Ali,) wrote a letter from Constantinople, to which city he had been banished, advising the Khedive to give up all, honestly, to his creditors, to retrieve his character and regain the position which he had so disgracefully lost. He recommended to him to give up all the private property of his family, to place his financial matters fully and honorably in the hands of European financiers, and to leave no means untried to repair the faults and errors of his past. The letter, which was long, ended thus: "These are, briefly stated, Monseigneur, the principal measures which I implore you to undertake sincerely, and without delay. As for the results to be obtained therefrom, they will be beneficial to you and to all, beyond your expectations. You will have lost, it is true, the free disposal of immense sums; but you will allow Egypt to lift up her head, and face the claims upon her, which she can, with regular administration, amply satisfy. The confidence of Europe and the affection of your people will be yours once more. May your Highness be convinced that my present conduct is that of a relative devoted to you, and anxious for your welfare.

"I am, Monseigneur, your Highness's most devoted servant and uncle,

"HALIM."

This letter produced such an effect in Egypt that Prince Halim would have been hailed with joy could he have been placed as a ruler over his rightful heritage.

In March, 1878, the famous Commission of Inquiry was instituted by a decree. The Khedive opposed it in every way possible, but in spite of his machinations it was fully carried out, and the whole investigation completed in four months' time.

The report of this inquiry was a surprise even to those who had best understood the state of the case before. It perfectly confirmed all that had been alleged regarding the matters of appropriating the lands of the people; the fearful extravagance of the reigning family; the extreme oppression of the taxes, and the terrible cruelty employed in collecting them; in short, the half had not been told.

Following this report, Nubar Pasha, Mr. Rivers Wilson and M. DeBlignières were made a Controlling Ministry, and it was believed that a step had now been taken which would compel the Khedive to outward honesty, if nothing more.

But, alas for the infatuation of associating the idea of honor with Ismail Khedive. In the face of all the guards which could be placed about him, he seized the money which was brought from the villages and perverted it to his own uses. The moudirs were in the service of their master, and when accused they publicly declared that they knew no law but the will of the Khedive.

At the beginning of the year 1879 it seemed that the affairs of Egypt were in a proper train to be controlled for the best. This control was threefold: first, the International or Mixed Tribunals for the purpose of enforcing and protecting the claims of foreigners against the Government of the Khedive; second, a Ministry in which were an Englishman and a Frenchman, without whose consent the Khedive could do nothing; third, special officials charged to see that the arrangements made with public creditors were fulfilled. Of course there are many details which go to fill out this outline, but it embraces the principles upon which the whole work was carried on. Much hope was felt that this arrangement would prove sufficient to meet the exigencies of the Egyptian crisis, but early in the year the Khedive quarrelled with Nubar Pasha and dismissed him summarily from the Ministry.

The Ministers remaining did not think it best to insist upon the restoration of Nubar Pasha, but when the Khedive wished to dismiss Riaz Pasha, a native official who was of great value, the Ministers did oppose him, and successfully too; they also insisted that whoever composed the Ministry, it should have a full power of veto upon any measure it disapproved. Their claims were enforced by a joint vote from the two Powers, which convinced the Khedive that he must yield this point or be dethroned.

Soon after this trouble was arranged the Khedive made a more decided stand, and peremptorily dismissed the whole Ministry, Mr. Wilson and

M. DeBlignières as well as the native officials, and appointed an entire Ministry of Pashas, men on whom he could rely, and thus threw down the gauntlet to England and France in a most cavalier sort of manner. This honest gentleman declared that he had plenty of money, but Mr. Wilson and M. DeBlignières would not allow him to pay it to those whom he owed. This action roused much feeling all over the world, and although the Khedive and his Pashas began immediately to have a very good time on their old plan, to oppress again the natives and to get everything for themselves at any cost, this endured but a few weeks.

All the European powers united, and as the Khedive would not resign, such an influence was brought to bear upon the Sultan that he deposed the Khedive and his eldest son, Tewfik Pasha, was made Viceroy. Thus ended the long and eventful reign of Ismail Pasha, and on the thirtieth of June, 1879, he left Alexandria for Naples. Many people crowded the city to bid him farewell, and he appeared as unconcerned as if he were merely going on a pleasure trip, while every possible mark of respect was shown him by the people. "The Saturday Review" of July twelfth, 1879, says:

"A special train, a guard of honor, a military band playing what is poetically termed the Egyptian Hymn, officials in full costume, and groups of affectionate residents clustering to render him the homage of a respectful farewell, combined to indicate that the outgoing Pasha was a very good man, and deserved, at least in the Turkish sense, well of his country.

"If he is doomed to pass the rest of his days in retirement, he will still be a striking example to all who are in a position to emulate him of what a first-class successful Pasha can be, do, and obtain. After a brilliant career, in which he has reduced the mass under him to beggary, has built more palaces than he could count, and very many more than he could inhabit, has fought unsuccessful wars, and has awakened numerous jealousies among Christian nations, he retires, amid lavish demonstrations of honor and respect, to pass the evening of his days in a delightful climate, with everything that wealth can command at his disposal. This seems to be the ideal career of a Pasha, and it is something for any man to have exactly realized the special ideal of the class to which he belongs."

It is said that the Khedive is to receive £50,000 a year, and his family are to receive the same

CALL TO PRAYER.

amount, and that this is all to be deducted from the £150,000 which is allowed to Tewfik Pasha.

At the same time that the Sultan issued the firman which deposed Ismail Khedive, he sent out a second one which annulled the firman of 1873, which conferred the power upon the ruler of Egypt to make treaties with foreign nations. By this decree the Sultan made it necessary for the Europeans to treat with the Porte concerning any arrangement to be made for the settlement of the Egyptian financial questions. This measure was very objectionable; it would cause great delays in the transaction of affairs, and would render it possible to even appeal from the decisions of the Mixed Tribunals to the authority at Constantinople.

The Powers therefore used their influence at Constantinople to the end that nothing should be done to complicate the already difficult matter of arranging the great debt which Egypt owed to Europeans. After much negotiation this matter was arranged in a manner which satified the Powers, and took nothing from the authority and dignity of the Sultan as Suzerain of Egypt.

One of the early acts of Tewfik Khedive was to send a peremptory letter to Nubar Pasha at Paris, commanding him not to attempt to return to Egypt. This outrageous act was so resented by the Powers, who had in reality given the young Khedive his authority, that he hastened to rescind this order and to send another letter to France which allowed the Khedive's late Prime Minister to return officially to Egypt before the end of the year—which letter was given to Nubar Pasha by M. Waddington, August 7, 1879.

Naturally many questions arose for consideration as to the formation of the government or cabinet of the new Khedive, and as under existing circumstances the European Powers, more especially England and France, were to be consulted and satisfied, several months were passed in preliminary *pourparlers* and correspondence.

Mr. Baring on the part of England, and M. de Blignières on that of France, were made Controllers of Egyptian Finance, and proceeded to Cairo in November, 1879.

It is of course impossible as yet to speak of Tewfik Khedive as a ruler of Egypt. But it is to be hoped that Egypt has seen her darkest days, and that they preceded a light which shall make the old "House of Bondage" a prosperous land.

The reports that have come of late (December,

1879) represent a hopeful state of things. A correspondent of the "London Times" writes that the fine crops of cotton, grain, sugar and beans have caused great activity and cheerfulness. He says: "The harbor is crowded with merchantmen, the railway is blocked with trains. Yesterday three long trains, all fully laden, were waiting outside the city while the others were being unloaded. The big canal is crowded with barges, the business streets are crammed with carts, and all these means of transport are laden with cotton and grain and cotton-seed. From eight in the morning to eight at night the merchants are in their stores or at the market, and many a worn face, made dull by bad times, is now bright and eager with the prospect of gain. The tradesmen, and more especially the purveyors of luxury, are looking up. Year after year of failing finance and feeble trade had told upon them. But they are doing well now, and if this present brimming Nile brings crops as it subsides as abundant as those we now profit by, all Egypt may fairly hope for a permanent return of the old prosperous times. The noble mansions and comfortable villas which Syrian capitalists, fearful of the variations of Egyptian stocks, and no longer caring to invest in them as they did, have run up round the city, may also find good rents and competent occupants. Indeed, all Alexandria is looking confidently, and with some reason, to material improvement."

Let us be grateful that our last words may thus be words of cheer, and let us hope that the time is not far distant when the poet's vision may become reality.

> " Out of all this a Presence comes, and stands
> Full-fronted, as who turns upon the Past,
> Modern among the ancients, and the last
> Of re-born, risen nations: in her hands,
> That once so many sceptres held, and rods,
> A palm leaf set with jewels: Princess, she —
> She has her palaces along the Nile,
> Her navies on the sea; —
> And in the temples of her fallen gods
> (Not hers — she knows but the One God over all),
> She hears from holy mosques the muezzin's call,
> "Lo, Allah is most great!" And when the dawn
> Is drawing near, " Prayer better is than sleep."
> She rides abroad; her curtains are undrawn —
> She walks with lifted veil, nor hides her smile,
> Nor the sweet, luminous eyes, where languors creep
> No more: She is no more Circassian girl,
> But Princess, woman with the mother breast;
> No Cleopatra to dissolve the pearl
> And take the asp — the East became the West!
>   Honor to Egypt — honor;
>   May Allah smile upon her!"

LIST OF NOMES OR ANCIENT DIVISION OF EGYPT.

(*As given in Brugsch's "Egypt under the Pharaohs."*)

KEMI (Egypt) and its Nomes, according to the List of the Monuments.

I.—PATORIS (the South Country, Upper Egypt).

   1st Nome.   *Capital:* Ab. (Elephantine).
                   Deities: Khnum and Sopet (Sothis).

   2nd Nome. *Capital:* Teb (Apollinopolis Magna).
                   Deities: Hor (Apollo) of Hut, and Hathor (Aphrodite).

   3rd Nome. *Capital:* Nekheb (Eileithyiapolis).
                   Deity: The goddess Nekheb.

   4th Nome. *Capital:* Ni or Ni-amon (Diospolis Magna).
                   Deities: Amon-ra (Zeus) and the goddess Mut.

   5th Nome. *Capital:* Qobti (Koptos).
                   Deity: Khim (Pan).

   6th Nome. *Capital:* Tanterer (Tentyra).
                   Deities: Hathor and Hor-samta.

7th Nome. *Capital:* Ha (Arab, Hou, Diospolis Parva).
Deities: Nebtha (Nephthys and Noferhotep.

8th Nome. *Capital:* Abdu (Abydos).
Deity: Anhur (Mars).

9th Nome. *Capital:* Apu (Panooplis).
Deity: Khim (Pan).

10th Nome. *Capital:* Tebu (Aphroditopolis).
Deity: Hor-mati.

11th Nome. *Capital:* Shas-Hotep (Hypsele).
Deity: Khnum.

12th Nome. *Capital:* Ni-ent-bak (Antæopolis).
Deities: Hor and Mati (Isis).

13th Nome. *Capital:* Siout (Lycopolis).
Deities: Ap-maten (Anubis) "of the South," and Hathor.

14th Nome. *Capital:* Qors, Qos (Cusae).
Deity: Mat (Themis).

15th Nome. *Capital:* Khimunu (Hermopolis).
Deity: Thut (Hermes).

16th Nome. *Capital:* Hibonou (Hipponon).
God: Hor.

17th Nome. *Capital:* Qasa (Cynonpolis).
God: Anup (Anubis).

18th Nome. *Capital:* Ha-Suten (Alabastronopolis).
God: Anup.

19th Nome. *Capital:* Pi-maza (Oxyrhynchus).
God: Set (Typhon).

20th Nome. *Capital:* Khinensu (Heracleopolis Magna).
God: Khnum called Her-shaf.

21st Nome. *Capital:* Smen-hor (Ptolemais?).
              God: Khnum.
22d Nome. *Capital:* Tep-ah (Aphroditopolis).
              Deity: Hathor.

II.—PATOMHIT (the North Country, Lower Egypt).

1st Nome. *Capital:* Men-nofer (Memphis).
              Deities: Ptah (Hephæstus), and Sokhet.
2nd Nome. *Capital:* Sokhem (Letopolis).
              God: Hor (-uër)
3rd Nome. *Capital:* Ni-ent-hapi (Apis).
              Goddess: Senti (Hathor-Nub).
4th Nome. *Capital:* Zoq'a (Canopus).
              Deities: Amon-ra and Neit (Athena).
5th Nome. *Capital:* Sa (Saïs)
              Goddess: Neit.
6th Nome. *Capital:* Khesuu (Xoïs).
              God: Amon-ra.
7th Nome. *Capital:* Sonti-nofer (Metelis).
              Deities: He, "Lord of the West," and Isis.
8th Nome. *Capital:* Thukot (Sethroï)
              Deities: Tum (Helios), and Hathor.
9th Nome. *Capital:* Pi-usir (Busiris).
              God: Osiris.
10th Nome. *Capital:* Ha-ta-hir-ab (Athribis).
              Deities: Hor-khont-khethi, and the goddess Khut.
11th Nome. *Capital:* Qa-hebes (Cabasus).
              Deity: Isis.
12th Nome. *Capital:* Theb-nuter (Sebennytus).
              God: Anhur (Mars).

13th Nome. *Capital*: Anu (On, Heliopolis).
    Deities: Hormakhu (Helios) and the goddess Iusas.

14th Nome. *Capital*: Zo'an (Tanis).
    Deities: Hor and the goddess Khont Abot.

15th Nome. *Capital*: Pi-thut (Hermopolis).
    Deities: Thut and the goddess No-hem-ani.

16th Nome. *Capital*: Pi-bi-neb-dad (Mendes).
    Deities: Bi-neb-dad (Mendes), and the goddess Ha-mehit.

17th Nome. *Capital*: Pi-khun-en-amon (Diospolis).
    Deities: Amon-ra and the goddess Mut.

18th Nome. *Capital*: Pi-Bast (Bubastis).
    Goddess: Bast.

19th Nome. *Capital*: Pi-uto (Buto).
    Goddess: Uto (Isis).

20th Nome. *Capital*: Qosem (Phacussa).
    God: Sapt, "the Lord of the East."

INDEX.

	PAGE.
Abbas Pasha, murder of	408, 410
Aboukir, battle of	357
Abraham, legend of	336
Abu Simbel	176
Abydos, temple at	166, 169
Achmed Pasha	357, 360, 368
Ai, the Holy Father	149
Alexandria, founding of	220
Alexandrian University	227
Alexandrian Library, destruction of	299
Alexandrian Library, founding of	227
Amru, story of	311
Ancient Divisions of Egypt	23
Apis Bulls, account of	199, 205, 213, 220
Arsinoë, founding of	233
Auletes, "the flute player,"	256
Baba, tomb of	95
Bakhatana, princess of	190
"Barrage du Nil,"	405, 414
Battle of the Pyramids	353
Bek, the architect	144
Belzoni's Tomb	156
Beni-Hassan, tombs of	69
Berenice, founding of	233
Bes, the god	63
Beyrout	176
Boulak, museum of	56, 80, 134
Brugsch-Bey	55, 63, 67, 90, 95, 128, 147, 172, 175, 209
Bubastis, temple at	197
Cairo, founding of	320
Canal from Nile to Red Sea	233
Caracalla, treachery of	281
Cheops	38
Cherif Pasha	449
Chosroes of Persia	306
Cleopatra's Needles	266
Commerce with India	65, 271
Constantinople	290

474   Index.

	PAGE.
Corvée, The	435
Crocodile, The	83, 89
Dastagerd, palace of	309
Doric Column, origin of	71
Edfou, temple at	99
Educational System	400, 430
Egypt, highest prosperity of	242
Egyptian Worship at Rome	265, 275
El-Kab, tomb at	99, 107, 141
Esneh, temple at	241
Exodus, time of	95
Gnosticism	278
Green Chamber, The	31
Hadrian and Antinous, visit to Egypt	276
Hall of Columns at Karnak	155
Hammamat, expedition to	188
Harris Papyrus	183
Hashop, Queen	109
Homer, temple of	245
Hyksos or Shepherd Kings	86
Ibis, the	97
Institute of Egypt	361
Ismaïla, city of	438
Ismaïl Pasha	397
Ismaïl Sadyk Pasha	450
Joseph, time of	94
Joseph's Well	338
Judæan War	198
Julian Year, introduction of	264
Khafra, statues of	50
Khedive, the late, gift to America	266, 419, 427, 454, 461
Khnumhotep, tomb of	75
Khuaten, tomb and sculptures of	145, 146
Kleber, General	372
His Proclamation, 373; Assassination of, 376.	
Labyrinth, wonderful	84
Makoukas, treachery of	312
Mamelukes, slaughter of	382, 389, 391
Manetho, writings of	38, 207, 209, 234
Medinet Abu	184, 188
Mena, King	27
Memnon, statues of	134
Memnonium, The	155, 160, 166

	PAGE.
Memphis, founding of	27
Menou, General	376, 380
Mineptah II., Pharaoh of the Exodus	178
Mœris Lake	80
Mohammed	310
Mohammed Ali	378, 381, 386
Goes to Mecca, 395, 399; Private Life, 401; Death, 406.	
Monasteries	293, 299
Monastery of St. Catherine	303
Musical statue	137
Mut, the goddess	141
Napoleon Bonaparte	344, 345
Famous Proclamation, 349; Enters Cairo, 355; Battles with the Mamelukes, 356; Syrian Campaign, 365; Surrender of Jaffa, 366; Siege of Acre, 368; Again at Jaffa, 369; Return to Cairo, 370; Leaves Egypt, 371.	
Negroes, as artists	149
Nicopolis, founding of	263
Nilometers	20
Nilometer at Elephantine	264
Nimrod, statue of, at Florence	194
Nitocris, story of	59
Nubar Pasha	443, 459
Oasis of Ammon	220, 223
Obelisks, removal of	128
Obelisks removed to Rome	263
Omar, destruction of books	317
Osymandyas, statue of	161
Paper, origin of word	251
"Papyrus Judicaire"	187
Parchment, origin of word	251
Pashas, magnificence of	332
Patah, the god	28
Pentaur, poem by	174
Pergamus, library at	251
Persecution of Christians	289
Philæ, temple at	238
Pompey's Pillar	289
Port Saïd — Great Sea-walls	438, 442
Prince Halim	423, 457
Prisse-papyrus	54
Ptolemais, city of	233
Ptolemy Soter, works at Alexandria	228
Punt, land of	61
Pyramid, the great	42

	PAGE.
Ramses III., riches of	184
Ramses VI., tomb of	189
Riaz Pasha	450, 460
Rosetta Stone	16, 246
Rougé, M.	175
Saïd Pasha	413, 417
Saladin	320
Scribes	35
Serapis, worship of	234
Sesostris, tomb of	178
Set, the god	89
Shadoof, The	23
Silsilis	103, 152, 198
Slave Trade	436
Smith, Sir Sidney	375
Sphinx, the great	50, 132
Sphinxes, avenue of	138
Stage Temple, The	112
Statues of the Nile	20
St. Macarius	296
St. Mark in Egypt	272
St. Mary of Egypt	293
Strabo's Journey	265
Suez	441
Suez Canal	362, 417, 425, 437, 441
Syenite Granite	45
Tables of Sakkarah and Abydos	36, 38, 49, 53, 59
Tell-el-Amarna	143, 150
Tewfik Pasha	461
Thebes, ruin of	255
Thi, Queen	142
Thut or Thoth, the god	96
Ti, tomb of	53
Translation of the Scriptures into Greek	234
Treasures carried to Rome	263
Turin, musuem at	150, 191
Triumphs	119
Turin Papyrus	36, 38
Ulema, The	341
Una, story of	56
Wahabis, The	390
Zenobia, account of	288
Zoan-Tanis	169
Zodiac at Denderah	266

www.ingramcontent.com/pod-product-compliance
Lightning Source LLC
Chambersburg PA
CBHW051900300426
44117CB00006B/467